PORTRAIT OF A
PALM BEACH
PLAYER
1000 FIRST DATES

JOHNNY DEPTH

PORTRAIT OF A PALM BEACH PLAYER
1000 FIRST DATES

Written by Johnny Depth and Kerry Lutz

Editing and cover by George Verongos

ISBNS
Paperback: 978-1-970521-02-3
Hardback: 978-1-970521-03-0
Digital: 978-1-970521-04-7

Library of Congress Control Number: 2025925198

FIRESTARTER
publishers

ACKNOWLEDGMENTS

This book would not exist without the hard-earned truths, brutal honesty, and unwavering clarity of a few men who refused to lie to themselves—or to the rest of us.

To Corey Wayne

You taught me that strength isn't about domination—it's about walking away when self-respect is on the line.

"The strongest negotiating position is being able to walk away and mean it." That line changed everything.
understandingrelationships.com

To Strong Successful Male

For the support, the eye-opening insights, and the steady, grounded dialogue. You gave countless men—myself included—the framework to rebuild themselves with clarity and purpose.

Your calm delivery hits harder than outrage ever could.
YouTube Channel

To Rollo Tomassi

You cracked the code and forced men to see what we were never supposed to notice.

The Rational Male didn't just explain the game—it exposed the entire stadium. Your work made me dangerous—in the best possible way.
therationalmale.com

To Rich Cooper

For reminding every man that chasing excellence will always beat chasing tail. Your voice is a mirror and a sword.

"Do the work" isn't a catchphrase—it's a lifestyle.
richcooper.ca

To Coach Greg Adams

For unmasking the modern dating marketplace with surgical precision—and brutal humor. *The free agent lifestyle* isn't a fallback plan. It's a power move.
gregadamsone.com

And finally—to the men still waking up, still rebuilding, still remembering who they were before the world told them who to be—

This book is your war journal. Your wake-up call. And your permission slip to never be average again.

Stay sharp. Stay dangerous. Stay free.

—Johnny Depth

CONTENTS

INTRODUCTION

I never set out to become a serial dater. It just sort of…happened. One app turned into two, two turned into ten, and before I knew it, I was swiping my way through South Florida like it was my second job.

The thing about dating in this era is that it's easier than ever to meet someone—and yet, somehow, harder than ever to truly connect. Maybe it's the paradox of choice. Maybe it's the gamification of romance, where we keep swiping in search of something just a little better. Maybe it's just me.

But let's be real here—I am a catch. A retired attorney, a Renaissance man, an intelligent gentleman with a great sense of humor and some serious dance moves. And, let's not be bashful—my lovemaking skills are near the top of my gender. I inhabit a target-rich environment.

That being said, I'm not a conventional player. I don't date women just to get them into bed and disappear. But if they want it and I feel a spark, why not? Maybe it leads to something more, maybe it doesn't. That's the gamble.

Over the years, I've gone on an average of two dates per week. More than a thousand first dates. The number that led to a second date? Maybe 5%. The ones that turned into something more? Say, 1 to 2%. The odds aren't great, but hey, I like the game.

I've met women from all walks of life—some amazing, some forgettable, some just in it for the free dinner. I don't mind being used for a meal or two, but I will never be someone's personal ATM. I'm generous to a fault, but I'm not a sucker.

This book isn't about any one woman or any one date. It's about the experience. The thrill, the frustration, the humor, and the absurdity of it all. It's about what it means to be single in a world where you're always just one swipe away from another possibility.

It's been a wild ride. And it's not over yet.

THE ART OF INTIMACY
(AND THE LACK THEREOF)

South Florida is filled with women who, on the surface, seem to have it all together. They've aged gracefully—polished, fit, confident, and undeniably attractive. Many are financially independent, socially savvy, and know exactly how to work a room. But scratch the surface, and something's missing. Beneath that well-curated exterior is a yearning they don't fully understand, a restlessness they can't quite explain. Because when it comes to true intimacy—not just sex, but deep, soul-awakening connection—most of them have no idea what that actually feels like.

It's not really their fault. These are women who've spent decades in long-term relationships, usually marriages that checked all the respectable boxes but left them empty between the sheets. They were faithful. Dutiful. Emotionally invested. But they weren't fulfilled. Their sex lives became transactional, obligatory—a marital duty to perform rather than a shared experience to savor. Over time, they stopped expecting anything different. They settled into routine, convinced that passion was a thing of youth or fiction.

And so now, newly single in their 40s, 50s, even 60s, they've returned to the dating world carrying decades of repressed desire. They swipe, they chat, they dress up, and go out, hoping for something—but unsure what that "something" really is. They talk about finding companionship or a decent man, but the truth—the unspoken, burning truth—is that they need a good fuck. They don't even realize it until it happens. Until someone touches them with intention, looks at them with hunger, makes them feel like a woman again.

Most of these women are sexually underfed, whether or not they acknowledge it. They've had sex, sure—sometimes a lot of it. But it's been years, maybe decades, since they've had the kind of experience that leaves them trembling, breathless, and genuinely satisfied. I know this because they tell me. Quietly. Sometimes after the first night. Sometimes, weeks later, when they've processed what they felt. I've lost count of the number of women who've whispered to me that they never really understood their own bodies until we were together. And I don't say that to brag. I say it because it speaks to something much deeper than performance.

This is about presence. About a man knowing how to be in the moment, how to read a woman's body like it's speaking a secret language—and responding accordingly. Most men never learn this. Especially not the ones who spent years in a marriage where sex became predictable, perfunctory, or infrequent. They stop exploring. They stop asking. And eventually, they stop caring.

Meanwhile, their wives carry on, quietly resigning themselves to mediocrity. Some learn to fake it. Others just go numb. But the result is always the same: a lifetime of going through the motions without ever being truly awakened. And that becomes their normal.

Then, someone like me shows up. Someone who doesn't treat her body like a checklist, but like a canvas. Someone who listens—not just with his ears, but with his hands, his breath, his eyes. And for the first time in years, maybe ever, she feels seen. Desired. Taken.

I'm not a sex therapist. I'm not here to fix anyone. But if there's chemistry, if that electric current flows between us, I lean in. And more often than not, it leads to something transformative. For her. And sometimes, for me, too.

I've had women tell me that they didn't know they could feel that way. One woman in her late 40s told me—tears in her eyes—that she'd never had an orgasm during sex. Not once. Her ex-husband never asked, never explored, never tried. Another woman, who'd been divorced for three years, said she felt like her body had been in hibernation until I touched her. These aren't isolated stories. This is the silent epidemic of sexual dissatisfaction that no one talks about.

And the saddest part? They don't even know what they're missing until someone shows them. That's why they keep dating. That's why they stay on the apps. They're not just looking for company. They're looking for *themselves*—for the version of them that's still vibrant, sensual, alive.

But here's where it gets complicated. Because even when they find it—even when they wake up to the pleasure they didn't know they were capable of—most don't stay. They take the experience, thank you for it in their own way, and move on. Sometimes it's confusion. Sometimes fear. Sometimes a sense that they don't quite deserve it yet.

And me? I'm still here. Still dating. Still showing up. Still waiting to meet the woman who's not just looking for a taste of something better—but one who's actually ready for the full course.

That's the paradox of being a man who understands women better than most. I know how to unlock them. But very few are ready to stay open.

I keep hoping one will.

THE ART OF SEDUCTION

I used to believe that being a "nice guy" was the key to a woman's heart. I thought that kindness, patience, and consideration were enough—that if I showed up consistently, listened attentively, and treated her well, she would see my value and choose me. I operated under the illusion that love was a reward for good behavior. That if I just proved I was reliable, respectful, and emotionally available, she'd see me as the one.

But that fantasy shattered over time. Because no matter how thoughtful I was, no matter how much effort I put in, it never worked the way I wanted it to. I watched time and again as women gravitated toward men who seemed, frankly, unworthy. Men who were emotionally unavailable, selfish, and sometimes downright cruel. These weren't rich or particularly attractive guys. They weren't geniuses or gentlemen. But they had something I didn't yet understand: *pull*.

So I asked myself, what's really going on here? What do these men have that I don't? That question sent me down a path of discovery. I started reading books, watching videos, listening to psychologists, and dating coaches. I studied male-female dynamics, pickup artistry, evolutionary biology, and interpersonal psychology. Some of it was nonsense. But buried beneath the surface-level tactics was a truth that changed everything: *I am the catch.*

That realization flipped the switch.

I stopped chasing. I stopped trying to be chosen. I stopped contorting myself into what I thought women wanted. I started showing up as myself—authentic, confident, grounded in my own worth. And that's when everything shifted.

Women don't respond to logic. They respond to energy. To emotion. To presence. The men who stir something *in* them are the ones they choose, not the ones who quietly wait on the sidelines. Attraction isn't built on checklists; it's sparked by feeling.

And the truth is, women don't fall for résumés. They fall for men who make them feel something—curiosity, excitement, tension. They fall for a man who can hold a moment, who looks at them like he sees something rare, who creates an atmosphere that invites them to surrender…just a little. It has nothing to do with what you say and everything to do with how you *say* it—your tone, your timing, your body language, your eye contact.

Seduction is not about deception. It's about presence. It's the art of inviting someone into an emotional experience and letting them lose themselves in it. It's knowing how to hold her gaze just a beat longer than expected. It's brushing her hand at the right moment, letting silence stretch just enough to heighten the anticipation. It's speaking in a voice that's calm, measured, slightly teasing. It's creating space for the possibility of pleasure without forcing it.

Once I understood that, my whole approach to women changed. I became more direct—not aggressive, but deliberate. I stopped waiting for signals. If I was interested, I said so. I didn't play games or make excuses. I simply let my intention be known, and I did it in a way that made her feel desired, not pressured.

That subtle but crucial shift changed everything. Women responded. Because at the end of the day, every woman wants to feel wanted. Not just admired, but claimed. Not in a possessive way—but in a way that says, *I see you, I want you, and I'm not afraid to show it.*

Now, I don't chase. I don't beg. I don't audition. I walk into every interaction knowing that I bring value. If she sees it, great. If she doesn't, I move on. I never try to convince someone to want me. I show up as I am and see who responds.

And that confidence? That non-neediness? It's magnetic. Because nothing is more attractive than a man who is rooted in himself. A man who knows his worth and doesn't seek validation.

Some men think seduction is manipulation. It's not. It's alignment. It's stepping into your masculine energy and allowing her to step into her feminine. It's polarity. And when it's real, it doesn't need to be forced. It happens naturally.

The best part? Seduction doesn't end with the first kiss. It's a dance. A slow burn. A steady rhythm of curiosity and connection. It's making her laugh, making her wonder, making her think about you long after you've left the room. It's keeping the tension alive—not with tricks, but with presence.

And once you understand that, the entire dating game changes. Because you're no longer trying to "win" anyone. You're simply allowing attraction to unfold. And you trust that the right women will feel it.

So yes, I used to be a nice guy. And there's nothing wrong with being kind, generous, and respectful. But those things alone won't make her want you. You have to make her *feel*. And when you master that art, the whole world opens up.

THE POWER OF THE MOMENT

When a woman agrees to get in my car after a date, it's not just transportation—it's transition. From surface to depth. From pretense to presence. It marks a silent understanding that something more is about to unfold. Most women don't realize it at the time, but by the moment they cross that threshold and hear the car door click shut behind them, a shift has already occurred. They've left behind the rules of modern dating, the stiff conventions of the dinner table and stepped into a space where intimacy doesn't wait for permission—it reveals itself with intention.

I have a saying: when she gets in my car, she's already mine. She may not know it yet. She may still be playing coy or weighing her options. But I know the moment is coming, and I know how to guide her there. It's not about dominance in the crude, performative sense. It's about leadership. About creating a frame so secure, so compelling, that she naturally softens into it. And in that frame, she feels safe enough to explore the side of herself that rarely sees daylight.

The car is a sacred space. It's where walls come down. It's confined, quiet, and loaded with possibility. There's something primal about being alone together in the dark, with the engine idling and the streetlights glowing dimly through the windshield. It strips away social posturing and brings you back to instinct. Most women have spent their entire lives burying that instinct under layers of expectations and caution. In that car, with me, those layers start to peel away.

The anticipation doesn't come from pressure—it comes from possibility. A slow shift in energy. A lingering glance. The silence stretches just long enough to charge the air. A hand on the thigh that doesn't grope but anchors. A voice in her ear that doesn't demand but declares. That's when it happens. That's when the hesitation disappears, and the permission is given—not with words, but with breath, with body language, with the surrender in her posture.

That's the power of the moment. Not the act itself, but everything leading up to it. The pacing. The subtle cues. The build-up. It's not about rushing. It's about letting her feel the gravity of what's about to happen. And when she does, she leans into it. Eagerly. Desperately. Not because she's been seduced by trickery, but because she's been given a rare gift: the chance to let go without shame.

And make no mistake—most women have never truly let go. They've performed. They've complied. They've tried to be what their partners wanted. But very few have experienced the raw, unfiltered pleasure of being desired without reservation. Of being taken without judgment. Of being seen—not just as a partner, but as a deeply sensual being whose pleasure matters.

There's no script for what unfolds next. Sometimes, it's frantic, rushed, full of heat. Other times, it's slow, languid, dripping with anticipation. But it's always mutual. Always electric. Always laced with a sense that something real is happening. That, for once, she doesn't have to think. She can just feel.

And no, I've never been caught. Maybe I'm lucky. Maybe I'm just that discreet. But part of me thinks that the world quietly makes space for this kind of intimacy. That it respects the sacredness of it—even when it happens in the most unexpected places. The backseat. The passenger side. A quiet cul-de-sac. It becomes a stage for something timeless. Something elemental.

But what keeps me coming back to these moments isn't the thrill of conquest. It's the transformation. The shift I see in her face, in her breathing, in the way she clings to me when it's over. It's not about getting laid. It's about witnessing a woman come alive. Seeing the tightness in her shoulders melt. Watching the guarded look in her eyes turn to softness. That's the reward.

So when I say she's mine, I don't mean possession. I mean connection. For that moment, in that space, she is fully present with me. No past. No future. Just two people locked in the most primal of dances. And when it's done, whether she stays or disappears into the fog of modern dating, we both know something happened. Something rare. Something neither of us will forget.

The Power of Pleasure

Pleasure is the most underrated force in the universe. We chase money, power, status—but at the root of it all, we are pleasure-seeking creatures. And nowhere is that more apparent than in the quiet, urgent moment when a woman finally lets herself feel.

The kind of pleasure I'm talking about isn't about friction or frequency. It's about depth. It's about taking a woman somewhere she's never been before—not just physically but emotionally, mentally, spiritually. It's about unlocking something inside her that she didn't even know was there. And once she tastes that level of surrender, of safety, of stimulation—she can never go back to anything less.

That's the real high for me. Not the act itself, but the aftermath. The trembling. The gasps. The look of disbelief on her face. The whispered, "I didn't know I could feel like that." That's the moment I live for. That's when I know I've done more than fuck—I've *freed* her.

Pleasure starts long before the clothes come off. It starts with attention. With tone. With the way I say her name. The way I take her chin in my hand, tilt her head toward me, and kiss her slowly—like I have all the time in the world. It's in the teasing. The near-misses. The brush of fingers down her spine. The words I whisper in her ear. "You're mine tonight. I'm going to take my time." That's when she exhales. That's when she lets go.

I've had women tell me, "No one's ever kissed me like that." Not because I have magic lips, but because I'm *there*. Fully. Present. Focused. Most men are distracted, performance-driven, too eager. I'm not. I'm in no rush. I let her rise to the edge and stay there. I want her begging. I want her so hungry for release that when it comes, it floods her like a dam breaking.

I remember one woman, 47 years old, divorced, three kids, successful in business, composed and polished. She told me she had never had a proper orgasm in her life. I was stunned. Not even once? She swore up and down. Never solo. Never with her ex-husband. Never with any partner. So I took it as a challenge. Through fingers, tongue, timing, and complete, unwavering attention, I brought her to the edge again and again until she shattered in my arms.

Her body convulsed. She cried. She held me like I had just saved her from drowning. And in a way, maybe I had. I had introduced her to herself—her *real* self. The version that lives underneath the armor, the achievements, the roles she plays. I gave her access to something that had always been inside her but had never been claimed.

That's the power of pleasure. It's not just orgasm. It's revelation. It's awakening. It's healing.

And yes, sometimes the pleasure is purely physical. Sometimes it's dirty, raw, explosive. But even then, it's not meaningless. Because in that moment, she knows I want her—not just her body, but *her*. All of her. And that kind of desire? It heals. It affirms. It elevates.

Most women don't even know how much they crave this until they experience it—until someone finally treats their pleasure not as a goal but as a gift—a process—a language.

And once they do? They never forget it. Even if they leave. Even if it was one night. That moment stays with them. Etched in their memory like a secret. A benchmark. A reminder of what's possible.

And for me? That's more than enough.

THE SUBTLE ART OF LOWERING INHIBITIONS

Alcohol has always had a reputation—sometimes feared, sometimes worshipped—as a catalyst for transformation. And in the world of seduction, it plays a unique role. It's not about clouding judgment or distorting reality. Not when used responsibly. For me, it's about softening the sharp edges of the day, quieting the internal monologue, and allowing both parties to slip into the ease of presence. Just one or two drinks, no more, are enough to shift the atmosphere from cautious to curious, from structured to sensual. I've always maintained a strict boundary—I don't want a woman who's too drunk. Sloppy, incoherent, numb? That's not seduction. That's negligence. I want her lucid, aware, and fully embracing the experience—not just passively along for the ride.

The magic happens in that narrow window—after the first sip, but before the inhibitions fall too far. It's where eye contact lingers, where laughter spills more freely, where the body begins to open before the mind catches up. I have a simple line I use when we first sit down: "This place is loud, and my hearing's not what it used to be—mind if we sit next to each other?" It's practical, innocent, even considerate. But it does more than move her closer. It signals something else: that I'm comfortable taking the lead. That I want proximity. That I plan to engage not from across the table but side by side. And that changes everything.

Once we're seated together, the energy shifts. The wall of formality crumbles. What began as polite conversation over menus becomes a dance of body language—her shoulder brushing mine, her knee resting against my thigh, the warm weight of her hand lingering a beat longer when I pass her a glass. I touch her gently, deliberately, like a question without a question mark. And when she doesn't pull away, that's her answer. We've crossed the first threshold.

Every move is subtle, but nothing is accidental. As the night unfolds, her posture softens, her laugh deepens, and her eyes stay locked on mine longer than they need to. She's relaxing into it—not just the drink, but the feeling. The dynamic. The tension I've built not through pressure but through calibrated, intentional presence. By the time the entrees are cleared, we're no longer strangers at a table. We're two people sharing a story, writing new lines in real time with every glance, every touch, every playful tease.

Here's what most men get wrong: they think seduction is about escalation. It's not. It's about atmosphere. If you do it right, the desire builds itself. You don't have to force anything. You just have to allow the space for it to bloom. And that's where alcohol, used sparingly and thoughtfully, can help. It's not about getting her to say yes. It's about helping her want to.

But let's be clear—I'm not taking every woman to bed. That's not the goal. In fact, I'd say, more often than not, I don't. And I'm okay with that. Because for me, the win isn't in the act. It's in the awareness that, if I wanted to, I probably could. That sense of mutual recognition—that heat behind the eyes, that electric charge across the table—that's often more intoxicating than the physical act itself.

When I do choose to go further, it's never about convincing. It's about confirming. Confirming that the moment is right. That the energy is aligned. That she's not just open but eager. That she wants this as much as I do—maybe more. And when that happens, it doesn't feel like conquest. It feels like gravity. Like inevitability. Like the moment was always coming, and we're just finally catching up to it.

Seduction is not about taking. It's about leading. Creating a space where she feels safe enough to want, to explore, to surrender. Where she doesn't feel pressured but instead feels powerful—because she's choosing this. Choosing me. Choosing the moment.

16

And yes, sometimes that moment begins with a drink. But what it really begins with is trust.

The Illusion of Choice

Ask a woman what she's looking for in a man, and she'll give you a polished list of desirable qualities: tall, handsome, confident, successful, kind, maybe even funny. And she's not lying—not consciously, anyway. But if you observe her actual choices, if you trace her dating history, you'll find a disconnect between her stated preferences and her lived behavior. Why? Because women don't choose based on logic. They choose based on emotion.

Seduction begins with understanding that truth. Attraction doesn't come from checking off boxes. It comes from energy. From the way a woman feels in your presence. That's why the bad boy, the rogue, or the mysterious stranger gets more attention than the reliable, predictable, nice guy. Not because he's better on paper, but because he makes her feel something.

It's not her fault. It's biology. Women are wired to respond to emotional stimuli. They want to be excited. To be uncertain. To be curious. They want to feel a flutter in their chest, a pull in their gut. And that's not created by your job title or your credit score. It's created by your presence. Your command. Your subtle tension between restraint and pursuit.

Here's the paradox: every woman wants to be seduced, but she also wants to believe that she's the one doing the seducing. That she's choosing, not following. That she's in control—even as she surrenders. And the art of seduction lies in giving her that illusion. Not to deceive her, but to protect her. To make her feel safe enough to open, to trust, to explore.

When I guide a woman into desire, I'm not forcing her hand. I'm leading her into her own hunger. Into the part of her that's been starved for sensation, for danger, for depth. And I let her feel like she discovered it all on her own. That's not manipulation. That's mastery.

That's how you meet her where she is—and then take her somewhere she didn't know she wanted to go.

Because the truth is, she's already made up her mind. Within thirty seconds of meeting you, a woman knows whether or not she'll sleep with you. Everything else is just a dance—a performance, a ritual, a slow stripping away of social expectations until nothing's left but instinct.

I've studied that dance. I've memorized the steps. And I don't rush them. I enjoy them. The tease. The mystery. The power of a shared glance that lingers too long. The moment she leans in when she doesn't have to. The subtle shift when her voice lowers, her breath quickens, her resistance becomes curiosity.

That's when I know she's ready. Not because she says so, but because her body does. Her eyes say it. Her posture says it. Her silence says it. And I don't need words to translate any of it. Because when a woman is in that state, she doesn't want logic. She wants leadership.

So, I give her both the illusion of choice and the certainty of direction. I let her feel like she's discovering me, even as I'm orchestrating the entire experience. And she loves it. Because deep down, every woman wants to surrender. Not to a man who demands it, but to one who's earned it. Who's strong enough to guide her and sensitive enough to make her feel like it was all her idea.

And that's the secret. That's how seduction becomes seamless. Not a trick. Not a tactic. But a shared experience built on emotional honesty and primal instinct.

Because in the end, seduction isn't about control—it's about connection. And the man who understands that never needs to beg, never needs to chase. He simply offers the experience.

And she, inevitably, takes it.

THE POWER OF DANCE

Dance didn't just change the way I move—it changed the way I live. I didn't start taking lessons because I thought it would be a good way to meet women or because I wanted to use it as a slick seduction technique. I did it for me. I did it because I was tired of being locked inside my own mind, tired of the social anxiety that gripped me like a chokehold every time I walked into a room full of strangers. I needed to break free of that internal paralysis, and something about dance felt like the right place to start.

In the beginning, I was stiff. Self-conscious. I needed two or three drinks just to convince myself to get out on the floor, and even then, I moved like I had weights strapped to my limbs. Every step felt scrutinized. Every turn felt clumsy. I was hyper-aware of everything and everyone. But I kept showing up. Week after week, class after class, I let the rhythm sink into my body. Slowly, the music began to drown out the noise in my head. The beat became louder than the inner critic. And one night, without thinking, I danced without fear. No drinks. No hesitation. Just motion, presence, and ease.

That night marked a turning point. It wasn't just that I had learned to dance—it was that I had stopped giving a damn about what other people thought. For the first time, I was truly comfortable in my own skin. That confidence seeped into other areas of my life. Conversations flowed more easily. Eye contact held longer. I carried myself differently—not because I had something to prove, but because I no longer felt like I had anything to hide. I had unlocked a part of myself I didn't even know was buried.

And then, something else became clear. Women love to dance. Almost universally. It doesn't matter if they're any good. What matters is that they're willing—willing to move, to be led, to surrender to the music and to the man guiding them. That willingness reveals a lot. It shows openness. Femininity. A desire to connect. I began to realize that dance wasn't just a hobby or a skill—it was a gateway. A portal to deeper understanding, intimacy, and magnetism.

When a woman steps into your arms on the dance floor, something primal happens. You feel her heartbeat align with yours. You guide her steps, and she follows—not out of obligation, but because she wants to. That moment, that shared rhythm, is a microcosm of a relationship. It's a dance of trust, leadership, and surrender. If she can't follow you on the floor, what makes you think she'll follow you anywhere else? For me, dance became a filter. If we couldn't find flow together in motion, chances were we'd struggle in every other aspect of connection.

And here's the kicker: most men can't dance. Or more accurately, most men won't even try. They're too afraid of looking foolish, of losing control, of not knowing what to do. So they stand off to the side, nursing drinks, scanning the room, hoping to impress someone from a distance. But while they're waiting, I'm already on the floor, guiding her through turns, twirls, dips, and close embraces. While they're watching, I'm touching. Leading. Engaging. That difference is everything.

I don't even have to speak. The moment my hand touches the small of her back and we fall into sync, the seduction begins. Not through words, but through motion. Through presence. Through the unspoken promise of, "I've got you." That's the kind of message women don't hear often enough. And when they do, their bodies respond before their minds even have time to catch up. They smile differently. They hold on tighter. They look at you like you just gave them permission to feel something they didn't even know they missed.

Dance is, at its core, embodied communication. It's where leadership and sensitivity coexist. If you're too forceful, she resists. If you're too hesitant, she flounders. But if you lead with clarity and stay attuned to her responses, she flows with you. She melts into you. She trusts you. And that trust, once earned, carries into everything else.

I've had nights where I didn't exchange more than a few sentences with a woman, yet the chemistry was undeniable. All it took was a few songs. A few moments of perfect alignment. When the music ended, she looked at me like we had just shared something sacred. And in a way, we had. Because in those three-minute bursts, we weren't strangers anymore. We were collaborators in a kind of erotic ritual that most people never even get to experience.

But make no mistake—dance isn't just about seduction. It's about healing. It's about finding your own rhythm and inviting someone else into it. It's about rediscovering your body as something expressive, powerful, and magnetic. Most men live in their heads. Dance brings you back into your body. And when you inhabit your body fully, women notice. They can feel it. And they're drawn to it.

There's something profoundly masculine about being able to lead well. To take a woman's hand, guide her to the floor, and give her an experience she'll never forget—not because you dazzled her with footwork, but because you made her feel seen, supported, and safe. That's the essence of attraction. That's what women crave. And that's why dance is such a potent, overlooked superpower.

You don't have to be a professional. You don't need choreography or a decade of training. You just need rhythm, presence, and the courage to step forward and say, "Trust me." Because when you do, and she does, the rest takes care of itself.

The truth is, I don't dance to pick up women. But women do get picked up. Not because I try—but because I'm present, I'm playful, and I'm confident in a way that most men aren't. That combination is irresistible. It transcends words. It bypasses logic. It goes straight to the gut. And once you understand that, once you feel the power of leading a woman through a dance that leaves her breathless, you'll never go back to the sidelines.

So yes, dance changed my life. And if you're smart enough, brave enough, and open enough to embrace it, it'll change yours too.

AMERICAN WOMEN VS.
THE REST OF THE WORLD

Over the years, I've dated women from all over the globe—Spanish, Brazilian, Russian, Thai, American—and I can tell you that cultural context matters more than people want to admit. While no woman fits neatly into a box, and exceptions exist in every country, patterns absolutely emerge. Culture shapes attitude. Attitude shapes behavior. And behavior is everything in relationships.

Let's begin with American women. For many of them, particularly those raised in urban, educated environments, femininity has become an optional accessory rather than an identity. I'm not just talking about physical appearance or style—though even that has shifted dramatically—but about energy. The rise of women's liberation, the explosion of higher education, and increased financial independence have fundamentally changed the way many American women view men. And not always for the better.

In today's America, it's not uncommon for a woman to earn more than her male counterpart, to hold more degrees, and to be far more entrenched in ambition and achievement. On paper, that's progress. But in relationships, especially romantic ones, it has introduced a new tension. Too often, this power shift translates into disdain—especially toward middle- or working-class men. If a man doesn't measure up on every axis of success, he's considered disposable. Invisible. Irrelevant.

The problem is simple: as women's standards continue to rise, the pool of men who meet those standards shrinks. And instead of adjusting expectations, many women double down. They swipe past perfectly decent men who are hardworking, loyal, and grounded because those men don't "excite" them. They mistake masculinity for toxicity. They confuse submission with weakness. And they convince themselves that any dynamic where the man leads must be oppressive. It's no wonder so many of them are single, frustrated, and bitter.

Hence the birth of the so-called "passport bros." These are men—smart men—who've decided to opt out of the American dating game. They're not angry. They're not misogynists. They're just tired of the combative energy, the endless tests, the rejection of traditional roles. So, they go abroad. Or they date foreign-born women right here in the States. And having done both myself, I can't blame them.

When I dated Spanish women, the difference was immediately noticeable. They were more sensual, more open, and less burdened by social dogma. There was a natural rhythm to the interaction—a mutual enjoyment that didn't feel like a negotiation. Brazilian women? Even more so. There's a playful femininity in Brazilian culture that's practically extinct in the U.S. These women understand the power of softness. They take pride in pampering their men, not because they're subservient, but because it brings them joy to make their man feel good.

But there's a trade-off. These women often expect to be taken care of in return. And I don't mean just emotionally. I mean financially. The dynamic is clear: she'll make you feel like a king, but she expects to be treated like a queen. And honestly? That's fair—so long as both sides understand the agreement. With Brazilian women, you get warmth, beauty, and attention—but it comes with a price tag.

Russian women? They take this dynamic to another level entirely. Stunning. Seductive. Alluring. But always calculating. With them, everything is a transaction cloaked in romance. They'll charm you, thrill you, and leave you spinning. But make no mistake—they're playing the long game. They're looking for security, for status, and for the lifestyle they believe they deserve. And if you're not paying attention, you'll fall right into it.

In contrast, other Eastern European women—Ukrainian, Polish, Czech—seem less hardened, less strategic. Still traditional, still feminine, but not quite as transactional. There's a sincerity to their affection that feels more grounded. More rooted in connection than in commerce. It's a welcome shift when you've been dealing with the high-stakes poker faces of Moscow and St. Petersburg.

And then there's Thailand.

I've spent time there, and it's unlike anything else. Thai women are, without question, transactional. They know why you're there. You know why they're there. And yet, it doesn't feel seedy. Because Thai women don't just take—they give. They serve, nurture, care. They'll bring you meals, massage your feet, laugh at your jokes, and treat you like royalty. And while the unspoken agreement is clear—money for companionship—it's wrapped in a level of genuine warmth that makes it feel less like a transaction and more like a partnership.

For many men, that's a deal worth making. Not because they can't get women at home. But because in Thailand, the rules are clearer. The expectations are aligned. And the reward is immediate. You feel appreciated, admired, even adored. That feeling is addictive.

Now, I'm not saying all American women are damaged. That would be unfair. There are still some traditional, feminine, nurturing women here. Women who take care of themselves, who want to support their man, who understand and value polarity. But they're few and far between. Needles in a haystack of empowerment jargon and Instagram platitudes.

I remember being at a bar one night, chatting with two Jewish women (like me)—smart, attractive, mid-40s. I casually mentioned my recent trip to Thailand. Their faces changed instantly. They got defensive. One made a snide remark about sex tourism. The other rolled her eyes and muttered something about "mail-order brides." I just smiled.

I told them, "A Thai woman's greatest pleasure is giving pleasure to her man. And by that, I don't just mean sexually. I mean emotionally. She finds fulfillment in making him happy. What's so wrong with that?"

They got angry. Visibly upset. But beneath the hostility, I saw something else—curiosity. Interest. Maybe even arousal. Because when you challenge someone's worldview with confidence and clarity, you stir something deep. And even when they push back, a part of them wants what you're describing. A part of them craves the dynamic they've been taught to reject.

That's the irony. The same women who preach independence and equality are often the ones most drawn to masculine leadership. They say they want partnership, but what they really want is polarity. They want to feel safe enough to let go. To soften. To be led. But pride, ideology, and social conditioning keep them locked in combat with their own desires.

So when I say I prefer foreign women, it's not about exoticism or fetish. It's about energy. Femininity. Reciprocity. I want a woman who makes me feel like a man—not because I dominate her, but because she appreciates me. Honors me. Supports me. And in return, I do the same.

That's the essence of a good relationship. Mutual admiration. Mutual service. Mutual satisfaction. And if I have to go halfway around the world to find it, so be it.

THE TIMELESS NATURE OF ATTRACTION:
WHY FEELINGS TRUMP LOGIC EVERY TIME

More than thirty years ago, my mother—a strong, intelligent, no-nonsense woman—fell deeply for a man who, by almost every rational standard, was entirely unworthy of her. He was charming, certainly. Physically attractive, yes. Tall, fit, with a crown of white hair that gave him the nickname "the Jewish Cary Grant." But beyond those superficial charms, the man was inconsiderate, unreliable, and absolutely not what you'd call dependable. Still, none of that seemed to matter. My mother, a woman who prided herself on her discernment and shrewd judgment, couldn't resist him. And when my siblings and I questioned her about it, all she would say—slightly embarrassed—was, "He makes me laugh."

That was it. That was the entire explanation for why she kept seeing a man who didn't show up when he said he would and didn't treat her with the kind of care she deserved. He made her laugh. And while it seemed absurd at the time, it taught me one of the most important lessons about attraction I've ever learned: when it comes to desire, emotion always beats logic.

Women, regardless of how educated, accomplished, or independent they may be, don't choose men with a spreadsheet. They don't weigh pros and cons in some rational formula and select the "best man." Attraction doesn't work like that. Women are wired to respond to how a man makes them *feel*—not how he looks on paper. You can be successful, respectful, dependable, and loyal and still be passed over for the guy who's fun, unpredictable, and emotionally engaging. Because the truth, whether men want to hear it or not, is that women chase the feeling, not the résumé.

This wasn't some new revelation that came with modern feminism or social media. My mother was born in 1925. She was raised in an era when women were taught that their primary roles were wife, mother, and homemaker. Her generation valued stability and security. Yet even she couldn't help falling for a man who sparked something emotional in her, even if he lacked every other quality she logically should have required. That's the universality of this truth: generations may change, but the nature of attraction stays the same.

Men have a hard time accepting this because we process decisions differently. We look for stability. We evaluate whether a woman is kind, loyal, attractive, nurturing, capable. Our assessments are practical, often logical. But women? Women don't ask, "Does he check the right boxes?" They ask, "How does he make me feel?" And if the answer is thrilling—even if it's volatile, risky, or borderline reckless—then she's in.

This emotional priority explains why women often fall for men who are chaotic, unavailable, or unreliable. It explains why the "bad boy" archetype has never gone out of style. It's not that women *want* to be mistreated. It's that they crave excitement, unpredictability, a sense of adventure. They want to feel alive, not bored. And if the price of feeling alive is a little inconsistency, many will gladly pay it—at least for a while.

Men who lead stable lives often find themselves frustrated. They think, "I have a great job, I'm polite, I treat her well—why won't she choose me?" The answer lies in emotional chemistry. If you're not making her *feel* something intense, she will not stay interested—no matter how many boxes you check. You're offering safety, but not spark. Reliability, but not electricity.

This dynamic has only intensified in today's dating landscape. Back in my mother's day, women had fewer options. Financial dependence often forced them to settle for the stable man, even if he wasn't the most exciting. But now? Women don't need men for survival. They can pay their own bills, buy their own homes, raise children on their own. That means they no longer have to prioritize practicality. They can chase what *feels* right.

And they do. In droves.

This is why so many men feel lost. They've been told to be good providers, to be respectful, to listen, and to be patient. And when they do all that, they still lose to the guy who rolls up late, flirts with the waitress, and disappears for three days. Why? Because the latter triggers emotion. He's unpredictable. He's mysterious. He's frustrating—but exciting.

Of course, this isn't to say that all women are blind to long-term consequences. At some point, most will crave stability. But here's the catch: even then, they still want to *feel*. They don't want a safe man who bores them. They want a man who gives them both security and stimulation. And if you can't provide both? You won't last.

This is why emotional stimulation is the most underrated trait a man can cultivate. It's not about being a clown or a manipulator. It's about mastering the ability to create emotional impact—through humor, storytelling, unpredictability, confidence. If you can make a woman feel something she doesn't feel with anyone else, she'll keep coming back. That's the hook.

Take confidence, for example. Not arrogance—true confidence. The kind that says, "I know who I am, I know what I want, and I'm not afraid to walk away." That kind of energy is magnetic. It creates tension. It keeps her guessing. And guess what? The more she has to guess, the more invested she becomes.

Or consider humor. It's not just about making her laugh. It's about creating rapport, lowering defenses, and showing her that you don't take yourself—or her—too seriously. It's disarming. It builds intimacy. That's why my mother kept seeing a man who didn't deserve her. He made her laugh. He gave her emotional contrast. He pulled her out of her own seriousness and into play.

Men who understand this don't compete on looks or status. They compete on *vibe*. On connection. They walk into a room and immediately create curiosity. Who is this guy? Why does he seem so at ease? Why do I want to know more? That's the emotional reaction women chase.

So what can men do today to adapt?

First, stop thinking that your accomplishments are enough. They aren't. No one gets laid for having a 401(k). Learn to cultivate presence. Learn to speak in a way that draws people in. Learn to listen— not passively, but with intention. Most importantly, learn to make her feel.

Second, embrace unpredictability. Not in a flaky or cruel way, but in a playful, engaging way. Don't always be available. Don't always respond instantly. Let her wonder a little. Let her reach out first. Let her feel the tension of anticipation. It's in that space—between certainty and doubt—that attraction thrives.

Third, own your flaws. Stop trying to be perfect. Perfection is sterile. It's boring. Show your edges. Be real. Women want a man who's *human*, not a checklist. They want someone who can lead, but also laugh at himself. Someone who's strong, but also emotionally accessible.

And finally, don't beg to be chosen. Be the chooser. Know your worth. Move through the world like a man who has options—because when you do, women will sense it. They'll feel your energy before you speak. They'll be drawn to it without knowing why.

Looking back, I see my mother's behavior for what it was: completely normal. Completely human. She wasn't weak. She wasn't naive. She was simply responding to what all women respond to—emotion, tension, and presence. And the man who gave her those things, despite all his shortcomings, held her attention.

That's the timeless truth every man must understand: people don't change. Not at the core. Styles change. Roles evolve. Technologies advance. But when it comes to attraction? We are the same creatures we've always been. Emotional. Reactive. Deeply driven by how someone makes us feel.

So, if you want to win in the modern dating world, forget the formulas. Forget the list of what women say they want. Watch what they do. Study their behavior. Learn what excites them. And most importantly, learn how to create the emotional experience they can't forget.

Because, in the end, logic never stood a chance.

HOLDING THE KEYS: WHAT MEN NEED TO UNDERSTAND ABOUT DATING

Let me set the record straight: this isn't a dating strategy manual. I'm not here to hand out tactical tips or turn you into a pickup artist. There are already more than enough so-called experts with YouTube channels and Instagram reels promising to teach you the "ten secrets to get her hooked." That's not my lane. What I want men to understand is something much deeper—something foundational. You hold the keys. You, not her. Especially as women age and the dynamics of the dating world begin to shift dramatically.

The truth is, many women, particularly those who married young and banked on lifelong love, find themselves suddenly single later in life. They've been cast aside, replaced by younger models, and thrust back into a dating scene they don't understand. For many of them, it's their first time dating in decades, and it shows. They're disoriented, unsure of the rules, unsure of themselves. But, despite that, many of them carry an outdated belief: that they still hold all the power. And that's where men need to wake up.

Most guys, especially those who got married early and then divorced later in life, enter the dating pool with a mix of confusion and desperation. They were never particularly successful with women to begin with, and now they're older, maybe a little out of shape, maybe financially depleted from the divorce. They want connection. They crave intimacy. But they don't know how to play the game. So they fall into the same traps, make the same mistakes, and end up being used, discarded, or friend-zoned.

That's why this chapter exists. Not to give you game, but to remind you that you have value—more value than you probably realize. As men age, we become more distinguished. Our careers peak. Our emotional intelligence improves. If we've taken care of ourselves, we retain our physical appeal well into our 40s, 50s, and even beyond. Meanwhile, women's options narrow with age. Their sexual power diminishes, especially in a culture obsessed with youth. And while there are exceptions, the overall trend is undeniable.

But too many men still act like they're the ones chasing. Like they have to impress her. Like they're the lucky ones to be on the date. And that mindset will sabotage you every time. If you want to succeed, you need to act like the prize. Not in an arrogant way, but with quiet confidence. You need to walk into every interaction knowing you bring something valuable to the table—and that you get to choose who sits across from you.

Part of that process is learning what to avoid. Because not every woman is worth your time, your energy, or your attention. In fact, steering clear of the wrong ones will save you years of frustration, emotional damage, and financial pain. So let's get into some real talk. These are the women you need to avoid, no matter how attractive they might be on the surface.

First, there's the "What Do You Do?" woman. If one of her first three questions revolves around your job, your income, or where you live, consider that a red flag. She's not interested in you—she's interested in your resources. It's not curiosity; it's calculation. She's sizing you up like a spreadsheet, not a human being. And if you pass the test, it won't be because she likes you—it'll be because you can provide. Don't mistake gold-digging for interest. They often look very similar at the beginning.

Then we have the middle-aged woman who's never been married. Now, this isn't a hard and fast rule. There are always exceptions. But generally speaking, if she's in her 40s or 50s and has never had a long-term relationship, there's usually a reason. And that reason is often rooted in selfishness. She's spent decades putting herself first, doing what she wants, when she wants, how she wants. That's not inherently bad—until you try to build something with her. Because compromise?

Sacrifice? Shared goals? Those muscles are underdeveloped, if they exist at all.

Add to that the only child syndrome. Again, not universal, but patterns exist for a reason. Only children often grow up never having to share. Never having to negotiate. Never having to accommodate someone else. That kind of upbringing leaves a mark. It breeds entitlement. It fosters a mindset where their needs always come first. And unless they've done serious self-work, they'll drag that mindset into every relationship.

Next up: broke women. This one's delicate, because it's not about judging someone's financial status. But if a woman is constantly struggling, in debt, living paycheck to paycheck—or worse, living off others—proceed with caution. It's not just about money. It's about mindset. Financial instability often comes with emotional instability. And even if she's sweet, even if she's gorgeous, even if she makes you feel alive—you'll never really know if she's into *you* or into what you can do for her. If she's looking for a rescue mission, don't sign up to be her savior. You want a partner, not a dependent.

Now let's talk about appearance. I always make it a point to look sharp on a date. Pressed shirt. Clean shave. Nice shoes. Because presentation matters. And I expect the same in return. If a woman shows up looking like she just rolled out of bed—chipped nails, greasy hair, sweatpants and no effort—that's not casual. That's disrespect. It says, "You're not worth dressing up for." And if she doesn't care enough to put in effort for a first impression, it won't get better later. You deserve someone who sees the date as special. Who wants to impress you, too.

On the flip side, guys—we've got to clean it up, too. I can't tell you how many times I've seen men show up to dinner in shorts and flip-flops. Unless you're at a beachfront tiki bar, that's unacceptable. Women notice. And they judge. If you want to attract quality, you have to present quality. A crisp pair of jeans and a button-down shirt go a long way. Show her that you respect yourself—and that you respect her time.

Then there are the personality red flags. These are the women who might pass the initial screening but reveal their dysfunction quickly. Cat ladies who treat their pets better than people. Women with endless therapy talk and no healing. Narcissists who need constant validation. Borderline personalities who swing from love-bombing to rage in 48 hours. And of course, substance abusers who think a date isn't complete without five drinks or a joint in the car. These are not just red flags—they're sirens. Run.

Because at the end of the day, dating is about discernment. It's about realizing that you, as a man, have power. Too many men walk around like beggars, hoping a woman will choose them. But the truth is, you get to choose, too. You don't have to tolerate disrespect, drama, or dysfunction. You don't have to settle for someone who drains your energy instead of fueling it.

You're not a second-class citizen in the dating world. You're not past your prime. If you've taken care of yourself—mentally, physically, emotionally—you're just hitting your stride. And the women who are truly worth your time? They'll recognize that. They'll appreciate it. And they'll meet you with the same energy.

So hold your head high. Keep your standards. And remember this: you hold the keys. Not because you're better, but because you know your value. And that makes all the difference.

CONFIDENCE, STRENGTH, AND THE POWER TO WALK AWAY

There's a line I've come to live by, and it's something every man needs to internalize: in any relationship, the person who is willing to walk away at any moment holds all the power. It sounds harsh, maybe even a little manipulative, but it isn't. It's reality. And it's not about games—it's about boundaries. It's about knowing your worth and refusing to let anyone diminish it. I learned this the hard way, through painful experiences that chipped away at my confidence until I had no choice but to rebuild it from the ground up.

There must be a limit to how much disrespect you're willing to tolerate. If you don't draw that line, no one else will. This isn't about being combative or difficult—it's about preserving your dignity. When someone treats you poorly, when they put you down, belittle your efforts, or make you feel small, you owe it to yourself to walk away. And not just walk—walk tall. Too many men stay in relationships out of fear. Fear of being alone. Fear of starting over. Fear of not finding anyone else. But nothing is lonelier than sharing your life with someone who doesn't respect you.

Confidence doesn't come from validation. It doesn't come from external praise. It comes from knowing, deep down, that you are enough. That you have value, independent of anyone else's opinion. A confident man doesn't need to beg, prove, or explain himself. He simply *is*. And ironically, that's exactly what makes him so attractive. Women say they love confidence, and they're not lying—but what they're really responding to is the man who isn't afraid to leave. There's power in that. A subtle, unnerving power that keeps her guessing, keeps her invested.

Because the moment she knows you're in it, no matter what—no matter how she acts, how she treats you, how many lines she crosses—you've lost. That's when the dynamic shifts. That's when she starts testing you, disrespecting you, seeing how much she can get away with. It's not that she's evil. It's that you've removed the consequences. And when there are no consequences, bad behavior flourishes. You teach people how to treat you. And if you teach her that she can do whatever she wants and you'll still be there, guess what? She'll do whatever she wants.

But let's not confuse confidence with arrogance. Confidence isn't loud. It's not boastful. It's not about pretending you're something you're not. Real confidence is quiet. It's grounded. It comes from competence—from knowing you've built yourself into a man of strength, value, and integrity. It's the result of overcoming adversity, pushing through fear, and learning from failure. You can't fake that. But you *can* grow it. One decision at a time.

The best advice I ever heard? "To be confident, act confident." It's deceptively simple, but powerful. Confidence is a muscle. You don't develop it by waiting until you feel ready. You develop it by stepping up when you're scared, by speaking up when it's uncomfortable, by walking away when it hurts. Each time you choose yourself over validation, that muscle grows. And once you've got it? Guard it. Protect it. Because someone will try to take it from you. Someone will try to make you doubt yourself. Don't let them.

Confidence isn't just sexy—it's survival. It's what keeps you from sinking into relationships that drain you, from tolerating people who don't deserve you. It's what allows you to walk away with your head held high, knowing you didn't lose anything—you gained your freedom.

How to Deal with Gold Diggers

Let me be clear: I don't play games. I don't run manipulative scripts or play hard to get. But when it comes to gold diggers? I make an exception. Because one thing I cannot stand is being used. And if you've ever been on the receiving end of that—if you've ever opened your wallet or your heart only to be left empty-handed—you know exactly what I mean.

I used to think that being generous was the path to a woman's heart. That if I bought her things, made her life easier, showed her I could provide, she would love me for it. That belief got me walked on. And walked over. I remember the look in their eyes—not love, not gratitude, but calculation. I was useful, not special. And when the use ran out, so did they.

But here's what I eventually figured out: gold diggers aren't just greedy. They're *insecure*. A woman who truly values herself—who knows her worth and respects yours—doesn't need to manipulate. She builds. She partners. But a gold digger? She leverages the one asset she believes she has—her looks. She doesn't build. She extracts. And if you let her, she'll suck you dry.

They're smart, too. The good ones don't ask about your finances on the first date. They don't need to. They watch. They observe. They notice the car, the watch, the way you tip. They listen for clues. And if you're not careful, you'll give them all they need to formulate a plan. They won't ask for money—at first. They'll make you want to give it. That's the trap.

I remember one woman in particular. Russian. Twenty years younger. Absolutely stunning. Wild in bed, intelligent, charming. She played it perfectly. Never asked a single question about my finances. Never hinted at needing anything. But she was watching. She saw the house. The car. The lifestyle. And she knew exactly how to act. She gave me everything I thought I wanted—attention, affection, unforgettable sex. For a while, I was hooked.

But I have rules. One of them? I don't take any woman seriously until we've been seeing each other for at least three months. No commitments. No emotional investments. Just observation. And around the three-month mark, I started to notice something. She was trying too hard. Not in the sweet way—in the calculated way. She gave me the best sex of my life one night, then the next day, hit me with a sob story about needing to move and asked if I could help her out financially.

Done.

No fight. No explanation. Just blocked. Deleted. Gone.

I didn't owe her a conversation. Because she had already revealed her intentions. And once I know a woman is trying to use me, I don't just walk—I slam the door behind me. That's not cruelty. That's clarity. When someone reduces you to a dollar sign, you don't owe them empathy. You owe yourself freedom.

Too many men get sucked into the fantasy. They confuse attention for affection. They think amazing sex equals emotional connection. But real connection isn't transactional. If a woman is into you, she doesn't need your money. If she's asking for help early on, she's not looking for love—she's looking for a lifeline.

The smart gold diggers are dangerous because they don't look like gold diggers. They look like dream girls. They say the right things. Do the right things. And if you're not vigilant, you'll fall. That's why discipline matters. Emotional discipline. Sexual discipline. Financial discipline. Because once you cross that line—once you become her provider—you're no longer her partner. You're her ATM.

And here's the worst part: there's no coming back from that. You can't reclaim the dynamic. Once she sees you as the guy who will pay her bills, that's all you'll ever be. And even if she stays, it won't be because she loves you. It'll be because she's comfortable. And comfort, without respect, is death.

So here's the bottom line. Pay attention. Stay sharp. Know the signs. Don't get swept up by beauty or performance. Watch her behavior over time. And the moment she starts talking about her problems—especially financial ones—cut her loose. Not because you're cold, but because you're wise. You worked too hard for what you have to give it to someone who didn't earn it.

Be generous with a woman who builds with you. Who shows up for you. Who invests emotionally and doesn't ask for anything in return. But with anyone else? Hold the line. Walk away. And never apologize for doing so.

Approach Anxiety and The Modern Dating Landscape

There was a time in my life—before my first marriage, back when the world felt like it turned just for me—when I had absolutely no fear of approaching women. Bars, clubs, social events—it didn't matter. I'd walk up, make conversation, lay on the charm, and more often than not, things would go my way. Confidence wasn't just something I had—it was the air I breathed. I didn't second-guess myself, didn't hesitate, didn't flinch. And it worked. The game was alive, spontaneous, and fueled by energy.

But today? That version of me feels like someone else entirely. I'm not that guy anymore—not because I couldn't be, but because I don't want to be. The whole ritual of in-person cold approach—the rehearsed lines, the feigned interest, the mindless small talk—it bores me. The juice isn't worth the squeeze. There's no anxiety behind it, no fear of rejection, no crisis of confidence. It's just indifference. The return on investment is too low for the energy it demands.

That's why I've fully embraced dating sites and apps. Online dating, for all its flaws, offers something no bar or lounge ever could: efficiency. With a few swipes, a few messages, I can connect with multiple women at once, filter through options, and choose who I want to spend my time on. There's no need to play the peacock, no need to wait for the right song or perfect moment. It's direct. And in a world that's increasingly fast-paced and transactional, directness is a gift.

Now, don't get me wrong. I know online dating isn't perfect. It strips away the spontaneity. It reduces chemistry to pictures and punchlines. It's filled with ghosts, bots, and people who are more addicted to the attention than they are serious about meeting. But even knowing all that, I still prefer it. Because at least I know what I'm getting into.

The ambiguity of in-person flirtation—the cat-and-mouse, the mixed signals—that just doesn't do it for me anymore.

Rejection has never been my issue. I've been rejected more times than I can count, and I wear those rejections like badges. Each one taught me something. Thickened my skin. Shaped my approach. So when I say I don't bother with in-person cold approaches anymore, it's not out of fear—it's out of choice. I could walk into any bar, scan the room, and strike up a conversation with the most stunning woman there. I just don't care to.

There is, however, one exception to this rule: dance venues. For some reason, that setting still makes sense to me. There's no pretense. No pressure. It's just rhythm and movement. You don't need a clever line or flashy outfit. All you need is timing and a willingness to lead. Asking a woman to dance bypasses all the usual nonsense. It's a physical invitation, not a verbal one. And when it works, the chemistry is immediate.

That's why, in many ways, dancing remains my favorite form of in-person connection. It's honest. It's unfiltered. There's no hiding on the dance floor. If the rhythm is right and the connection is there, you feel it. And if it's not, you move on to the next song, the next partner, the next chance.

Maybe one day I'll dive back into the world of live, spontaneous flirtation. Maybe I'll walk into a bar for no other reason than to see if I still have it. But even if I don't, I'm not losing sleep over it. There's no hole in my life where pickup artistry used to be. I'm not suffering. I'm not lonely. I'm just choosing my battles. And the truth is, there are more effective ways to meet women than relying on luck and body language.

At the end of the day, every man has to find the approach that works for him. Some thrive on the hunt. They love the adrenaline, the improvisation, the thrill of the chase. Others, like me, have outgrown the game. We still play—we're just smarter about how and when. And if that means casting a wide net from behind a screen instead of wading through loud bars and forced banter, so be it. Because dating isn't about impressing the crowd. It's about connecting with the one who matters.

WOMEN AND THEIR PETS: A GROWING OBSESSION

Something strange has happened in modern dating—and it has four legs, fur, and usually shows up in the first photo of a woman's dating profile. I'm talking, of course, about pets. More specifically, the increasing tendency of women to lead with their animals. It's no longer unusual to scroll through a profile and find that the star of the show isn't the woman herself—it's her dog. Or cat. Or three cats. Sometimes, you don't even see the woman until the third or fourth photo. And by then, the message has already been sent.

Now, let me be clear: I love animals. Especially dogs. I've had them my whole life. They're loyal, affectionate, and often better company than most people. But there's a difference between loving animals and replacing human relationships with them. And that's exactly what I'm seeing more and more of—women who have poured so much emotional energy into their pets that they've left little, if any, room for a man.

The dog-in-the-profile-pic phenomenon isn't just a quirk. It's a signal. A red flag. It tells me that she's either been burned so badly she's chosen a creature who can't hurt her, or she's become so emotionally dependent on her pet that she sees it as her primary relationship. Either way, I'm swiping left. Because if your identity is so wrapped up in your animal that you lead with it instead of yourself, we're already incompatible.

There's a fine line between animal lover and emotional crutch. The former is healthy and admirable. The latter is concerning. When I see a woman who's clearly prioritized her pet over meaningful human connection, I have to ask myself: what kind of relationship is she really capable of? If your dog comes before everything, what role does a partner play in your life? Backup caretaker? Occasional plus-one? Emotional support human when the pet's asleep?

We all have wounds. We all carry baggage. But there's a difference between coping and avoidance. Too many women are using their pets to avoid vulnerability. They've traded the risk of heartbreak for the guaranteed affection of something that can't reject them. And while I understand the appeal, it's not something I'm signing up for.

When I date a woman, I want to feel like a priority. I want to know that I matter. That my presence is valued, not just tolerated between dog walks and vet appointments. I want to be seen as a partner, not a guest in a life that revolves around a golden retriever. And if I have to compete with a schnauzer for her attention, I'm out.

Call it old-fashioned, but I believe people should come first. My dog will never outrank my girlfriend or wife. Never. And I expect the same in return. If you're more emotionally invested in your Labrador than you are in building a relationship with a man, then why are you even on a dating site?

So here's the takeaway: if her profile opens with a pet, you better believe that pet will dominate the relationship dynamic. Dinner plans will revolve around feeding schedules. Vacations will be canceled over kennel anxiety. And heaven forbid you're not a "dog person"— you'll be treated like a monster. It's not worth it.

Swipe left. Move on. Let someone else play second fiddle to a Pomeranian. You deserve to be the main event.

Beware of Drinkers and Substance Abusers

If you spend enough time in South Florida—and I mean really spend time, not just visiting the beach or sipping cocktails on vacation—you'll begin to notice a darker undercurrent. Substance abuse is everywhere. You can't swing a yoga mat without hitting a rehab center. Recovery houses dot the landscape. Entire zip codes seem built around getting clean, staying clean, and—far too often—falling off the wagon again. Addiction here isn't an anomaly. It's a business model.

Now, before anyone jumps down my throat, let me make something clear. I have deep sympathy for people who are battling addiction. I've known people—good people—who've fought those demons. Friends, acquaintances, even family. And I've seen the toll it takes. The wreckage. The cycles. I hold no judgment for anyone genuinely trying to recover. But with that said, I am not in the rehab business. And I refuse to make someone else's problem my mission.

That's a hard line I've drawn, and I encourage other men to do the same. If you're in a relationship, it should lift you. Empower you. Complement your life. It should not become a full-time job of managing someone else's chaos. A partner is not a project. And if a woman's relationship with substances—alcohol, weed, pills, whatever—overshadows her relationship with you, then you are not her partner. You're her buffer. Her enabler. Her safety net. And eventually, her scapegoat.

I don't need perfection. I'm not some puritan expecting a woman to swear off margaritas or avoid weed like it's the plague. I'm fine with a couple of drinks on a night out. Getting buzzed now and then? No problem. Casual use of weed? Go for it. But when getting high or drunk becomes a recurring theme in her lifestyle—when it bleeds into her personality, her behavior, her choices—that's when I'm out. And you should be too.

You have to be vigilant. I pay attention from the very first date. I watch how much she drinks. I listen to how she talks about partying, her social life, her past. When I greet her with a kiss or a hug, I take a discreet breath. Can I smell the wine or the vodka before we've even sat down? Is there a whiff of weed clinging to her clothes or hair? These things matter. They don't tell you everything, but they tell you enough.

I'm not confrontational about it. I don't interrogate or lecture. But I will weave a few stories into the conversation—maybe something about a friend who couldn't stop drinking, or someone who always seemed to have a joint in hand. And then I wait. I watch how she responds. If she gets defensive or laughs it off a little too hard, I file that away. Because people reveal themselves when they don't think you're watching.

It's not about playing detective. It's about protecting your peace. Because if you get involved with someone who drinks too much or uses too often, you are signing up for a life of volatility. One minute you're in love, the next you're cleaning up emotional—or literal—vomit. One moment you're planning a weekend getaway, the next you're arguing because she's blacked out and didn't call you back. And then come the apologies. The promises. The excuses. Wash, rinse, repeat.

If you're a man who values your time, your energy, and your sanity, then you cannot afford to ignore these red flags. I don't care how beautiful she is. I don't care how good the sex is. I don't care how fun she is when she's "just a little tipsy." That fun turns to dysfunction faster than you can say "rehab intake."

Now, if you struggle with addiction yourself, that's a different story. Maybe you'll find someone who shares your journey. Maybe you can support each other. Maybe. But that's a whole different path. That's not the road I'm on, and it's not the one I'm writing for. I'm writing for the men who have their shit together, or at least are trying to. The men who understand that a woman should enhance your life, not hijack it.

You're not a therapist. You're not a 12-step sponsor. You're a man building a life. And that life deserves someone who can meet you on stable ground—not someone whose idea of Friday night is a blackout and a bar tab the size of your rent. So trust your gut. Listen to the signals. And above all, remember this: you're not here to save anyone. You're here to thrive.

FINDING WOMEN AT THE GYM OR WHOLE FOODS: MYTH OR REALITY?

Some dating advice sounds so logical, so crisp and convincing, that you almost feel dumb for not following it. One of the all-time favorites? "Go to the gym or Whole Foods. That's where the quality women are." It's practically gospel in certain circles. Fitness-conscious women at the gym, health-conscious women at Whole Foods. What could go wrong?

In theory, it makes perfect sense. You're not going to meet many feminine, fit, driven women hanging out in dive bars or chain-smoking on park benches. The gym is where the disciplined gather. Whole Foods is where the nutrient nerds shop. Both places are populated with women who are at least paying some attention to their health, their appearance, and—by extension—their life. Add to that the price tag of shopping at Whole Foods, and you've also got a pretty good proxy for financial stability or higher income.

But for me? It's never worked. Not once. Not even close.

Let's talk gym culture first. When I go to the gym, I'm there to get it done. Focused. Zoned in. Headphones on. I'm not looking to make small talk between sets or figure out whether the girl in the Lululemon leggings is giving me a signal or just doing Romanian deadlifts. The gym, for me, is personal time. It's sacred. And from what I've seen, a lot of women feel the same way. Sure, some might welcome the attention. But most? They're there to sweat, not to flirt.

It's not about fear of rejection or approach anxiety. It's about vibe. The gym is not a social setting—it's a performance arena. You don't interrupt a guy mid-bench press to ask where he's from. Same principle applies. So while I've heard the stories of guys who met their wives between incline sets, that's not my story. And I'm okay with that.

Now, Whole Foods. Oh, the mythos of Whole Foods. I've lost count of how many podcasts and dating blogs swear by it. "Strike up a conversation in the produce aisle!" "Ask for a recipe recommendation at the olive bar!" Sounds great—if you're into flirting while holding a $15 bottle of organic kombucha. But here's the truth: when I'm in Whole Foods, I'm locked in. I'm reading labels, comparing ingredients, planning meals. I'm not scanning the aisles for my next date. And judging by the faces I see, neither is anyone else.

Could it work? Maybe. If you're naturally extroverted. If you enjoy spontaneous social interactions. If you know how to slip a clever comment into someone's cart without seeming creepy. But me? I like intentionality. I like knowing that when I'm engaging with someone, we're both there for the same reason. Dating apps do that; they remove the guesswork.

Still, I'm not dismissing the gym or Whole Foods entirely. The logic still tracks. Women in these places tend to be health-conscious, which often means more attractive, more disciplined, and more intentional about how they live. These are good signs. And if you're the type who can strike up a conversation anywhere—gym, store, sidewalk—go for it. It's just not my thing. At least not yet.

Maybe one day, I'll shake things up. Maybe I'll start chatting with women by the kale display or crack a joke in the supplements aisle. Maybe. But for now, I'm sticking with what works for me—focused fitness time, efficient shopping, and intentional dating. Because at the end of the day, whether it's Tinder, Trader Joe's, or the treadmill, what matters most isn't where you meet—it's how you connect.

HOW FAR TO GO ON THE FIRST DATE?

Let's cut through the nonsense—I generally prefer not to sleep with a woman on the first date. That's not some moral stance or romantic idealism. It's simply a matter of long-term strategy. I've learned, through experience, that when things move too quickly, they tend to burn out just as fast. That initial intensity, while thrilling in the moment, often fizzles before there's even a chance to establish anything meaningful. The chase ends before it even begins, and suddenly, there's no excitement left. What could have been a slow burn of growing connection turns into a one-night flash that barely leaves a mark.

But let's be real—just because I prefer not to doesn't mean I always follow my own advice. I've lost count of how many times things moved fast, sometimes faster than I anticipated. The chemistry was there, the spark undeniable, and before either of us could name what was happening, the clothes were on the floor. And in a lot of those cases? The next morning marked the beginning of the end. Because what starts with a sprint usually doesn't make it to the marathon.

That's why I've come to believe that while it's smart to take things slow when there's real potential, you still have to maintain a certain level of momentum. "Slow" doesn't mean passive. It doesn't mean neutered. Women aren't looking for platonic companions—they're looking to *feel*. Excitement. Suspense. Tension. The unspoken promise of more. You have to keep that energy alive. You have to touch, tease, escalate. You have to build anticipation like a slow-boiling pot, always keeping it just below the point of overflow.

The worst mistake you can make is letting things go flat. That's when you land in the dreaded friend zone—a place no man wants to be. A place where sexual tension goes to die. Once you're there, it's almost impossible to climb out. That's why every interaction, especially early on, has to walk the line between interest and intent. You have to touch her with purpose, speak with confidence, and carry the under-current of masculinity that lets her know she's dealing with a man—not a buddy, not a therapist, not an asexual clown who's trying to "just get to know her."

I don't believe in arbitrary rules. I'm not one of those "three-date min-imum" guys or someone who believes in holding out for a month. Every situation is different. Every woman is different. The only rule I follow is this: once mutual orgasms are happening, there's no point in waiting further. By then, you've crossed the Rubicon. But before that line is crossed, you have to keep things simmering. Keep her guessing. Keep the pace seductive—not stalled.

Because here's the truth—sexual tension is the engine of early dating. Kill that engine, and the whole thing stalls. It's not just about sex. It's about polarity. Masculine and feminine energy colliding, dancing, teasing. The moment she stops wondering what might happen next is the moment she stops caring. Predictability is the death of attraction. So don't be predictable. Don't be static. Keep her on her toes.

Now, there's a personal story that proves just how tricky this balance can be. I was only ever truly friend-zoned once in my life. It was a unique situation—complicated, layered, and, in many ways, unavoid-able. I met a woman who was everything I was drawn to: over twenty years younger, stunning, smart, full of life. The chemistry was imme-diate and intense. But there were two major obstacles—I was married at the time, and she was my employee. Not exactly a setup that lends itself to romantic development.

Despite those limitations, we maintained a connection. Over the years, we've stayed in touch. And while we've never crossed the line, the energy between us never really disappeared. There were mo-ments—charged, heavy moments—where the possibility hung in the air like a storm that never quite broke. I could have made a move. I felt the pull. I saw it in her eyes. But for one reason or another, I never did.

I believe that one day we will. When the timing's right. When the stars finally align and the circumstances shift. But I've also learned that there's a kind of power in restraint. In knowing something could happen, and choosing not to force it. Because forcing it? That's how you lose it entirely.

Timing is everything. And trying to push when the timing is wrong—when life, emotions, or circumstances are in flux—can shatter the potential for anything lasting. Sometimes, what looks like a missed opportunity is really just a delayed one. And in the meantime, I'd rather have a solid connection that lives in that delicious space of potential than destroy it by trying to scratch an itch at the wrong time.

So what's the lesson? Keep the tension alive, but respect the tempo. Don't rush to the bedroom unless it's mutual, electric, and unmistakable. And whatever you do, don't let things go cold. Because once the heat fades, so does the connection.

WHAT TO DO ON YOUR DATE: THE POWER OF PLANNING

If there's one piece of advice that every man should tattoo onto his brain, it's this: planning matters. A great date doesn't just happen—it's designed. Crafted. Orchestrated like a piece of music. You don't just show up and wing it. You lead. You create an experience. And the man who does this well doesn't just get the girl—he leaves a lasting impression.

For me, dates are easy to plan. I'm a foodie. I love discovering new restaurants and sharing that excitement with someone else. A perfectly curated meal, followed by dancing and a long walk under the stars? That's my idea of a great night. But the secret isn't the venue—it's the intention. It's the fact that I've thought it through. That I've taken the time to build something memorable.

Women hate uncertainty—especially on a date. The moment you ask her, "So, what do you feel like doing?" with no plan in place, you've killed the vibe. That question signals indecisiveness. Lack of leadership. And whether she admits it or not, a woman wants to feel like you're capable of creating a moment worth remembering. Confidence is not just about posture and voice. It's about preparation.

That doesn't mean everything has to go perfectly. Sometimes, things fall apart. A reservation gets canceled. The place is unexpectedly closed. Weather ruins your outdoor plans. Life happens. But here's where most men miss the mark—when the plan goes wrong, and you don't have a backup, she doesn't just see a change of venue. She feels *let down.*

Because women don't just plan outfits for dates. They plan feelings. They imagine the flow of the evening, the story they'll tell their friends, the emotional beat of every interaction. When you disrupt that fantasy without a graceful pivot, you leave her with a single, powerful association: disappointment. And the cruel truth about dating is this—women remember how you make them feel. If the dominant emotion from your time together is frustration or disarray, that's the story she'll replay.

You may think, "It wasn't my fault the kitchen was closed" or "I didn't know the concert was sold out." Doesn't matter. She won't just remember the problem—she'll remember that you didn't solve it. And that memory becomes your new identity in her mind. The guy who couldn't keep the night on track. The man who didn't deliver.

That's why planning is more than just logistics—it's reputation management. It's branding. You're saying, "I care enough to think this through." You're telling her, without words, that she matters. That this evening isn't a placeholder—it's a moment.

So here's the strategy: plan in layers. Pick a restaurant you know will hit the mark. Make a reservation. Have a secondary spot in case the first one tanks. Choose a location that's walkable, with somewhere quiet nearby. Dancing is great, but even a lounge or cozy wine bar can do the trick. Something transitional. Something that allows the energy to evolve.

And be prepared. Know the area. Know where to park. Know what time the kitchen closes. Know what the dress code is. These small things might not seem like a big deal, but they add up. They show competence. And competence, especially in a man, is a massive turn-on.

Planning isn't about control. It's about care. It's about saying, "I've got this," so she doesn't have to. And in a world full of chaos, that kind of steadiness is rare—and sexy.

So next time you set a date, don't leave it to chance. Treat it like something that matters. Because it does. Not just for her—but for you, too. The man who leads with purpose always wins.

LET'S TALK POLITICS—OR BETTER YET, LET'S NOT

If there's one conversational landmine that can destroy the vibe of a date faster than a whiff of bad breath or an ill-timed joke, it's politics. In this age of hyper-polarization, political affiliation has morphed from a casual topic of discussion into a defining character trait—almost a tribal identity. What once might have been a mild difference of opinion has now become, for many, a declaration of war. Rational conversations are rare, and emotional landmines are everywhere. If you're not walking on eggshells, you're walking into crossfire.

But it wasn't always this way. I remember a time when people could disagree and still remain civil—hell, even attracted to each other. Forty years ago, when I first started dating, you could be a Democrat and date a Republican without it being treated like a betrayal of your values or heritage. You didn't need perfect political alignment to share a meal, a bed, or even a life. But somewhere along the way, that mutual tolerance disintegrated. Politics now operates like religion once did—rife with zealotry, dogma, and unrelenting certainty.

This evolution has affected every arena of life: families are divided, workplaces are tense, and romantic partnerships are increasingly being filtered through the lens of ideological compatibility. It's no longer "Do you like wine and long walks on the beach?" It's "What's your stance on immigration reform and gender identity policy?" The dating world has become a minefield of political tests, and a single wrong answer can torpedo your chances before dessert is even ordered.

Now, there are three basic ways to navigate this mess when dating. First, you can address politics upfront. Be transparent. Put it on the table early. If you know you won't tolerate someone with opposing views, save yourself the headache and make your stance known from the beginning. It might cost you a few dates, but it will save you from long-term drama. Second, you can declare politics off-limits. Some people manage to pull this off—agreeing to never bring it up, treating politics like that crazy uncle at Thanksgiving: everyone knows he's there, but no one wants to talk to him. Third, you can stick to dating people who already share your views. It's the safest route, but it also severely limits your pool.

Personally, I have strong political views, but I also view politics with a hefty dose of cynicism. I've been around long enough to know that most politicians—regardless of their party—are full of it. I've met them. I've studied them. I know the game. And because of that, I'm able to listen without losing my mind. I don't get rattled when someone disagrees with me. But that level of detachment is becoming rare. Most people can't discuss politics without becoming combative, defensive, or downright hostile. And that's where the problem lies.

In relationships, emotional compatibility matters. And if a particular topic consistently throws one or both of you into a state of tension or conflict, it's a problem. If you know you can't respect someone whose views differ from yours, that's your boundary—and it's okay. But don't lie to yourself. Don't pretend it doesn't matter, only to end up resenting them later. Be honest. And be strategic.

The bottom line is this: politics will come up, eventually. Whether you want it to or not. Whether it's a passing comment, a news headline, or an election cycle, it will surface. And when it does, you need to be prepared. Either steer the conversation gracefully, change the subject, or be ready for the fallout. But don't let it blindside you.

Most importantly, don't take it personally. If you go out with someone and discover they're on the other side of the political aisle, don't make it a moral indictment. They're not evil. They're just different. And if that difference is too big to bridge, then wish them well and move on. Life's too short to waste time trying to convert someone who doesn't want to change—or being converted yourself just to keep the peace.

Never Take Anything Personally—A Dating Essential

If there's one philosophy that can radically change not only your dating life but your entire approach to relationships, it's this: never take anything personally. In the modern world, we're constantly bombarded by opinions, reactions, and unsolicited commentary. Everyone has something to say. And more often than not, it has nothing to do with you—and everything to do with them.

In today's climate, people seem almost addicted to outrage. An off-handed comment becomes an act of aggression. A joke can spark a firestorm. Someone doesn't return a text, and it's treated like emotional warfare. We live in an era of hyper-sensitivity, where people search for offense like it's a hidden treasure. But here's the truth: what others say or do is almost never about you. It's about their worldview, their trauma, their expectations, and their projections. When you internalize that truth, you become bulletproof.

One of the most powerful pieces of wisdom I ever came across comes from the book *The Four Agreements* by Don Miguel Ruiz. Based on ancient Toltec wisdom, it lays out four rules for living a grounded and authentic life. And while all four are valuable, the one that changed everything for me is this: never take anything personally. Because the moment you do, you give away your power. You allow someone else's words or opinions to dictate your internal state.

This is especially true in dating. When you put yourself out there—on apps, at bars, on dates—you're going to face judgment. Rejection. Criticism. Women might tell you that you're too intense, too serious, too sarcastic, too aloof. Some might mock your clothes, your hairline, your laugh. Some might just disappear without a word. And every one of those experiences has the potential to shake your confidence. If you let it.

But here's what you have to understand: when someone rejects you, criticizes you, or ghosts you, it's not a referendum on your value. It's a reflection of their tastes, their baggage, their expectations. Maybe you remind them of their ex. Maybe they're not in the right emotional place. Maybe you're just not their type. That doesn't make you wrong or flawed. It makes you human. And it makes them human too.

When you take things personally, you start bending yourself to fit into other people's boxes. You edit your personality. You second-guess your instincts. You start dating like a politician—saying whatever you think will win the vote, instead of being authentic. And that's when the real damage happens. Because you can't attract the right person by being someone you're not.

Instead, adopt emotional detachment. Not apathy—just clarity. When someone criticizes you, take a breath. Ask yourself: is this about me? Is this useful? Or is it just noise? If it's valid feedback, great—grow from it. If it's nonsense, let it roll off you. Either way, don't absorb it like gospel.

One of the greatest emotional skills a man can have is the ability to walk away from an insult without carrying it like baggage. Learn to laugh at yourself. Learn to deflect without bitterness. If a woman takes a shot at you, smile and pivot. If she's nasty, disengage. If she doesn't respond to your message, shrug it off. Because when you stay calm, when you stay in your frame, you win.

Of course, not all comments are harmless. Sometimes, someone will say something that stings because, deep down, it hits a nerve. Maybe there's a little truth in it. Maybe it exposes something you haven't dealt with. And in those moments, you have two choices: spiral into self-doubt, or use it as a mirror. If there's something you need to fix— fix it. But don't let it break you.

In the end, the world is full of people projecting their insecurities onto others. The stronger you become, the less any of it matters. You stop taking offense. You stop chasing approval. You start moving through the world with the quiet confidence of someone who knows who he is.

So don't let rejection shrink you. Don't let criticism harden you. And never let a stranger's opinion dictate your worth. In dating, as in life, the most powerful move you can make is simple: don't take it personally.

CONTROL YOUR REACTIONS, CONTROL YOUR OUTCOME

People say dumb things. We all do. It's part of being human. An awkward moment, a poorly phrased comment, or a misread situation—these things happen all the time. Most of the time, they don't mean anything. They're not attacks. They're not threats. They're just blips in the rhythm of human interaction. So if you're the kind of man who wants to get ahead in dating—and in life—you've got to learn to let the small stuff slide.

But what if someone crosses the line? What if the comment isn't just awkward—it's rude? What if the behavior isn't just clumsy—it's controlling or manipulative? That's when your reaction matters most. Not the other person's behavior—your reaction. Because you don't control what other people say or do. You only control how you respond. And your response determines your outcome.

This is one of the core truths every high-value man must understand. You will be tested. You will be poked, prodded, and provoked. Whether it's a woman on a date, a colleague in a meeting, or a stranger in traffic, people will try to get a reaction out of you. And the moment you give them what they want—whether that's anger, frustration, or desperation—you've handed over your power.

There's a phrase used in military circles that I've come to love: "Charlie Mike." It means "Continue Mission." In other words, stay the course. Don't get thrown off. Don't let a setback derail you. If someone insults you, shrugs you off, mocks your ideas, or ghosts you—Charlie Mike. Continue Mission. Let it bounce off your armor and keep moving forward.

Because the truth is, people can only control you if you let them. The second you lose control of your emotional state, you become reactive.

And a reactive man is not a powerful man. A reactive man is at the mercy of others. He's dancing to someone else's tune. That's not where you want to be—not in dating, not in business, not in life.

The best men I know, the ones who truly embody masculine strength, all have one thing in common: emotional discipline. They don't lash out. They don't break down. They don't let the world dictate their mood. They respond with clarity, calm, and purpose. And it's not because they're emotionless—it's because they've trained themselves to respond instead of react.

So how do you develop this kind of strength? It starts with awareness. Pay attention to your triggers. Notice what sets you off. Is it being ignored? Disrespected? Challenged? Whatever it is, identify it. Then reframe it. When someone pushes that button, see it for what it is: an opportunity to sharpen your control. Instead of reacting, breathe. Pause. Smile, even. And then decide, with intention, how you want to proceed.

This kind of emotional control is magnetic. Women sense it. They feel it. They respect it. A man who can maintain his composure under pressure is infinitely more attractive than a man who's emotionally volatile. Why? Because he's safe. Not in a boring way—but in a "this man knows himself" kind of way. And in a world full of weak, reactive men, that kind of stability is rare.

Now, none of this means you should tolerate disrespect. Quite the opposite. If someone is genuinely rude, manipulative, or controlling, you don't owe them your time or energy. You don't need to argue, explain, or retaliate. You just exit. Gracefully. Decisively. A calm exit is more powerful than a dramatic confrontation. It says, "You're not worth my peace." And believe me, people remember that.

This principle is especially important in dating. You're going to meet people who test you. Sometimes intentionally, sometimes subconsciously. A woman might push your buttons just to see how you respond. She wants to know if you can handle yourself. If you lose your cool, she'll see you as weak. If you shut down, she'll see you as emotionally unavailable. But if you stay centered? That's when she leans in. That's when she starts to trust your strength.

Let's say you're on a date and she makes a sarcastic comment about your job or appearance. Instead of snapping back or getting flustered, try this: smile and change the subject. Or throw it back playfully. Deflect without defensiveness. Because what she's really doing is checking for your frame. Are you solid, or are you shook? And if your frame is strong, you've passed the test.

Controlling your reactions also protects your long-term happiness. If every rude comment or rejection sends you into a spiral, you're going to live in constant turmoil. You'll dread dating. You'll fear failure. But if you learn to see those moments as noise—as irrelevant distractions—you'll move through the world with freedom. You'll take more risks, engage more fully, and recover more quickly.

The most successful men aren't the ones who never fail—they're the ones who recover fastest. Rejection, failure, and friction are baked into the game. You're not going to avoid them. But you can choose how you respond. You can keep moving forward. You can continue mission.

And when you do? You become unstoppable.

A man who controls his reactions controls the room. He controls the energy of the conversation. He controls the tone of the date. He sets the rhythm. He leads. And women crave that. They want to be with someone who can hold it together, no matter what life throws their way.

This doesn't mean you become cold or robotic. You're not hiding your emotions—you're mastering them. You still feel things. You still connect. You still care. But you express those emotions with intention. You speak with purpose. You act with strength. And that makes all the difference.

Let's say someone ghosts you after two great dates. Instead of chasing or venting, you simply move on. No texts. No follow-ups. No drama. Just silence. That silence says more than any angry message ever could. It says, "I'm good with or without you." And that's power.

Or maybe someone tries to provoke you with politics, religion, or a personal jab. Instead of engaging in a fruitless debate, you keep your cool. You smile. You change the subject. Or you end the conversation entirely. Again, it's not about winning the argument—it's about winning your own peace.

When you stop reacting emotionally, you start seeing clearly. You stop chasing validation. You stop needing to prove yourself. You start living on your terms. And that shift changes everything—from the way you date to the way you lead your life.

Control is freedom. Control is attraction. Control is power.

So the next time someone tries to get a rise out of you, remember: your reaction is your responsibility. Not theirs. Yours. And when you master that, the rest of the world has no choice but to respect it.

Charlie Mike. Continue mission. Because nothing—not rejection, not insult, not friction—can stop a man who stays in control.

Go With Your Gut—
It's Never Wrong

There's a voice inside every man. A subtle, persistent whisper that says, "Something isn't right here." Most of us hear it. Fewer of us listen. And almost all of us have paid the price for ignoring it. That voice is your gut. Your intuition. Your built-in radar for people, situations, and decisions that don't align with who you are or where you're headed. Ignore it at your peril.

It hasn't happened to me often, but when it does, it's unmistakable. I'll be on the phone with a woman I matched with, and something just doesn't feel right. There's no obvious red flag. No outrageous behavior. But underneath the surface, something hums with tension. A tone. A hesitation. A way of answering a question that doesn't sit well with me. And every single time I've pushed past that feeling—every time I've silenced my instincts—I've regretted it.

The thing is, we're trained by society to override our gut. We're told to give people the benefit of the doubt. To be "open-minded." To not judge a book by its cover. And while that sounds noble, it can also be dangerous. Because your gut is your evolutionary safeguard. It's the product of millions of years of survival instincts. It exists to protect you from harm, not just physical, but emotional, psychological, and even spiritual. When you feel that subtle tension, that internal resistance, it's not your imagination—it's information.

This doesn't just apply to dating. It applies to everything—business, friendships, partnerships, major life decisions. Every time I've gone against my better judgment in any of these arenas, I've ended up wishing I hadn't. Whether it was hiring someone I had doubts about, investing in a deal that felt shaky, or entering a relationship that gave me pause—I paid the price. And the common denominator in all those situations? I knew better. I felt it. But I ignored it.

There's a story I always go back to when people ask me how I learned to trust my gut. It involves a woman I spoke to on the phone a few years ago. She seemed attractive. Intelligent. Reasonably normal on paper. But from the moment we started talking, something was off. I couldn't name it. I couldn't pin it down. It was just a vague sense that we weren't compatible. That she wasn't who she appeared to be. But like a lot of men, I talked myself out of my own intuition. I figured I was being too picky. Too sensitive. So, I agreed to meet her for lunch.

But something kept gnawing at me. The next day, I decided to cancel. I sent her a polite message saying I was busy and wouldn't be available for the next couple of weeks. That's when it all unraveled. Her response was instant and accusatory: "I think you were playing me." Red flag confirmed. But she didn't stop there. She looked up my phone number, found my full name, and let me know she had it—as if that were a power move. She hadn't asked for it. She'd weaponized it. That was all I needed to see.

I blocked her immediately. Didn't think much of it afterward. Chalked it up to a bullet dodged. Until a couple of years later, when I ran into her at a concert. She spotted me, marched right up, thrust her arms out, and with a thick New York accent, shouted, "You see what you're missing?" I was so caught off guard, I laughed and reflexively gave her a quick hug. Bad idea. She screamed, "DON'T TOUCH ME!" and bolted into the crowd. My friends and I laughed about it for months.

But the punchline came later. I found out she had multiple restraining orders. Several arrests. A rap sheet that explained everything I had felt from that very first phone call. My instincts had been screaming. And I had almost overridden them. That story has stuck with me ever since. Not because it was traumatic, but because it was such a clear example of how right the gut can be—and how wrong we are to ignore it.

Today, I listen to my gut without hesitation. If I talk to a woman and don't feel that initial spark of compatibility—or worse, if I feel an underlying discomfort—I end the conversation with kindness and clarity. I don't need to explain. I don't need to debate. I trust that the energy I'm feeling is telling me something my rational brain hasn't caught up with yet. And more often than not, it saves me from unnecessary drama and/or trauma.

We live in an age where people are constantly taught to suppress instinct in favor of logic. We overanalyze. We rationalize. We seek second opinions. And in doing so, we drown out the one voice that always knows the truth—our own. I'm not saying don't use your brain. I'm saying use your gut as your first filter. If something feels off, pause. Investigate. Don't dismiss that feeling. It's there for a reason.

The biggest lies we tell ourselves happen in that gap between gut and action. "She's probably just nervous." "Maybe I'm being judgmental." "It's just one date." These are the thoughts that lead to wasted time, emotional energy, and sometimes worse. Because while your gut is rarely wrong, your mind will lie to you all day long. Your mind wants to be polite. Your mind wants to see the best in people. Your mind wants to follow rules. But your gut wants to keep you safe. Which one do you think is more valuable in the long run?

There's also a deeper confidence that comes from trusting yourself. When you get in the habit of listening to your gut, you stop second-guessing. You stop explaining yourself. You become unapologetically aligned with your own judgment. And that self-trust radiates. Women notice it. Business partners notice it. Friends and family notice it. You become the man who knows himself—and that's magnetic.

Let's say you're messaging with someone online and everything looks good on paper. She's attractive. She's articulate. Her profile hits all your boxes. But something about her tone is cold. Or her jokes don't land right. Or there's an edge in her responses that feels off.

That's your cue. Don't ignore it. You don't owe her a meeting just because she looks good on your screen. Swipe left. Move on.

Or let's say you're already on a date, and midway through the conversation, you start to feel drained. Or annoyed. Or disconnected. That's not you being picky. That's your gut telling you this woman is not for you. You can finish the drink, thank her for her time, and leave without guilt. Because your time is valuable. Your energy is sacred. And your gut is the gatekeeper of both.

People will tell you you're being too critical. Too harsh. Too quick to judge. But those same people won't be there to clean up the mess when you ignore your instincts and it all goes sideways. Only you have to deal with the fallout. Only you carry the emotional scars. So why would you let someone else's opinion override your internal guidance?

Going with your gut doesn't mean you never take chances. It doesn't mean you avoid every uncomfortable situation. It means you trust your inner compass. You know when something feels right—and when it doesn't. And instead of trying to rationalize or explain away that feeling, you honor it. You let it guide you. You let it protect you.

The most powerful men I know don't waste time explaining their decisions. They don't ask for permission to follow their instincts. They move through life with quiet conviction. And when people ask why they made a certain call, their answer is simple: "It didn't feel right." That's all the explanation they need. That's all the explanation you need, too.

So the next time you get that feeling—that tightening in your chest, that slight discomfort, that whisper of doubt—pause. Listen. Trust it. Because your gut is never wrong. And every time you ignore it, you're betting against yourself.

In dating. In business. In life.

Go with your gut. Every single time.

IT'S THE JOURNEY, NOT THE DESTINATION

If you're anything like me—going on lots of dates, maybe borderline serial dating, maybe even stepping into what some would call "player" territory—there's one truth you need to embrace: enjoy the journey. Don't just focus on the outcome. Don't obsess over whether this next woman is "the one." Because the truth is, most of them won't be. And if you define success solely by whether or not you've found your forever partner, you're setting yourself up for constant disappointment.

This mindset shift is not only important—it's essential. When you start seeing every date as an opportunity instead of an audition, you change the entire energy of the experience. It's no longer about vetting, judging, or passing a checklist. It becomes about curiosity. Connection. Discovery. The ability to sit across from a stranger (or next to her because you're hearing ain't what it used to be) and see what she reveals—not just about herself, but about you.

Most men make the mistake of putting so much pressure on the outcome that they sabotage the present moment. They're tense. They're calculating. They're trying to read signs and figure out next steps before the appetizer hits the table. That kind of pressure is exhausting—for both of you. And ironically, it kills attraction. Women can feel when you're forcing it, and nothing is less sexy than desperation.

The truth is, the process of dating—especially if you're doing it often—should be something you look forward to. Not because you expect every night to be magical, but because you understand that each interaction adds something to your life. Sometimes it's a good story. Sometimes it's a new perspective. Sometimes it's just a great cocktail and a lesson in patience. But if you stay open to the experience, you never walk away empty-handed.

Your attitude going into a date shapes everything. If you're expecting disappointment, you'll find it. If you're dreading the interaction, it will show. But if you treat the evening as a unique moment in time—an opportunity to learn, laugh, flirt, and connect—you've already won. Even if you never see her again.

And here's the real kicker: that detachment from outcome? That lightness? That presence? It makes you more attractive. Women can feel it. When you're not fixated on where the night is going, you're more fun to be around. When you're relaxed and engaged, she relaxes too. And when she senses you're not trying to force anything, she's far more likely to lean in, especially if you're sitting next to her.

It's a paradox, but it's true: the less you try to "get" something from the date, the more you're likely to get. Whether it's a kiss, a second date, or something more, it tends to happen more naturally when you're not clinging to expectations. This is emotional abundance in action. And it's a game-changer.

This isn't to say you shouldn't have goals. If your long-term vision includes a committed relationship or marriage, great. Keep that in mind. But don't carry that goal into every date like it's a resume review. That energy is heavy, and it turns people off. No one wants to feel like they're being measured or evaluated. They want to feel seen. They want to feel chemistry. They want to have fun.

There's also a deeper truth here. Every woman you date, even briefly, becomes part of your story. She may not be your forever, but she plays a role in shaping the man you're becoming. Maybe she challenges you to level up. Maybe she inspires you in some way. Or maybe she just reminds you of what you don't want—and that's valuable, too.

Dating is rarely linear. You'll go forward, backward, sideways. You'll connect with someone for a week, a month, maybe longer, only for it to fizzle. You'll ghost and be ghosted. You'll misread signals and have your signals misread. It's messy. But it's also part of the human experience. And if you can embrace that mess without resentment, you'll not only have more success—you'll enjoy yourself along the way.

There's also something to be said for gratitude. Think about how lucky you are to even have the opportunity to meet new people. To go out. To explore chemistry. There are millions of people who would love to be in your shoes. So don't squander the gift by sulking through the process. Appreciate the moments, even the awkward ones. Even the ones that end with a handshake and a "thanks, but no thanks."

Remember, you're not just dating to find someone. You're dating to refine your taste. To sharpen your skills. To understand what works for you and what doesn't. To grow. And when you shift your mindset from acquisition to exploration, everything changes. You stop seeing dates as tests and start seeing them as opportunities for connection.

So take the pressure off. Laugh a little more. Be curious. Be playful. Share stories. Order dessert. And when the night ends, let it end without clinging. If there's magic, it'll flow. If there's not, you move on with a smile and a better sense of what fits you.

Dating is not a transaction—it's an adventure. And like any great adventure, it's the journey that teaches you the most. So enjoy it.

ARE YOU THE PILOT OR THE PASSENGER?

Life—and dating—is all about perspective. You can either be the pilot or the passenger. The one steering the experience, or the one watching the clouds go by, hoping for a soft landing. And the truth is, too many men have handed over the controls. They've given up agency. They're waiting for something to happen instead of making it happen. And then they wonder why they feel powerless, frustrated, or confused.

Being the pilot means owning your mindset, your actions, and your direction. It means showing up to dates with a sense of purpose—not just to impress, but to connect, to explore, to lead. It means deciding that your experience matters, regardless of the outcome. Because if you're not in charge of your own energy, someone else will be. And when that happens, you become reactive instead of intentional.

Think about how many people live like passengers. They swipe endlessly, go on dates without clarity, stay in bad relationships out of fear, and let outside circumstances dictate how they feel. One bad date ruins their week. One unreturned text ruins their confidence. They've outsourced their emotional stability to strangers. And that's a terrible trade.

But when you choose to be the pilot, everything shifts. You start viewing each experience as something you get to create, not something that just happens to you. You control the tone, the pace, the energy. You don't show up wondering if she'll like you—you show up wondering if you'll connect. If the chemistry will flow. If it's mutual.

Being the pilot doesn't mean controlling the other person. It means steering your own experience. It means bringing your best energy, staying grounded in your values, and navigating with clarity. You don't have to fake anything. You don't have to convince anyone of your worth. You simply show up with presence, lead the interaction, and stay unattached to the outcome.

One of the most powerful shifts you can make is realizing that your emotions are your responsibility. If a date goes sideways, you don't have to spiral. If a woman isn't into you, that doesn't change your value. If the night doesn't end with fireworks, it doesn't mean it was a failure. You're still the pilot. And the next flight is already boarding.

Think about how much time we spend waiting for external validation. For someone else to say, "You're good enough." "You're attractive." "You're worthy." It's exhausting. And it's unnecessary. Because when you step into your own authority, you don't need that validation anymore. You already know who you are.

This applies to every part of life—not just dating. Career. Friendships. Fitness. You can either steer or drift. And drifting might feel easier, but it always leads to regret. Steering takes effort. It requires attention. But it leads somewhere. And even if you don't reach your ideal destination right away, at least you're moving with intention.

There's also joy in the journey when you're the pilot. You get to choose the route. You get to take detours. You get to learn along the way. Every experience becomes valuable because you're actively participating in it. You're not waiting—you're living. You're not hoping—you're doing.

When it comes to dating, this mindset is everything. Instead of fearing rejection, you embrace exploration. Instead of chasing, you connect. Instead of getting discouraged by one bad experience, you see it as part of the flight path. And you trust that the right connection will align when it's meant to—not because you forced it, but because you stayed on course and weathered the inevitable turbulence along the way.

So ask yourself: are you piloting your dating life, or just going along for the ride? Are you choosing the energy you bring to each interaction, or reacting to whatever comes your way? Are you grounded in your values, or bending to fit into someone else's frame?

Because the man who pilots his own experience never loses. Even if the flight gets bumpy. Even if the destination changes. He's in control. And control, in this context, doesn't mean rigidity. It means awareness. Presence. Power.

When you decide to be the pilot of your life—and your dating journey—you stop hoping for the perfect woman to show up and "complete" you. You start living as a complete man. And that kind of energy? That's what draws the right people in.

So take the controls. Plan the route. Enjoy the ride.

Because it's not about where you land—it's about how you fly.

Don't Endure a Miserable Journey for an Uncertain Destination

Some people trudge through the dating world like it's a grueling marathon they never signed up for—bad dates, awkward silences, emotionally draining encounters—endured all in the hope that maybe, just maybe, the destination will make it all worth it. They put their heads down and keep grinding, believing that if they suffer enough now, the universe will eventually reward them with a perfect partner. But here's a harsh truth worth absorbing: a miserable journey doesn't guarantee a happy ending. Life doesn't work that way. Dating certainly doesn't.

Too many people treat dating like a job they hate but won't quit. They tolerate disrespect, settle for lackluster conversations, and compromise on values just to "see where it goes." They put up with low energy, bad vibes, or plain incompatibility, as if logging hours will somehow increase the chances of a positive result. But why? Why endure when you could simply redirect? Why slog through something that drains you when you could reframe the entire experience as an opportunity to enjoy, learn, and grow?

You don't owe anyone your time, your energy, or your emotional bandwidth if the interaction is clearly misaligned. And you certainly don't owe it to yourself to keep showing up to experiences that rob you of joy. Your dating life should be a reflection of your standards, your values, and your emotional well-being—not a punishment for being single. If you're treating dating as a chore, it will feel like one. If you're treating it as a creative adventure, that's exactly what it becomes.

Even if you never find the exact relationship you envision, what if you lived fully and freely throughout the process? What if you found joy in each interaction, regardless of outcome? That shift in perspective doesn't just make dating more enjoyable—it makes *you* more attractive. Because nothing draws people in like a man who is at peace with himself, enjoying the moment for what it is.

Take the pressure off. Seriously. Stop trying to script the outcome. Instead, show up curious, grounded, and willing to flow with whatever the night brings. Maybe it's romance. Maybe it's a hilarious story. Maybe it's a lesson wrapped in awkwardness. All of it is useful. All of it adds texture to your life.

And when it doesn't work out? When the conversation falls flat, or the energy just isn't there? Don't see it as a failure. Just reset your course and keep flying. One awkward date doesn't define your journey. Ten of them don't. A hundred of them still don't. Because dating isn't a linear path with guaranteed rewards—it's an ever-changing landscape of experiences that you get to navigate with curiosity and discernment.

There's a certain kind of liberation in detachment. When you stop clinging to specific outcomes and start focusing on the experience itself, you become more present. And presence is powerful. Presence says, "I'm here because I want to be, not because I need something from you." That energy is magnetic. Women feel it. They respond to it. They lean into it.

This mindset doesn't just make dating more enjoyable—it makes life more enjoyable. You stop being a slave to outcomes. You stop waiting for happiness to arrive in the form of another person. Instead, you start creating it now. In the moment. In the date. In the connection, however brief.

Finding the Good in Any Date

Back when I was married to my first wife, I learned a lesson that's stuck with me far beyond the marriage. She was an artist, a highly creative woman who worked in advertising. We went to the movies constantly. And like anyone who sees a lot of films, we encountered everything—from absolute masterpieces to unwatchable trainwrecks.

But what stood out was her ability to find something redeeming in even the worst films.

If the script was terrible, she'd comment on the lighting. If the acting was wooden, she'd appreciate the costumes. If the story made no sense, she'd notice the camera angles or set design. She had trained her eye to find beauty, creativity, and effort—even in failure. And over time, I found myself doing the same. No longer was a bad movie a waste of time; it was a study in craft, a glimpse into someone's effort, an exercise in perspective.

Dating is exactly the same. Not every date will entertain you. Not every woman will be your match. Some conversations will go nowhere. Some evenings will feel like forced social interviews. But if you choose to look deeper, to find value even in the lack of chemistry, you shift from judgment to appreciation—and that changes everything.

You won't connect with everyone. That's inevitable. Some people will be too quiet, too loud, too superficial, too intense, too whatever for your taste. And that's okay. But even when it's clear there's no romantic future, you can still find something to respect. Something to acknowledge. Some glimpse of what makes them human.

I've been on dates where I knew within five minutes there was no spark. Still, I've seen women come alive when talking about their children, their work, or their passions. I've seen warmth in their laughter, resilience in their stories, and intelligence in their opinions. Just because we weren't a match doesn't mean there wasn't something there to appreciate.

I've sat across from women who were completely self-absorbed, only to later learn that they were highly skilled professionals saving lives or running complex businesses. I've been out with women who barely asked me a question the entire night, only to realize that they were socially anxious or burned out from previous dating experiences.

These realizations didn't excuse bad behavior—but they provided context. And context invites empathy.

Let's be clear: not every person has redeeming qualities. Some people are toxic. Some radiate negativity like a bad cologne. And when you encounter those people, you don't have to find a silver lining—you just have to exit gracefully and keep moving. But in most cases, a little effort to see beyond the surface reveals something worthwhile.

You might meet someone who isn't your type but tells you a fascinating story. Someone you'll never date again but who recommends a great book or restaurant. Someone whose worldview challenges your own, expanding your thinking. These small gifts are often overlooked because we're too busy measuring dates by outdated standards: chemistry, attractiveness, romantic potential.

But if you can release the pressure to find "the one" and start finding value in "the moment," your dating life becomes infinitely richer. Every interaction becomes an opportunity—not just to meet someone, but to meet *yourself* in new ways. How do you respond to awkward silences? How do you handle disappointment? What do you learn about your preferences, your triggers, your standards?

This isn't just philosophical—it's practical. When you walk into a date looking to find something good, you're more relaxed. You're more open. You're more fun. And that, paradoxically, makes a good outcome more likely. People want to be around those who enjoy themselves. Who listen. Who stay present.

And even if the night ends with no fireworks, you've still exercised a muscle that makes you a better man: the ability to hold space, to find meaning, to stay grounded. That's attractive. That's masculine. That's powerful.

So the next time you're on a date that doesn't feel like it's going anywhere, pause. Look again. Listen deeper. Find something to appreciate—not because it will change the outcome, but because it changes *you.* You become someone who doesn't need constant validation or excitement to enjoy himself. You become someone who can create meaning out of any moment.

That's the real win in dating—not the perfect match, but the evolved mindset. Not the flawless connection, but the constant growth. Not the guaranteed destination, but the meaningful journey.

Stop enduring. Start appreciating. The view is much better from here.

A Shift in Perspective

A wise philosopher once said, "I am the better of every man in at least one aspect of my character, and every man is the better of me in at least one area of his." That one line shifted the way I view people—especially in dating. Because let's face it, when you're going on date after date, especially if you've been through hundreds like I have, it's easy to start categorizing people. You start seeing patterns. You become quick with your judgments, your red flags, your disqualifiers. And sometimes, if you're not careful, you stop seeing people altogether. You just see data points.

But here's the thing: everyone you meet has at least one thing to teach you—whether it's how they carry themselves, how they overcame something, or how they light up when talking about a topic they love. That doesn't mean you need to like everyone. It doesn't mean you need to see everyone as a potential partner. But it does mean that you can choose to view people through a more generous lens—one that looks for nuance, not just flaws.

This is especially powerful when you run into someone you don't particularly like. Maybe they're abrasive. Maybe they're boring. Maybe they say something that rubs you the wrong way. That's usually when most people shut down and mentally check out. But what if, instead of reacting, you asked yourself, "What is this person good at? What do they care about? What can I learn from them—even if we'll never go out again?"

It's a subtle shift in perspective, but it's life-changing. Because suddenly, dating isn't just about finding someone—it's about becoming someone. Someone who listens more. Judges less. Learns faster. And lives better. It turns the entire experience of dating into a growth journey instead of a draining grind. That's how you protect your energy. That's how you stay in the game without becoming jaded.

Psychologists have a name for this kind of mental reframe: projection. Often, what bothers us most in others is something we're wrestling with in ourselves. The arrogant guy reminds you of times you've felt insecure. The oversharer makes you uncomfortable because you struggle to open up. The flaky woman hits a nerve because, deep down, you fear being rejected. It's not always obvious. But it's worth exploring.

The next time you find yourself irritated by someone on a date—pause. Ask yourself if your reaction is about them...or about you. That kind of self-awareness doesn't just improve your dating life. It makes you a better communicator, a better friend, a better man. Because once you stop being triggered by everything, you start connecting to what really matters.

This doesn't mean tolerating rudeness or disrespect. It just means that before you decide someone's "the worst," you take a breath and consider the possibility that they're just doing the best they can with what they've got. And that maybe, just maybe, your job isn't to fix or change them—but to understand what you're meant to see and move forward with clarity.

Every person you meet becomes a mirror, showing you where you've grown...and where you still need work. That doesn't just make you more self-aware. It makes you unstoppable. Because suddenly, even the dates that "don't go anywhere" become wins. They become lessons. They become perspective.

Dating, when done right, becomes one of the most powerful self-development tools in the world. You learn to read people. You learn to hold space. You learn how to handle rejection, how to stay grounded, and how to walk away with grace. But only if you keep your ego in check. Only if you let go of the idea that every date has to lead somewhere.

Because here's the truth: most of them won't. But all of them can teach you something—if you're open.

When It's Time to Walk Away

Now let's get one thing straight. While every interaction might have something to teach you, that doesn't mean you have to stick around for all of it. Not every date is worth finishing. Some are flat-out miserable. Some are toxic. Some drain you so hard you wonder why you ever left the house in the first place. And when that happens, you're allowed to tap out.

There's a difference between open-mindedness and self-sacrifice. Between patience and self-betrayal. If you're sitting across from someone who's rude, cruel, chronically negative, or just clearly not aligned with your energy, you don't owe them the rest of your night. You don't have to sit through an appetizer, a drink, or even the second half of the sentence they're speaking. You can simply say, "This isn't a good fit," leave money for your portion of the check, and walk out with your dignity intact.

There's nothing noble about suffering through a bad date just to be polite. And there's no payoff at the end of the night that's worth compromising your peace. In fact, the longer you stay in those misaligned situations, the more you damage your own self-trust. You start second-guessing your instincts. You start convincing yourself that maybe it's not that bad. And before long, you're stuck in a pattern of tolerating way more than you should.

Walking away early isn't rude—it's mature. It means you respect your own time and energy. It means you don't need drama or closure or endless justification to honor your boundaries. And it sets a precedent. Because once you start leaving what doesn't serve you, you start attracting what does.

Still, how you walk away matters. Whenever possible, leave gracefully. You don't need to be cold or cutting. You can be kind and direct. "Hey, I appreciate your time, but I don't think we're a match." That one sentence is a game-changer. It's clear, honest, and respectful. And if the other person takes it badly? That's not your problem. That's confirmation you made the right call.

Don't be afraid to block, delete, and move on when needed. Not every connection deserves follow-up. Not every awkward exchange requires analysis. You're not a therapist. You're not a rehab center. You're a man on a journey—and you get to choose who walks alongside you.

That said, don't throw everyone away at the first sign of friction. There's a balance. Some conversations start rocky and evolve into something meaningful. Some people are nervous and take time to open up. But if you're two drinks in and still feel like you'd rather be anywhere else, listen to that voice. It's your gut, and it's usually right.

The best thing about walking away is that it gives you room to walk *toward* something better. When you stop forcing dead-end connections, you create space for real ones. When you stop tolerating poor treatment, you raise your standards. And when you walk away early, you preserve your energy for the people and experiences that are actually aligned.

Dating is a numbers game, sure—but it's also an energy game. You have a limited supply of emotional fuel. Don't waste it on people who suck the air out of the room. Invest it in connections that give back. That energize you. That challenge you in a good way. That feel light even when the conversations go deep.

Walking away doesn't mean you failed. It means you chose peace. And peace, in today's dating landscape, is the ultimate power move.

So here's the real takeaway: respect yourself enough to leave. Value yourself enough to stop explaining. And trust yourself enough to know when it's time to go.

Because every time you do, you sharpen your instincts, you reinforce your worth, and you step a little closer to the kind of connection you actually want.

You don't just get better at dating—you get better at *being*.

WOMEN AND SEX:
A TRUTH LONG REPRESSED

There's a common misconception—one that's been passed down through generations, bolstered by movies, religion, outdated norms, and plain ignorance—that men enjoy sex more than women. That somehow, male desire is primal, powerful, and constant, while female desire is secondary, delicate, or conditional. But anyone who's spent real time in the bedroom with a woman who's fully in her body, fully in the moment, and fully uninhibited, knows that's complete bullshit. Because when a woman is truly unlocked—when she feels safe, desired, respected, and turned on—there is no comparison.

Men may have the drive, but women have the depth. Men may initiate more often, but women can go longer, feel more, and reach higher peaks. The female body was quite literally designed for pleasure. Anatomically, psychologically, hormonally—everything about it is built for climax after climax, for extended erotic experiences that most men, frankly, can't physically match. A man may be "one and done," but a woman? She can ride that wave over and over until sunrise— and then go again.

And yet, our culture has done women a disservice. We've told them to suppress their desire. To be modest. To be cautious. We've made them feel that to own their sexuality is somehow to lose their value. That to love sex is to be "promiscuous," "easy," or "less than." So what happens? They repress it. They bury it. Or they only let it out in secret—if at all.

This repression isn't just cultural—it's systemic. It starts young. From the time a girl becomes aware of her body, she's told to cover it. Hide it. Be careful. Boys will be boys, but girls must be proper. Girls who explore their bodies are shamed. Girls who talk about pleasure are silenced. And by the time they're grown, many women don't even know what they like—let alone how to ask for it.

But here's the beautiful truth that no amount of repression can erase: women love sex. Not all of them. Not all the time. But when they do? They *really* do. And it's not just physical. It's emotional, psychological, even spiritual. When a woman surrenders fully to the experience, it becomes a symphony of sensation, connection, and release. It's not about performance. It's about presence. It's not about chasing orgasm—it's about allowing it.

I've known many women who were vocal about their enjoyment of sex. Not crude. Not vulgar. Just honest. They knew what they liked. They weren't shy about it. They didn't feel guilty about wanting to be touched, kissed, licked, entered, worshipped. They reveled in it. And it wasn't about needing a man—it was about expressing a part of themselves that had often been denied. These women didn't view sex as transactional. They viewed it as transformational.

And that's what makes being with a fully expressed woman such a powerful experience. Because once she trusts you—once she knows you're not going to judge her, rush her, or shame her—she becomes unstoppable. The sex becomes electric. The room disappears. Time becomes irrelevant. You're no longer just two people doing something physical. You're two energies merging, colliding, combusting.

For me, there's no greater thrill than watching a woman unravel in the bedroom—not because I "scored," but because I was able to guide her somewhere she rarely gets to go. A place where she loses control. A place where she stops thinking. A place where she feels everything. That's why I always insist on her coming first. Because once she's there—truly there—she stops holding back. And when she stops holding back, it's game over.

It's not about ego. It's about connection. It's about mastery. It's about knowing that she walked in as one woman and will leave as another. Not because of me—but because of what she allowed herself to experience in my presence. And yes, I take pride in that. Because it's not easy to get a woman there. It takes patience. Presence. Sensitivity. And a real love for the feminine.

The truth is, most men don't know how to unlock a woman. They're too focused on themselves. Too focused on "getting off." Too focused on mechanics. And that's why so many women fake it. They fake moans. They fake orgasms. They fake interest. Because they've been conditioned to prioritize the man's experience over their own. And that's a tragedy.

But when you flip the script—when you center *her* pleasure—everything changes. The energy in the room shifts. She softens. She opens. She starts trusting. And the deeper that trust grows, the more uninhibited she becomes. That's when the magic happens. That's when you realize she's been starving for this. Not just the touch—but the reverence.

Because deep down, every woman wants to be taken—but not in a way that depletes her. In a way that elevates her. She wants to feel desired, devoured, and still respected. She wants to surrender—but only to someone strong enough to hold her through the surrender. She wants to let go—but only if she knows you won't take advantage of it.

This is why sex with a woman is never just sex. It's a psychological event. A spiritual ceremony. A full body reset. And the men who understand this—who treat it as sacred—are the ones who get the best of her. Not just sexually, but emotionally. Because when a woman feels safe enough to be herself in bed, she bonds. She blooms. She becomes more of herself.

This is also why it's such a gift to focus entirely on her pleasure. There's something primal about driving a woman crazy. Not for dominance—but for delight. Watching her writhe. Hearing her gasp. Feeling her nails dig into your back. Seeing her lose track of time, space, and even language. That's the reward. That's the drug. Not the orgasm. Not the ego stroke. But the witnessing. The knowing that you were the conduit.

In my experience, the women who love sex the most are the ones who have freed themselves from cultural shame. They've done the work. They've claimed their desires. They've stopped apologizing. And as a result, they radiate a kind of sexual confidence that is unmistakable. They don't need you—but when they choose you, they go all in. No holding back. No games. Just fire.

And yet, many men are intimidated by these women. They don't know how to handle that kind of intensity. They mislabel it. They judge it. Or worse, they try to suppress it. But here's the secret: if you honor it, you win. If you meet her fire with your own grounded strength, she'll go deeper than you ever imagined. Because she doesn't want to dominate. She wants to *co-create.*

Women aren't complicated—they're layered. They're multi-dimensional. And their relationship to sex is tied to their relationship with themselves. When they're shut down, disconnected, or ashamed, their bodies tighten. Their desire shrinks. But when they're honored, seen, and fully accepted, they become limitless. They become the embodiment of erotic energy.

So to any man reading this: stop believing the lie that women don't like sex. They do. Sometimes more than you. But you have to earn your way in—not with gifts or words, but with presence and respect. You have to prove that you can hold the intensity. That you're not afraid of her fire. That you're not going to use her, judge her, or shame her for something that was never shameful to begin with.

Women are built for pleasure. They're wired for waves. And when you understand this—truly understand it—your entire approach to intimacy changes. You stop chasing. You start creating. You stop demanding. You start guiding. You stop taking. You start giving.

And the irony? That's when you receive the most.

Because a fully satisfied woman is the greatest gift a man can receive—not just sexually, but energetically. She'll feed you. Fuel you. Inspire you. And if you're lucky, she'll invite you into a world that most men never get to experience.

But only if you're man enough to let her come first—in every sense of the word.

NEVER ARGUE WITH A WOMAN

Here's a hard-earned truth that every man needs to learn, preferably sooner rather than later: never argue with a woman. I'm not saying this as a joke. I'm not saying this out of bitterness. I'm saying it as someone who has argued in courtrooms before some of the most demanding, combative judges in the country—and I'd take that over an emotionally charged argument with a woman any day of the week. Court is difficult. Court is rigorous. But at least in court, logic is king, rules are respected, and there is a chance that reason will actually prevail.

With women, especially when emotions are running high, reason becomes irrelevant. Logic gets drowned out by waves of emotion, history, tone, and body language. You can make the most bulletproof point in the world, and it still won't land if she's not in a space to receive it. And let's be honest—most arguments don't even begin with the issue at hand. They begin with a feeling. A perceived slight. A miscommunication. And before you know it, you're not just talking about what happened five minutes ago—you're talking about something that happened five years ago.

In court, there are rules. There are procedures. There are lines that cannot be crossed. In a courtroom, if the opposing counsel brings up irrelevant evidence or starts character assassinating you based on past unrelated mistakes, the judge will shut it down. But when you're in an argument with a woman, all the rules go out the window. For her, nothing is off-limits. For you, everything is. If you raise your voice, you're the aggressor. If you try to walk away, you're accused of abandoning the conversation. If you stay and defend yourself, you're being argumentative.

This isn't to say that women are inherently unreasonable or that they can't handle conflict maturely. Many women can. But when things escalate emotionally—especially in romantic relationships—you're no longer dealing with just her intellect. You're dealing with her entire emotional archive. Every feeling she's ever suppressed, every resentment she's ever held onto, every insecurity she hasn't voiced—all of it can surface in a single conversation. And when it does, no amount of reason or evidence will save you.

The male brain and the female brain are wired differently when it comes to conflict. Men tend to compartmentalize. They want to address the issue, solve the problem, and move on. Women, on the other hand, often process things relationally. They want to explore the emotional landscape, revisit patterns, and ensure that you truly understand how your actions made them feel—not just in the moment, but historically. This is not a bad thing. It's just different. And if you try to handle a female emotional argument like it's a legal deposition, you're going to lose every time.

The truth is, once you allow yourself to be pulled into a heated argument, you've already lost. The moment it becomes a shouting match, or worse, a trade of insults, the dynamic shifts. It's no longer about resolving anything—it's about emotional dominance. And in that arena, you can't compete. Women are masters of emotional warfare. They have a memory for details you've long forgotten. They know exactly which buttons to push. And they aren't constrained by the male instinct to "stay on topic."

A woman in an emotionally charged state has access to a verbal arsenal that would make a prosecuting attorney blush. She will bring up the time you forgot her birthday three years ago, the way you looked at the waitress last month, and the sarcastic tone you used during an argument last week. Nothing is too far back, too minor, or too irrelevant. It's all on the table. And the more you try to steer the conversation back to the original issue, the more she'll remind you that *this* issue is just the tip of the iceberg.

And God forbid you actually get angry. Because once you show real frustration—once you raise your voice, pound your fist on the table, or let your face twist into anything that looks like rage—you've stepped into the trap. She might cry. She might go cold. She might accuse you of being emotionally unsafe. And in that moment, it doesn't matter how calm and collected you were up until now. You're the bad guy.

That's why I always say: don't argue. Don't engage. Don't escalate. The minute you feel the energy turning south—when you can sense that this is no longer a conversation, but a collision—step back. Breathe. Say something neutral like, "I don't think this is going anywhere right now. Let's talk when we're both calm." And then walk away. Not storm out. Not slam doors. Just disengage. It's not weakness. It's wisdom.

Now, you might think walking away makes you look like you're avoiding accountability. And yes, she might say that. She might accuse you of not caring, of refusing to engage, of invalidating her feelings. But don't take the bait. You can always revisit the issue when things cool down. You can always come back to the conversation with calm, clarity, and focus. But you can't un-say the cruel thing you blurted in the heat of battle. You can't un-hear the words that were meant to wound.

Understand this: arguments are not debates. In a debate, the goal is to win through superior logic. In an argument—especially with someone you care about—the goal should be understanding. And understanding cannot happen when emotions are at a boil. No one listens well when they feel attacked. No one processes clearly when their heart rate is pounding out of their chest.

And here's the irony: the calmer you stay, the more emotional she may become. It's not manipulation. It's biology. When one person in an emotional exchange doesn't mirror the other's intensity, it creates tension. She may interpret your calm as coldness. As indifference. But that's her process, not yours. Your job isn't to match her emotion. It's to manage your own.

Let me be clear—I'm not advocating for silence or emotional suppression. I'm not saying men should never express anger or frustration. I'm saying there's a time and place. There's a way to voice your feelings without becoming reactive. And there's tremendous power in knowing when to speak and when to stay silent.

Think of it this way: arguing with a woman is like stepping into a storm. The winds will swirl. The temperature will rise. Debris from the past will start flying. And if you try to fight the storm, you'll get destroyed. But if you wait it out—if you stay grounded, calm, and centered—the storm passes. And once it does, the real conversation can begin.

Emotional intelligence means knowing when a fight isn't worth having. It means understanding that your need to be right is less important than your need to stay sane. It means realizing that sometimes, the best move isn't a clever comeback or a persuasive argument—it's simply walking away with your peace intact.

You'll find, more often than not, that the issue resolves itself when you give it space. Once the heat dies down, your partner might even come back with a clearer head, ready to talk without the fireworks. And if she doesn't? Then maybe you learned something important about the relationship. Maybe that kind of volatility isn't something you want to keep inviting into your life.

This approach doesn't make you passive. It makes you strategic. It makes you resilient. It makes you a man who knows how to handle chaos without becoming chaotic. And trust me—women respect that. Even if they won't admit it in the moment, they feel safer with a man who doesn't lose his cool. A man who can absorb the tension without amplifying it.

So next time you feel an argument brewing, remember this: you're not in court. You're not on trial. There are no rules here except the ones you choose to live by. And the most important rule of all? Protect your peace. Guard your energy. Don't let anyone—no matter how beautiful, intelligent, or emotionally compelling—drag you into a battle you can't win.

Because when you argue with a woman in the heat of the moment, the outcome is always the same: everyone loses.

But when you stay calm, stay kind, and walk away with grace, you win.

Every time.

Why Dating Sites and Apps Almost Always Fail

Online dating is a lot like the pharmaceutical industry.

Think about it—Big Pharma has no real interest in curing cancer, diabetes, or heart disease. Their goal isn't to *eliminate* these conditions; it's to turn patients into lifetime customers. Lower your cholesterol, manage your blood pressure, control your blood sugar—but never *cure* you. Because if they cured you, you wouldn't need their products anymore.

Now, apply that same logic to dating apps. Their stated purpose is to help you find love, a lasting relationship, maybe even marriage. And yes, it happens. Occasionally. They're quick to parade around success stories, but the reality is that those stories are *extremely* rare. Because if their system *actually worked*—if people consistently found their perfect match and left the platform—dating apps would go out of business. That's why their success depends on *your failure*.

Ever notice how hard they make it to cancel your subscription? How everything is built around auto-renewal? How the algorithms seem to keep you engaged but never quite deliver what you're looking for? That's not an accident. It's by design. The entire industry thrives on *hope*. Hope that *this* match will be the one. That *this* swipe will change everything. That *this* date will be your last first date. And hope keeps people coming back, month after month, renewal after renewal, scrolling endlessly for "the one."

What Would Happen if Dating Sites Actually Worked?

Imagine if, overnight, every dating site user found their perfect match on day one. If every new subscriber got into a committed relationship within a week. What would happen? The industry would *collapse*. Just like if pharmaceutical companies miraculously cured all major diseases, they would no longer be needed, and their profits would vanish. Of course, you'll never hear this from a dating site's "About Us" page, but it's the uncomfortable truth.

So What Do You Do About It?

If you're the kind of person who prefers meeting women in person—at Whole Foods, the gym, a concert, a bar—then this entire discussion doesn't matter. You don't *need* dating apps. But if you're like most people, you've realized that the easiest, most time-efficient way to meet potential romantic partners is *online*. Does that mean you should change your approach? Maybe. But the reality is, humans are lazy. We like convenience. And it's *way* easier to swipe through 1,000 profiles than it is to go from place to place, hoping to strike up a conversation. Plus, let's be honest—bars and clubs are so loud these days that even if you *do* meet someone, you can barely hear what they're saying.

So, what's the solution?

It depends on *you*.

- If you're an extrovert and love meeting people in person, ditch the apps.
- If you value your time and want the widest possible selection, stick with them—but go in with *realistic expectations*.

Because in dating, as in life, you gotta kiss a lot of frogs to find the prince. Or, in this case, *the princess*. And for better or worse, as long as people keep searching for love, dating apps will keep giving them *just enough hope* to stick around.

Dopamine vs. Love—Never Mistake One for the Other

A wise doctor once said: "Dopamine is pleasure. Serotonin is happiness." And an even wiser recovering attorney once said: "If I can't find love, I will settle for dopamine every time." That second one? That's me.

Let's face it—we are pleasure-seeking animals. Given the choice between happiness and pleasure, most people will take pleasure every time. Maybe that's just me, or maybe it's human nature. But through years of experience, through countless dates and encounters, I've learned a crucial lesson: never mistake dopamine for love.

What is Dopamine? What is Love?

To understand why we so often confuse these two things, you need to understand the difference between them. Dopamine is the "feel-good" neurotransmitter that gives us a rush of pleasure and excitement. It's what drives addiction, what fuels our cravings, and what makes us chase that next high—whether it's sex, food, gambling, or even social media likes. Dopamine is immediate gratification. It's the thrill of the chase, the rush of winning, the high of desire.

Love, on the other hand, is something much deeper. Real love isn't just about excitement and passion—it's about connection, trust, stability, and emotional intimacy. Love isn't just about what someone makes you feel in the moment; it's about how they make you feel over time.

Dopamine is the first date with someone new. Love is the feeling of deep comfort and security when you've been with someone for years and still enjoy their presence. Dopamine is the fireworks. Love is the warmth of a steady flame that never burns out. And yet, most people—myself included—have fallen into the dopamine trap over and over again.

The Dopamine Trap: Why We Chase the High

I can't tell you how many times I've seen men—and women—mistake lust for love, infatuation for commitment, and dopamine for something deeper. It happens fast. You meet someone new. The chemistry is undeniable. Your heart races when you see them. The sex is electric. You feel like they were made for you, like you've finally found "the one." That's dopamine talking.

Dopamine makes you obsess over this person; makes you crave their presence like a drug. But what happens when the high wears off? That's when reality sets in. That's when you start to see the flaws, the incompatibilities, the things that were there all along but were blurred by the rush of excitement. The problem? Most people don't know how to differentiate between dopamine and real love. They chase the high, believing that this initial excitement is the foundation for a lasting relationship. And when the thrill fades, they panic.

- They think the relationship is broken.
- They assume they've "fallen out of love."
- They seek out a new source of dopamine—another partner, another high.

This is why so many relationships fail. Because people mistake infatuation for love, and when the thrill disappears, they assume the relationship wasn't meant to last. I know I used to do it all the time. They don't realize that love isn't about constant excitement—it's about something deeper.

Why Men Fall for the Dopamine Illusion

Men, in particular, are vulnerable to this trap. Our brains are wired to pursue, conquer, and win. We see dating as a challenge, a game to be played and won. The pursuit of a woman, the thrill of attraction, the rush of seduction—it's all dopamine. The problem is that most men don't understand that the game doesn't end when you win her over. They think once they sleep with her, once they make her theirs, that's it—the feeling will last forever.

But that's not how dopamine works. Dopamine is fleeting. The moment you get what you want, the thrill fades, and your brain starts looking for the next hit. That's why so many men who chase women endlessly lose interest the second they sleep with them. It's why men who crave the chase often find themselves stuck in an endless cycle of short-term relationships, hookups, and flings. They're addicted to the dopamine rush—but dopamine doesn't last. Real love? That's a different game entirely.

How to Tell If It's Dopamine or Love

So, how do you know if what you're feeling is real love or just a dopamine hit? Ask yourself these questions:

1. Do you still want to be around her when there's no sex, no excitement, no rush?
2. Do you enjoy the quiet moments, the simple conversations, the mundane parts of life with her?
3. Does she make you feel safe, secure, and understood—or just excited and aroused?
4. Do you actually like her as a person beyond the chemistry?
5. If the sex disappeared tomorrow, would you still want to be with her?

If your connection is built entirely on passion, attraction, and the thrill of the chase, then it's dopamine. If your bond is built on deep respect, genuine care, shared values, and mutual understanding, then it's love. And here's the key: Dopamine fades. Love grows.

The Role of Dopamine in Long-Term Relationships

Now, this doesn't mean that dopamine is the enemy, far from it. A healthy relationship still needs excitement, passion, and sexual chemistry. But the trick is learning how to balance dopamine with a deeper connection. Long-term relationships lose their initial spark not because the couple isn't meant to be, but because they stop doing the things that created dopamine in the first place. They stop:

- Flirting.
- Surprising each other.
- Taking each other on dates.
- Trying new experiences together.

When dopamine naturally fades, most couples assume that means the love is gone. But in reality, it just means you need to put effort into creating new sources of dopamine within the relationship.

- Try new things together.
- Go on an adventure.
- Surprise her with something unexpected.
- Keep flirting, keep teasing, keep the tension alive.

Dopamine may not last forever, but you can always create new spikes of it—if you're willing to put in the work.

Final Thoughts

Choose Wisely At the end of the day, you have a choice. You can chase dopamine forever—moving from one high to the next, mistaking every rush of passion for love, never truly settling into something real. Or you can recognize dopamine for what it is—a temporary thrill—and instead seek something deeper, something lasting, something real.

Most men never figure this out. They keep chasing pleasure, thinking they're chasing happiness. They keep confusing dopamine for love—and wonder why they never feel truly fulfilled. But you don't have to be one of those men. You can learn to recognize the difference. You can learn to seek real connection, not just momentary excitement. Because in the end, love is what lasts. Dopamine is just the ride that gets you there.

THE THREE WORDS THAT KILL
RELATIONSHIPS

The worst thing a man can say to a woman? "I love you." Not because love isn't real. Not because relationships don't matter. But because saying it first is almost always a mistake. Many men believe that expressing their feelings early will deepen a relationship, strengthen a bond, or prove their commitment. They think that by saying "I love you," they are creating security. But more often than not, saying it too soon does the exact opposite—it weakens the relationship and pushes the woman away.

Why Saying "I Love You" First Is a Mistake

I'm borrowing some wisdom here from Corey Wayne and Strong Successful Male, two well-known voices in the dating and self-improvement space. The truth is, when a man is more into a woman than she is into him, the relationship won't last. A woman has to feel like she's the one chasing you. She has to believe that she's slowly winning you over. The moment you make it clear that she already has you completely, the dynamic shifts.

She stops putting in effort. She stops feeling that subtle tension of uncertainty that keeps her attracted. She may even begin to lose respect for you without fully realizing why. It's human nature. When something is too easy, too predictable, too secure, we start to take it for granted. And this is where many men go wrong. They get caught up in the intoxicating mix of dopamine, oxytocin, and great sex. They feel the high of a new romance, the deep pleasure of intimacy, and they want to lock it in. They want to secure the relationship, so they declare their love too soon. But instead of bringing them closer, it has the opposite effect.

The Power of Uncertainty in Attraction

People are most attracted to things that are just out of reach. Think about it:

- The car you've always wanted but couldn't afford feels more desirable than the one you already own.
- The vacation spot you've never visited holds more allure than the one you've been to three times.
- The person who keeps you guessing is more intriguing than the one who lays everything out immediately.

Women are the same way when it comes to love and relationships. They need to feel like they are slowly winning you over, not that they have you completely from the start. That doesn't mean you should play games or be manipulative. It simply means that you should let the relationship develop naturally. Let her be the one to wonder where she stands. Let her be the one who starts to feel the need to lock things in. Because when she is the one saying "I love you" first, she has already invested emotionally. She has already decided that you are the prize. And that's where you want to be.

Why Men Say "I Love You" Too Soon

So why do men blurt out those three little words too early?

1. They mistake dopamine for love. The thrill of a new relationship, combined with physical attraction, can trick the brain into thinking something deeper is happening. But those feelings are often temporary.
2. They feel insecure and want reassurance. Some men use "I love you" as a way to get confirmation that the woman feels the same way—but the need for reassurance signals weakness.
3. They think it will make the relationship stronger. Men assume that by expressing love, the woman will feel closer to them. But most of the time, it lowers their perceived value instead.
4. They've been conditioned by movies and romance novels. Hollywood has sold men the fantasy that grand gestures

114

and declarations of love are the way to win a woman's heart. Real attraction doesn't work that way.

How to Avoid the "I Love You" Trap

So what's the right approach?

1. Let her say it first. The best relationships are the ones where the woman is chasing the man—not the other way around. If you feel the urge to say it, hold back and wait.
2. Show, don't tell. Love isn't just about words—it's about actions. Treat her well, make her feel desired, and create unforgettable experiences together. That will say more than "I love you" ever could.
3. Keep your emotions in check. If you feel yourself getting caught up in the excitement of a new romance, slow down. Don't make impulsive declarations. Enjoy the process without rushing into deep emotional commitments.
4. Maintain your self-respect. A woman should never feel like she is the center of your world. She should feel like she is earning your affection over time. Keep your focus on your own life, goals, and purpose.
5. Let her feel uncertainty. This doesn't mean playing mind games or being unavailable. It simply means allowing her to wonder where she stands, at least for a little while. The moment she feels like she has you completely, the attraction begins to fade.

Final Thoughts: The Real Secret to Lasting Attraction

At the core of all of this is a simple truth: Men who are too available, too eager, and too emotionally invested too soon lose their appeal. Women want a man who has options, a man who is confident, a man who values himself enough to let a relationship develop at the right pace. Saying "I love you" too soon kills mystery, eliminates uncertainty, and shifts the power dynamic in a way that rarely benefits the man. So be patient. Let her come to her own realization that she loves you. Because when she says it first—when she looks you in the eyes, vulnerable and open, and tells you that she loves you—you will know that she truly means it. And that is a love worth having.

Women Need Uncertainty—But Not Manipulation

A woman needs *some* level of uncertainty about you. Not full-blown fear that you'll leave her at any moment, but a *little* emotional ambiguity to keep her engaged. This doesn't mean you manipulate her. It doesn't mean you play mind games. It means that even when you *feel* the same way about her as she does about you, you keep your cards close to your vest. Take it from me—I've ruined more potential relationships with those three little words than you would ever believe.

Never Shower a Woman with Unearned Gifts

Another common mistake men make? Giving too much, too soon. Women *do* appreciate gifts, but only when they're earned. Randomly showering a woman with gifts doesn't increase her affection—it shifts the balance of power in the relationship and makes her too certain of your devotion. If she puts on an *incredible* dress, does her hair perfectly, and makes you weak in the knees just looking at her? If she surprises you with an amazing home-cooked meal? *That's* when flowers or a special gift is warranted.

Earned appreciation keeps a woman invested. Too many unearned gifts, and it all loses meaning. She stops seeing you as the catch, and you become just another guy trying to buy her affection. So, remember: dopamine is not love, "I love you" should never be rushed, and unearned rewards kill attraction. Keep your emotions in check, let her chase you, and make sure appreciation is always earned.

That's how you keep the balance—and the attraction—alive.

THE MYTH OF THE
DRAMA-FREE WOMAN

If you review 100 female dating profiles on any given app or site, you'll see it over and over again:

"No drama here."

"Drama-free lady."

"I don't do drama."

And I have no doubt that they *believe* it. But as with most things involving the female psyche, reality is rarely what it appears to be. A woman's operating system is emotion. They feel, therefore they are. And emotional states create *drama*. Even the most stable woman will have bouts of drama—she can't help it. It's part of her nature. The difference is that a highly emotional woman will go out of her way to create drama, while a stable woman will acknowledge it and try to control it. Either way, a woman is drawn to drama like a kitten is drawn to cream.

How to Handle Drama—And Why It's Necessary

This is where a man's patience comes in. A certain level of drama is baked into the cake. It's part of the deal. But when it starts spinning out of control, *you have to put your foot down*. Because if you don't, she will lose respect for you. That's a guarantee. Women need a man's **stability and rationality** to keep them grounded. When a man fails to provide that anchor—when he allows himself to get swept up in her emotional storms—she will no longer see him as strong. And once she stops seeing you as strong, it's only a matter of time before she stops seeing you as *desirable*.

That doesn't mean you go in guns blazing every time she gets emotional. **You can't come down on her too hard.** That will only escalate things and make her dig in. But you *do* have to set clear boundaries. If a woman sees that you're unwilling to engage in unnecessary drama, if she realizes that you won't let her emotional turbulence dictate your mood, she will adjust. Most importantly, if you put your foot down early, you'll avoid bigger problems later. The moment you start tolerating excessive drama, you set a precedent. She'll push the limits further, and before you know it, the relationship will be a never-ending cycle of chaos.

So when drama rears its head, recognize it for what it is. Address it calmly but firmly. Let her know that you're not signing up for the rollercoaster. And if she refuses to control it? Walk. Because a woman who respects you will always respect your boundaries.

WOMEN AND LINGERIE— OR THE LACK THEREOF

I grew up in the 1970s, an era where braless fashion was practically a movement. High school was a frustrating paradise for a breast man like me—so many girls *not* wearing bras, yet always just out of reach. Fast-forward to today, and while styles have changed, the underlying theme remains: less is more.

Younger women today wear outfits that push the boundaries of decency, keeping just enough fabric to avoid an indecent exposure charge. But let's be honest—a lot of what they wear is patently indecent. Beyond that, there seems to have been some unspoken, collective decision among women to abandon bras and panties altogether. Maybe it's the rise of implants, maybe it's a shift in comfort preferences, or maybe lingerie just doesn't hold the same appeal it once did.

Whatever the reason, I can't tell you how many women I've been with who were completely naked under their dresses or tops. And I love it. A woman dressing like that is sending a clear message, whether she consciously acknowledges it or not. She'll deny it all day long, but the truth is, a woman who steps out in a thin silk or nylon dress with nothing underneath is already thinking about pleasure. It's subtle. It's primal. And it's deliberate.

Reading the Signals

When I meet a woman, there's always the little hello hug and peck on the cheek. But during that moment, I'm also paying attention—I discreetly feel for a bra strap against her back. Then, as my hand slides down to her waist, I check for a panty line. Not in a crude or obvious way—always with the finesse of a gentleman. But that small bit of information tells me a lot.

A woman who walks into a date with no undergarments is, at the very least, in a sensual frame of mind. She may not even realize it herself, but her body does. And knowing this allows me to adjust my approach, reading her intent and guiding the night accordingly. In South Florida, I can tell you firsthand—Victoria's Secret must be struggling. Women have ditched their undergarments in droves.

And in my experience? It's a clear signal that things are about to get very interesting.

THE CAR—THE ULTIMATE TOOL OF SEDUCTION

Ever since the automobile was invented over a century ago, men have been using it as more than just a mode of transportation—it's been a *tool of seduction.* You've heard the term *chick magnet*—and while that usually refers to the allure of an expensive or flashy car, I've found that cars have an even greater power: they are magnets for getting women out of their clothes.

There's something about the intimacy of a car, the enclosed space, the shift from the structured setting of a restaurant to the private, unpredictable atmosphere of a moving vehicle. It's where the night takes on a new energy—where things really begin.

THE PALM BEACH POCKET PARK ROUTINE

Of course, every experienced man has his own little tricks. In Palm Beach, one of the wealthiest enclaves on the planet, I've refined my approach to take full advantage of the setting. Some of my favorite restaurants happen to be conveniently located near several pocket parks—small, quiet, tucked-away spots where privacy is just a few steps away.

The formula is simple:

- Dinner and conversation set the stage, the flirtation building throughout the meal.
- A walk afterward, tailored to her footwear—if she's in heels, we keep it short; if she's in comfortable flats, we take a longer route.
- A casual detour to a pocket park, where the ambiance shifts, the intimacy deepens, and things *heat up very quickly.*

By this point, the energy is undeniable. The lack of undergarments, the chemistry, the subtle signals—everything falls into place. And from there? The car becomes the next natural step. Somewhere between the flick of the door lock and the first kiss in the dim glow of the dashboard, the night takes on a momentum of its own.

Why Cars Still Work After All These Years

The car is a symbol of *freedom*—but in the right hands, it's also a *container* for desire. It removes distractions, creates an instant sense of privacy, and amplifies the moment. And for women who step into the night with nothing but a thin silk dress between them and the world? Let's just say Victoria's Secret *definitely* won't be getting their business that evening.

Surprise Is Always on My Side

I know I'm an attractive and appealing man, but I also know how most women initially perceive me—*unassuming*, not the type they expect to trigger their deepest desires. And that's exactly why surprise is my greatest advantage. After all, I'm a father of three. I raised them myself after my wife passed away many years ago. To the average woman, I probably come across as a well-mannered gentleman, the kind of guy who's stable, reliable, and maybe even a little predictable. But what they don't realize—at least not *yet*—is that beneath that composed exterior lies something they weren't expecting.

Women Love to Be Surprised

There's a common belief that women instinctively know within 30 seconds whether they'll sleep with a man. That may be true, but I've also seen plenty of women change their minds when they *discover* what they didn't see at first glance.

Because here's the thing:

- Women expect a predictable experience based on how a man *appears*.
- When he defies those expectations, *it ignites something in them.*

The slow realization that I'm not just another nice guy…that I understand *desire* better than most men they've ever met…that I can lead them into new experiences they weren't even looking for…That realization is electric.

The Hidden Advantage of Being Underestimated

Most women expect the "bad boys" to have the seductive edge. The ones who flaunt their intentions, act cocky, and make it obvious what they want. That's *not* me. My strength is in the *subtlety*. The unexpected shift from charming dinner conversation to a perfectly timed touch. The build-up they never saw coming. The gradual, deliberate escalation that feels natural but is anything but accidental. And when they finally realize what's happening—that moment when they're caught between curiosity and surrender—that's when they're *truly* hooked. Surprise is the ultimate seduction. And it's always on my side.

This Is Real

Now, you might be reading this and thinking, *This guy is full of himself. Full of shit.* But you'd be wrong. I wasn't always able to have my way with the ladies. It took years of **self-examination,** hard work, and course correction to figure out what I was doing wrong and how to fix it. I always did well financially, but let's be clear—I don't have a private jet. There are plenty of people in Palm Beach County far wealthier than I am. And that's exactly the point.

The False Promise of Wealth

A lot of men in my position use their wealth as a bargaining chip. They dangle the lifestyle, the luxury, the *promise* of a future payoff. And women—some of them, at least—will stick around for years, waiting for that golden reward. It works. But it was never what I wanted. I've been around wealthy people my entire life. Many of them are deeply unhappy, living lives that are filled with material success but completely devoid of meaning. Their relationships are transactional—just another extension of their business dealings. I wanted something different.

Mastering Desire—Without the Games

My goal was never to be a man women tolerated because of what I could *provide*. I wanted to be the man who **unlocked their rawest desires**, who could turn any woman into a *willing*—no, *eager*—partner in pleasure. Not because of money. Not because of status. But because she *couldn't resist*. It's not a head game—though maybe once it was.

Now, I don't have to **strategize** or **manipulate**. I simply act on my desires and let things unfold. I see who will play along, who will let themselves be guided, who will surrender to the moment. And you know what? Most of them do.

The Art of the Goodbye—Sealing the Night with Surprise

Like I said before, I have intimate contact with about 10% of the women I date. But if I wanted to, I could probably have it with virtually all of them—if I stretched things out over another date or two. Most of the time, the setup is the same. Maybe we hold hands as we stroll down the street after dinner. Maybe there's a light touch here, a shared laugh there. But regardless of how the evening unfolds, I always walk her to her car.

For two reasons.

1. **Safety.** I would never forgive myself if something happened to a woman I just spent the evening with—especially if I could have prevented it.
2. **Protection.** Women need to feel safe, to feel like the man they're with is capable of handling a situation if it arises. I'm not a fighter, but I am always armed, and I *wouldn't hesitate* to unleash hell on anyone who posed a threat.

And then comes the moment.

The Kiss That Leaves Her Shaken

I go in for the goodnight kiss—not too aggressive, not too soft. Just enough to make it clear who's leading. But that's never where it ends. As the kiss lingers, I slide down to her neck, a quick flick of my tongue, catching her off guard before she even realizes what's happening. Then, in a single motion, I take her earlobe into my mouth and start sucking.

Few women know what's happening until it's already underway. It drives them insane—their body's reaction betraying them before their mind catches up. Some instinctively try to push away, but I don't stop until I decide to. By the time we part, her world is shaken. She's unsteady, unsure, and completely disoriented by the moment.

Leaving Her Wanting More

If I like her, I might call her—in three or four days. Just long enough for her to obsess. To wonder. To replay the night in her mind. Just when she's about to give up all hope, her phone lights up. Because I'm full of surprises.

Why I Never Delete a Text

The reason is simple: I've been with so many women that I can't remember them all—and I don't even try. Instead, I let my phone do the remembering for me. I keep every single text conversation because, more often than you'd think, a woman I once dated will resurface years later on a dating site. To me, it's a fresh encounter. To her, it might be as well—time flows by, memories fade, and if I never followed up, she probably put me out of her mind. But the moment I enter my number to send a text, our entire texting history appears before me.

Revisiting the Past—Or Leaving It Behind

Sometimes, I scroll through the messages and think, *She looks great. We had a good time. Why not?* Other times, I read the conversation, shake my head, and leave the past where it belongs.

How I Keep Track

When I first started down this path, I just saved names and numbers. If I picked her up at her place, I'd store her address. I'd even add the name of the dating site where we met in the notes. But now? Now, I take image captures and store her picture on the contact card. I always say, I never forget a pretty face. And having her photo there really helps jog my memory—even when there was ample reason to forget.

TALES FROM THE 1000 DATES –
THE SUPERMODEL WHO COULDN'T GET ENOUGH

I've deliberately kept this book focused on the bigger picture—seduction, attraction, and the dynamics between men and women. But I know there's a part of everyone reading this that wants the prurient details. So who am I to withhold the goods? Here's a few of the more memorable events.

The Supermodel Who Couldn't Get Enough

She was a blonde, former supermodel—past her prime, but in the sexiest way possible. 5'9" with a killer build, large, billowing breasts, and the kind of elegance that only comes with experience. That night, she wore a silk strappy dress with no bra—a decision that didn't go unnoticed. We met at a waterfront restaurant in Fort Lauderdale. The waiters had seen me there many times before and nodded their approval when they saw who I was with.

She wasted no time, knocking back three glasses of wine in short order. By then, the electricity between us was undeniable. Touching. Stroking. Fingers lightly tracing hands, arms, and wrists. Brief kisses between sips of wine. The anticipation thick in the air. Dinner ended, and we took a slow, deliberate walk near the beach, eventually finding a bench tucked away from the crowd.

We sat down. Then the tension snapped. We were locked in a deep, desperate kiss, hands roaming, my fingers trailing down her body, over her breasts, teasing, caressing. Right there, in the open. A Broward County Sheriff's Deputy sat 25 feet away, parked, oblivious.

I discreetly stroked her breast, teasing her nipple through the fabric as she let out a barely stifled moan, her breath coming in short, heated bursts. We didn't stop. Not until it was too risky to continue. We got up, breathless, and walked back to my car—where the real action began.

The Car Scene

The moment we were inside, we didn't miss a beat. I reached for her straps and pulled them down, exposing her full, perfect breasts. She let out a deep, guttural moan as I took her nipple into my mouth, sucking like a baby who'd missed feeding time. Her fingers tangled in my hair, pushing me against her, arching into the sensation. She couldn't get enough. Then my hand slid downward. She felt it. She knew where this was headed. She lifted her hips slightly, eagerly helping me slide her panties down. By then, she was already dripping, ready, desperate. And then my fingers took over. And then my tongue.

I saw her a couple more times after that. But for whatever reason, nothing ever reached that level again. Maybe it was meant to be a one-time explosion. Maybe it was the thrill of almost getting caught. Or maybe some nights are just meant to be legendary.

THE ZOFTIG LADY WITH THE O SHOT

I had been out with this lady a few times prior. She was on the more zoftig side but still very attractive and clearly into me. That night, I took her to a local restaurant. She wore a **red, full**-length silky dress held together at the top by a gold clasp. Nothing was visible, but I knew that beneath that thin layer of fabric, there was nothing underneath.

Dinner unfolded as usual—touching, stroking, lingering kisses. When we left the restaurant, we both knew what was next. We agreed to go back to my place for a *"drink"* that neither of us actually wanted. While waiting for the valet, we were already making out. The valet attendant was visibly irritated, but fuck him. Let him be jealous.

Back at my place, we never bothered with the drink. We headed straight for the couch. As we kissed, I fumbled with the clasp but couldn't quite figure it out, so I took the next best route—pushing her dress up. Voila. No panties. I already knew from past experience that she never wore bras, but this time I was greeted with a perfectly smooth, hairless pussy. It was lovely.

I started with my fingers and felt how dripping wet she already was. That was my cue. I led her upstairs to my bedroom and told her to remove the clasp. The dress fell to the floor, and there she was, in all her glory. I positioned her on her hands and knees and started licking, but she quickly pushed me into position for more. She wasn't interested in rear action—she wanted direct attention.

As I worked her over, I noticed something unusual. Her clitoris was bulging, larger than usual. Then it hit me—she had the O Shot. This is a procedure where women have a permanent filler injected into their clitoris, making it hypersensitive and enlarged.

I went to town. She had a massive orgasm, shaking uncontrollably beneath me. But then, just as suddenly as she had given in to the pleasure, something changed.

Panic. Out of nowhere, she scrambled for her dress, threw it on, and ran out the door.

To this day, I don't understand what happened. Maybe it was overwhelming. Maybe it was something else entirely. Hell, maybe it was my breath. She called the next morning with some lame excuse about being ill. I didn't push for an explanation. Just another interesting experience. I chalked it up to the game and moved on.

THE WILD ONE WHO COULDN'T GROW UP

I spotted her profile on Hinge. She was stunning—a blend of Asian and Caribbean, with flawless caramel skin and a body that radiated sensuality. We exchanged texts, she gave me her number, and I called to arrange our first date. We met at a restaurant on Atlantic Avenue in Delray Beach, the nerve center of the town's nightlife scene. She walked in wearing Daisy Duke shorts and a tight-fitting top—hard to tell at first whether she was wearing a bra or not, but it didn't matter. Her presence was magnetic.

The First Date—Laying the Groundwork

Dinner was electric—flirtation, teasing, just enough physical contact to set the tone. Afterward, I walked her home, holding hands as we strolled through the warm Florida night. When we reached her doorstep, I gave her a quick kiss, said goodnight, and walked away. Three days passed before I called her. When she answered, the first thing she said was: "Oh, I thought you weren't interested."

Of course, she did. She was the kind of woman men called on the drive home from their date, desperate to lock things down. But the fact that I waited—that I didn't chase—made me ten times more interesting to her. Women always want the man who feels just out of reach.

Turning Up the Heat—The Barbecue Invitation

I told her to come over for a barbecue and to bring her bathing suit so we could take a dip in the pool. She arrived in another pair of Daisy Dukes, an open shirt, and just a bikini top. The moment she stepped inside, we started making out on the couch. The top came off. Then we moved to the bedroom.

I went down on her, and she had one of the most intense orgasms I've ever witnessed. She screamed so loud I was worried the neighbors would call the cops. That moment set the tone for what became a wild, no-holds-barred, month-long fling.

The Party Girl Who Never Grew Up

She was fun, uninhibited, and one of the kinkiest women I've ever been with. But she also drank like a fish and had a taste for harder substances. At first, I let it slide. The sex was too good. One night, she invited a few friends over for drinks and a barbecue. We all got shitfaced. At the end of the night, as her friend was leaving, she walked up to her, yanked off her panties, and tossed them onto my front lawn. They were still there the next morning. She was completely out of control, but she was also *wildly fun in bed*. So I let it ride.

Until Miami.

The Night It Fell Apart

We planned a weekend getaway—a show, dinner, a little partying. That first night, around midnight, she tried to call her daughter and son-in-law. No answer. Most people would assume they were asleep—because normal people sleep at 1 AM. Not her. She was wasted and immediately convinced that they had died in a car accident.

She was *hysterical*—beyond reason, beyond logic. I tried to talk her down, but nothing got through. So she called an Uber and left in the middle of the night to drive 60 miles to their house. Of course, when she got there, they were alive and well—sleeping, just like I told her they would be. She called me the next afternoon, acting like nothing had happened. Not even an apology. I was pissed off like never before.

Women don't usually get me that angry, but her complete lack of rationality was infuriating. The next day, she called, apologizing, but I was done. I told her, "We're over. Goodbye." And that was it. Well, mostly. A few more late-night roll-in-the-hay sessions followed, but I knew better than to get sucked back into the crazy. To this day, if I called her, she'd show up in a heartbeat. But I've learned my lesson. Some women are too wild to keep around. And no matter how good the sex is, you just can't be around crazy people.

THE POLARIZING PLEASURE:
WOMEN, ANAL SEX, AND THE ART OF CONVERSION

To say anal sex divides women is an understatement—it's a fault line, a lightning rod, a subject that sparks reactions as visceral and varied as opinions about the current occupant of the White House. Some women swear by it, reveling in its intensity, its taboo allure, its capacity to unlock a kind of pleasure that feels primal and uncharted. Others recoil at the mere mention, dismissing it as uncomfortable, unnatural, or simply not worth the effort. Like a controversial political figure, it's a topic that leaves little room for ambivalence: you're either in the fan club or you're emphatically not. And much like politics, the reasons behind these stances are often deeply personal, shaped by experience, trust, and—crucially—the skill (or lack thereof) of the person leading the charge.

I've seen this divide up close. I've been with women who've flat-out refused, their minds made up by a clumsy ex or a single bad encounter that left them wincing at the thought. I've also been with those who embraced it from the start, eager to explore every inch of what their bodies could feel. Me? I'm a fan—not just of the act itself, but of the challenge it presents: the chance to take someone from "never" to "more, please." There's something exhilarating about that shift, about guiding a partner past their doubts into a place of abandon and discovery. It's not about coercion—never that—but about patience, intuition, and a willingness to listen to what her body says, even when her words say, "no way."

Take Sarah, for instance. (Name changed, of course—she'd kill me if I didn't.) When we met, she was adamant: anal was off the table, a hard limit carved in stone. "I tried it once," she told me over drinks on our first date, her nose wrinkling like she'd smelled something sour. "He didn't know what he was doing, and I swore I'd never go

137

through that again." I didn't push—why would I? There's no fun in forcing anything, and besides, I figured if it ever happened, it'd be her idea, not mine. That's the trick: plant the seed, then let it grow on its own.

We clicked fast. By our second or third time together, the chemistry was electric—oral, penetration, the kind of rhythm that makes you forget where one body ends and the other begins. She came hard that night, her breath ragged, her skin flushed, her whole frame trembling in that post-orgasmic haze where the world feels soft and pliable. I saw my opening—not a calculated move, just a gut instinct. While she was still floating, I eased her onto her stomach, my hands gentle but sure. I started with a rim job, slow and deliberate, letting her adjust to the sensation. She tensed at first—old habits, old fears—but I kept it light, teasing, giving her space to pull away if she wanted. She didn't.

Instead, she melted. I guided her hand between her legs, encouraging her to touch herself while I worked. That's when the dam broke. She went wild—bucking, shaking, her moans turning into something raw and unrestrained. It was like watching a storm roll in, all that pent-up energy crashing through her. She came again, harder than before, her body quaking like it was rewriting its own rules. And she was still trembling when I reached for the lube.

One finger first, coated and careful, sliding in with a massage-like rhythm. No rush, no force—just an invitation. She didn't flinch. A second finger followed, more lube, a gentle stretch to ease her into it. Her breathing shifted—less shock, more curiosity. She was liking it, maybe even surprised she was liking it. Then came the main event: more lube, a generous amount on myself, and a slow, steady push. I watched her face, her body, ready to stop if she gave the word. She never did. Instead, she leaned into it, her hips tilting up, her gasps turning into pleas. She was loving every second—every inch—and I knew right then I'd made a convert.

Afterward, she lay there, spent and grinning, a far cry from the woman who'd sworn anal was a dealbreaker. "I can't believe I begged for that," she said, half-laughing, half-dazed. She didn't just enjoy it; she owned it, surrendering to her own pleasure in a way that felt like a triumph. For me, it wasn't about conquest—it was about witnessing that transformation, seeing someone rewrite their own boundaries in real time.

That's the thing about anal sex: it's not just physical. It's psychological, emotional, a dance of trust and vulnerability that can go spectacularly right or disastrously wrong. The haters—and there are plenty—often have a story behind their disdain. A lover who rushed in, heedless of prep or consent. A partner who treated it like a checklist item rather than a shared experience. Pain, embarrassment, a sense of being unheard—those are the scars that turn "maybe" into "never." I've heard it all: "It hurt too much," "He didn't care how I felt," "I only did it to make him happy." No wonder they hate it. When it's done wrong, it's not just uncomfortable—it's alienating.

But the lovers? They've got stories too. Women who've found the right pace, the right partner, the right moment—those are the ones who sing its praises. They talk about the intensity, the fullness, the way it hits nerves they didn't know they had. For some, it's a power thing—giving up control or taking it back. For others, it's pure sensation, a frontier beyond the usual playbook. And for a few, like Sarah, it's a revelation, a door they didn't know they wanted to open until someone handed them the key.

I don't ask permission in the moment—not out loud, anyway. That's a risk, I know, and it's not for everyone. But I read the signs: the way she moves, the sounds she makes, the absence of that sharp "stop." If Sarah had said no, I'd have backed off in a heartbeat—consent isn't negotiable. But she didn't, and I didn't need to beg forgiveness after. She was all in, her body telling me what her words hadn't yet caught up to. That's the art of it: knowing when to lead, when to pause, when to let her take the reins.

The Biggest Difference Between Guys Who Have More Women Than They Know What to Do With and Those Who Can't Find a Date

There is one fundamental difference between men who have a constant stream of women in their lives and those who struggle to even get a single date: mindset. That's it. It's not about looks, money, or status—although those things can help—it's about the way a man views himself and his place in the dating world.

Men who always have women chasing them believe in abundance. They know that women are everywhere, that attraction is a numbers game, and that no single woman is worth obsessing over. On the other hand, men who can't seem to find a date operate with a scarcity mindset. They believe that good women are rare, that every rejection is a catastrophe, and that if they don't immediately land a partner, they're destined to be alone forever.

This difference in perspective changes everything about how a man carries himself, how he interacts with women, and, ultimately, how women respond to him.

Abundance vs. Scarcity: Why Your Mindset Determines Everything

I always say about any woman I'm having second thoughts about, "There's ten waiting to take her place and a hundred I don't even know about." That's not arrogance—that's the reality for any man who has his life together and understands his value.

Contrast that with the guy who treats every first date like a make-or-break scenario. He thinks, *If this doesn't work out, I don't know when*

I'll get another chance. He puts pressure on the situation, overcompensates, and often turns women off because of the sheer desperation he exudes.

Think about it from the woman's perspective:

- One guy sits across from her, completely relaxed, flirting, enjoying the moment, and clearly not worried about the outcome. He's having fun, and his energy is contagious.
- The other guy is tense, nervous, and trying too hard to impress her. His body language screams that he needs her to like him.

Which one do you think she'll be more attracted to?

Women always gravitate toward the man who doesn't need them because he feels like he has options. And if he feels like he has options, it's usually because he does.

Why Men Who Struggle with Dating Keep Failing

The guys who struggle the most with dating are usually their own worst enemies. They don't believe they deserve better, they don't put in the work to improve themselves, and they carry around negative, self-defeating beliefs that sabotage every interaction they have.

Here's what I see over and over again with men who can't get dates:

1. They Overvalue Every Woman They Meet.
   o They see one woman as their only shot, so they cling too soon, act needy, or move too fast.
   o They become overly invested in text conversations, treating a match on a dating app like it's already a relationship.
   o They make women feel suffocated before anything even starts.
2. They Don't Work on Themselves.
   o They blame women, society, or bad luck instead of taking responsibility.

- They don't get in shape, they don't upgrade their style, and they don't improve their conversation skills.
- They expect women to like them for who they are instead of making sure they're actually likable.

3. They Play It Too Safe.
   - They fear rejection so much that they never take risks.
   - They wait for the "perfect moment" instead of making a move.
   - They hesitate, overthink, and overanalyze instead of just taking action.

4. They Take Rejection Personally.
   - A woman says no, and they internalize it as a personal failure.
   - Instead of learning from it and moving on, they sulk, complain, or quit trying altogether.
   - They don't understand that rejection is part of the game.

The Attitude of Men Who Always Have Women

Men who always have women carry themselves differently. They don't see any one woman as *special*—at least not until she's proven she's worth their time. They know that attraction is fluid, that there are always more opportunities, and that women are drawn to men who radiate confidence, certainty, and self-sufficiency.

Here's how they think and act differently:

1. They Know They Are the Prize.
   - They don't chase women—women chase them.
   - They set standards and expect women to meet those standards.
   - They let women prove themselves instead of trying to "win them over."

2. They Are Completely Comfortable with Rejection.
   - If a woman isn't interested, they don't care.

- o They don't beg for second chances or overanalyze what went wrong.
- o They move on instantly because they know there are countless other women out there.

3. They Lead in Every Interaction.
    - o They plan the date, they take control, they make decisions.
    - o They don't wait for the woman to make the first move or set the pace.
    - o They escalate when the moment is right instead of hesitating.

4. They Create Emotional Highs.
    - o They make women laugh, feel excitement, and experience adventure.
    - o They know that women want to feel something, not just have boring conversations.
    - o They flirt, tease, and keep things unpredictable.

5. They Never Act Desperate.
    - o If a woman cancels, they don't beg to reschedule.
    - o If a woman plays games, they drop her immediately.
    - o They treat every interaction as low stakes because they know they have options.

How to Shift from Scarcity to Abundance

Stop tolerating bad behavior. If a woman disrespects you, walk away. If you're a guy who struggles with dating, the first thing you need to do is change the way you see yourself. Women don't define your value—you do. The moment you start acting like the man you want to become, women will start seeing you that way, too.

Here's how you make the shift:

1. Change Your Internal Dialogue.
    - o Stop thinking, "Women don't like me." Start thinking, "I am the catch."

- o Stop telling yourself you don't have options. Start believing that you do.
- o If you don't see yourself as desirable, neither will women.

2. Expand Your Social Circles.
   - o Start meeting more people—at the gym, through hobbies, at networking events.
   - o The more women you meet, the more options you'll naturally have.
   - o Stop relying 100% on dating apps and start making real-world connections.

3. Take More Risks.
   - o Approach more women. Ask more women out. Make more moves.
   - o The more you try, the better you get—and the less you fear rejection.
   - o Repetition builds confidence. The guys who always succeed with women have simply failed more than you.

4. Upgrade Yourself.
   - o Improve your fashion. Hit the gym. Work on your communication skills.
   - o Learn how to tell better stories. Learn how to flirt.
   - o Get a professional photographer to take high-quality dating profile pictures.

5. Set Higher Standards.
   - o Stop chasing women who aren't interested. Only engage with women who show high interest.
   - o Scarcity-minded men accept whatever they can get. High-value men choose what they want.

Final Thoughts

At the end of the day, the only difference between men who are drowning in options and men who are stuck in a dating rut is the way they think. If you believe that there aren't enough women out there, you will always struggle. But if you believe that there are more women than you could ever possibly meet, then you will start to move through the dating world with ease and confidence.

The choice is yours. You can keep playing small and acting like love is scarce. Or you can embrace abundance and watch as women start chasing you for a change.

HIGH-VALUE MEN:
WHAT SEPARATES THEM FROM THE REST

The concept of a high-value man is something that gets discussed endlessly by dating coaches, YouTube channels, and self-improvement circles. But what does it really mean? Is it about money, looks, and status, or is there something deeper? While wealth and physical attractiveness play a role, being high-value is an internal game first and foremost.

A true high-value man is defined by his mindset, his presence, his confidence, and his ability to navigate relationships on his terms. He is not a man who chases after women in desperation, nor does he compromise his values to keep someone around. He knows his worth and, as a result, attracts the right kind of women who recognize that worth.

Throughout my life, I have met men who, by all traditional metrics, would be considered low-value. They weren't particularly wealthy, they weren't traditionally good-looking, and they didn't have prestigious careers. And yet, they had women fawning over them, fighting for their attention and doing everything in their power to keep them interested. How did these men manage to accomplish this?

The answer is simple: they mastered the not-so-subtle art of **not giving a fuck**.

The Core of High Value: Confidence and Indifference

The most attractive trait a man can have is confidence, and confidence is not something you can fake for long. It comes from knowing who you are, what you offer, and what you will and will not tolerate. The men who are always surrounded by women do not fear rejection, nor do they tie their self-worth to a woman's approval. They approach dating with an attitude of abundance, knowing that for every woman who isn't interested, there are ten more waiting to take her place.

On the other hand, men who struggle with dating exude the opposite energy. They care too much about what a woman thinks of them, they overcompensate to prove their worth, and they tolerate disrespect out of fear of losing someone they perceive as valuable. This is what sets low-value men apart from high-value men. The former operates from scarcity; the latter operates from abundance.

A high-value man does not put any one woman on a pedestal. He does not beg for attention. He does not jump through hoops to prove his worth. Instead, he lets women prove themselves to him. And because he is selective, women chase him.

The Power of Walking Away

If there is one lesson that every man should internalize, it is this: the person who is willing to walk away holds all the power. I have experienced this firsthand in my own dating life. When I was younger, I believed in the idea that if I could just convince a woman to like me, everything would work out. I tried to win them over with kindness, generosity, and attentiveness. I thought that being the "nice guy" who showed how much he cared would make a woman fall in love with me.

I was dead wrong.

It wasn't until I stopped caring about the outcome—until I became completely indifferent to whether a woman stayed or left—that everything changed. Women who would have previously lost interest suddenly became invested. They started working to keep my attention rather than the other way around. Why? Because when a man does not fear losing a woman, she fears losing him.

A high-value man has no problem walking away the moment he senses a woman is playing games, wasting his time, or treating him with anything less than the respect he deserves. He is not afraid of being alone because he knows he is perfectly fine with or without a woman.

The Role of Financial Stability in Being High-Value

Let's address the money aspect of being high-value. While financial success is not the sole determining factor, it is important. A man who is financially stable commands respect and independence, two traits that women find highly attractive. But the key distinction here is that a high-value man does not use his money as bait to attract women.

In places like Palm Beach, I have seen countless wealthy men who believe that flashing their wealth is the key to getting women. They drive the latest exotic cars, wear expensive designer clothes, and spend absurd amounts of money on women who have no genuine interest in them. And while this strategy may attract women initially, it does not command respect.

A man who uses money to lure women in will always find himself in one-sided relationships where he is being used rather than being truly desired. He becomes an ATM, not a man. The truly high-value man is financially secure but does not lead with his wallet. He does not feel the need to buy a woman's interest because he knows his presence alone is valuable. He provides a lifestyle, not a paycheck.

Improving Your Value: Practical Steps

The best part about being a high-value man is that it is something you can build. You don't have to be born into wealth, nor do you have to be genetically blessed with model-tier looks. You can increase your value through deliberate action.

Here's how:

1. Take Control of Your Physical Appearance—Get in the gym. Lose the extra weight. Build muscle. Dress well. A man who takes care of his body automatically separates himself from the majority of men who let themselves go.

2. Master Emotional Control—A high-value man never loses his composure. Women will test you. They will try to push your buttons. A weak man reacts emotionally. A high-value man remains unshaken.

3. Develop Financial Independence—You don't need to be a millionaire, but you do need to be self-sufficient. Women are biologically wired to be attracted to men who are providers and protectors.

4. Cultivate an Interesting Life—Have hobbies. Travel. Read. Learn. A boring man is an unattractive man. High-value men have rich, fulfilling lives that women want to be a part of.

5. Set Standards and Stick to Them—The moment you tolerate disrespect or poor behavior, you lower your value. A high-value man never compromises his principles for the sake of keeping a woman around.

Final Thoughts on Being a High-Value Man

Ultimately, being high-value is about self-respect. It is about knowing who you are, refusing to compromise on what you want, and carrying yourself with the confidence of a man who knows he is the prize. The world will always try to convince men that they need to chase—that they need to prove their worth to a woman. But the men who truly succeed in dating and relationships are the ones who understand that they are the prize, and women should be proving themselves to them.

I have lived both realities. I have been the man who chased, who tried to win over women, who put them on pedestals—and it led to nothing but failure. But once I embraced my own value, once I let go of the need to please women and focused on being the best version of myself, everything changed. I never wanted for a date again. And the same can be true for any man who is willing to step up, claim his worth, and live his life with the unshakable confidence of a man who knows he is high value.

Why I Consider Myself a High-Value Man

I don't play mind games. I don't fake confidence. I just know my worth. Here's what I bring to the table:

Above-average looks – I take care of myself.

Good health & fitness – I work out, stay active, and take care of my body.

Financial security – I don't need anyone to support me.

Intelligence & worldliness – I can talk about any topic and keep a conversation going.

Charisma & humor – I know how to flirt, connect, and entertain.

High-level inner strength – I never get rattled.

Great in bed – This one speaks for itself.

Emotional intelligence – I can read people like a book.

That's a complete package.

But here's the thing… Any man can increase his value. It's not something you're born with—it's something you develop over time.

How Any Man Can Become High-Value

You don't have to be rich. You don't have to be tall. You don't have to look like Brad Pitt. But you do have to work on yourself.

1. Get in Shape

There's no excuse for being out of shape.

- Hit the gym.
- Eat better.
- Lose weight.
- Build muscle.

Even if you don't become ripped, just being fit instantly makes you more attractive.

2. Upgrade Your Style

Most guys have zero sense of fashion.

- Wear clothes that fit.
- Ditch the oversized t-shirts and dad jeans.
- Invest in some quality pieces.

You don't have to be a fashionista. Just look like you give a damn.

3. Fix Your Mindset
   - Confidence isn't about being the best-looking guy in the room.
   - It's about knowing your worth and acting accordingly.
   - Women don't want a perfect man—they want a man who believes in himself.

4. Learn Social & Flirting Skills

If you don't know how to **start conversations, flirt, and make a woman laugh**, you're going to struggle.

Luckily, this can be learned.

5. Expand Your Horizons

A high-value man is interesting.

- Learn to dance.
- Travel and experience new cultures.
- Pick up a hobby that makes you unique.

Women love men who bring excitement and adventure into their lives.

Why Women Won't Settle for You If You've Settled for Yourself

If you're overweight, unmotivated, and lacking ambition, why would a high-quality woman want to be with you? Why should she settle for a man who has settled for himself? Women have endless choices—they are constantly being approached, pursued, and courted. If you don't stand out, you're invisible. And standing out doesn't mean being a millionaire.

It means:

- Having self-respect.
- Being confident in yourself.
- Bringing value to the table.

A high-value man doesn't chase.
A high-value man doesn't beg.
A high-value man walks away when he's not respected.

And because of that, women respect and desire him even more.

Final Thoughts: Level Up or Stay Stagnant

Every man has two choices:

1. Stay where you are. Keep doing what you're doing. Keep getting the same mediocre results.

or

2. Level up. Take control. Improve yourself. Demand better for yourself.

It doesn't take a lot of effort—but it does take consistent effort over time. And once you become the best version of yourself, you'll never have to chase women again.

They'll come to you.

LONG-DISTANCE RELATIONSHIPS— WHY THEY RARELY WORK

I've **never** engaged in a long-distance relationship, and I don't **plan to.** Not because I'm against them in principle, but because they **almost never work.** There are too many challenges, too many obstacles, and in most cases, they're just not worth the effort.

The Main Problem: Distance Kills Intimacy

Relationships thrive on **physical presence.**

- The quick touch on the arm.
- The goodnight kiss.
- The comfort of being together without even speaking.

That's impossible in a long-distance relationship. Instead, you get:

- Phone calls and texts trying to compensate for the lack of connection.
- Video calls that never feel the same.
- Long periods of waiting for the next visit.

In the short term, it may seem romantic, but over time, it wears people down. A relationship isn't just about feeling connected emotionally— it's about feeling connected physically. And no amount of FaceTime can replace that.

Travel Nightmares & Expense

Let's say she lives **two states away**, or even worse, **across the country.**

Now, every visit requires:

- Booking a flight
- Dealing with airport headaches
- Finding a hotel or staying at her place

- Spending a small fortune just to see each other

This adds up quickly—both in money and time. If you're constantly traveling, your life becomes centered around the relationship, and you end up sacrificing too much of yourself for something that might not even last. And what happens when:

- There's a flight delay or cancellation?
- Bad weather ruins your trip?
- She moves even further away?

Now, you're investing time and energy into something that is beyond your control. Relationships should enhance your life, not turn into logistical nightmares.

Trust Issues—Who's She with When You're Not Around?

Trust is hard enough in a normal relationship. Now, imagine a relationship where:

- You don't see her for weeks or months at a time.
- You have no idea what she's doing in her free time.
- You start wondering about every guy she works with or goes out with.

And let's be real—when the cat's away, the mice will play. I'm not saying every woman in a long-distance relationship cheats. But I am saying that if she's prone to cheating, the opportunity is always there. A woman who gets lonely and physically frustrated will eventually find comfort somewhere else. And it works both ways—men in long-distance relationships are just as likely to start looking elsewhere.

A relationship that requires blind faith to survive is not a strong relationship.

If You Have to Fly to See Her, She Better Be Close to a 10

This might sound shallow, but it's the **harsh truth.** If I'm jumping on a plane to see a woman, she better be exceptional.

She needs to be:

- A 10 in looks
- A 10 in personality
- A 10 in loyalty and effort

And even then...**why bother?** Because when I want a quickie, I don't want to book a round-trip ticket to get it.

Exception—When a Long-Distance Relationship Might Work

I won't say they never work, because there are some exceptions.

A long-distance relationship can work if:

- You have a clear plan to eventually live in the same city.
- The distance is temporary, not indefinite.
- You both have extreme trust and commitment.
- You're both financially and emotionally prepared for the challenges.

But even then, it's an uphill battle.

The longer the distance lasts, the harder it becomes to sustain. Why Long-Distance Relationships Aren't for Me

I need:

- Physical connection.
- Spontaneity.
- The ability to see my partner whenever I want.

A long-distance relationship **takes all of that away.** Instead, you get:

- Over-reliance on texts and calls.

- Constant scheduling issues.
- Doubt creeping into your mind.
- An unsustainable emotional burden.

That's not how I want to live. And that's why I will never entertain a long-distance relationship. Some people can do it, and more power to them. But for me? It's a hard no.

Distance—How Far Should You Go for a Date?

There was a time when I drove all over the state in pursuit of women. It was pointless—all it did was drive up my gasoline bill and waste my time. I've always enjoyed driving, and I don't mind Miami night-life at all. In fact, I go there often. I'm also a habitual speeder, but I speed responsibly. But here's the problem:

If a woman knows you're willing to drive 85 miles to meet her, she assumes you're desperate.

It gives off the wrong message—like you don't have options and are chasing instead of attracting. That never ends well.

When I'll Travel for a Date

These days, if I do go down to Miami, it's on my terms.

- I take my time setting up the date.
- I never appear too eager.
- She has to be something special—otherwise, I'm not bothering.

That doesn't mean I won't travel at all. For example, I love certain restaurants and dance spots in Fort Lauderdale. Even though it's a bit of a trek, I'll go if it's worth it.

The Real Issue—Most Women Won't Travel

Here's the problem: I might be willing to drive, but most women won't. Especially at night. Especially on I-95. I don't blame them—Florida highways at night can be a madhouse. So, this creates a logistical issue. If she's not willing to meet halfway, it probably won't work.

My Rule for Distance Dating

The best solution? Set a personal travel radius and stick to it.

- If a woman offers to meet halfway—driving 20-30 miles north to meet me—that shows potential.
- It means she's putting in effort.
- It tells me she's interested—not just looking for a free dinner.

Assuming I don't get a desperate vibe, I almost always say yes to meeting her. But if she expects me to do all the driving?

Not happening.

Final Thoughts

Distance is a personal thing. Some guys are willing to drive hours for a date. I won't. Because if a woman really wants to see you, she'll meet you halfway—literally and figuratively.

GOLD DIGGER STORIES FROM THE CRYPT

I've only gone out with three true gold diggers, and thankfully, never for long. Each one taught me the same lesson: If a woman expects you to pay for access, she's not worth the time or the money.

Gold Digger #1 – The One I Thought I Loved

At first, I really thought I was in love with her. I didn't mind paying for **dinners**—I'm old school like that. However, if a woman is seeing you regularly, she should offer to contribute something.

- Buy movie tickets
- Cover the popcorn
- Grab a round of drinks

Something.

Even a **fake gesture** would have been better than **nothing**. Instead, I found myself **constantly paying**—not in a sugar daddy way, but enough to make me wonder where this was going. I even bought her a bathing suit—a few hundred bucks on Lincoln Road. But by the time I realized the relationship wasn't going anywhere, my interest had completely evaporated.

My father used to say about **casino comps**: "If I'm gonna get screwed, I want to get kissed." And with her? I wasn't getting kissed.

Gold Digger #2 – The Mall Hustler

Met her at **Aventura Mall**—she was a **solid 9.** From the start, she was aggressive about asking me to buy her things. At first, I **said no**. Then, in a moment of **weakness**, I bought her a few things. And then a few more. Until finally, I looked in the mirror and didn't like what I saw. She was expecting me to drop $1,000 on her upcoming birthday. Two days before, I **ghosted her**. And you know what? I'm sure she found another sucker.

Gold Digger #3 – The Beauty with a Price Tag

This one was an African-American woman who was easily a 9.25. I was drawn in. Bought her shades and a bathing suit. Spent the day with her—got a couples massage. Played around in the massage room. But ultimately? Not worth it.

Final Lesson:

If a woman comes with an admission price, she can go find another sucker—and she probably will. Never again.

Choosing Which Women's Dating Profiles to Answer

This is **one of the biggest decisions** men face when using dating apps: Do you cast a wide net and see what comes in, or do you play it selectively? The answer? It depends on what you want.

Looks Matter—But Not as Much as You Think

Let's be honest: Men are visual creatures. Looks **will always be the first filter**—but they aren't everything. Personally, I believe that a woman's true beauty emanates from her heart and character. That said, there has to be some attraction.

For me, I'm willing to go down to a 6.5 out of 10, provided she has:

- A great personality
- Kindness and warmth
- A healthy lifestyle

What I **won't accept**:

Morbid obesity – In the **age of Ozempic and Monjaro,** there's no excuse for not at least trying to manage weight.

Laziness and lack of effort – If I work out and stay in shape, I expect my partner to do the same.

Bad energy or negativity – Physical beauty fades, but a bad personality never improves.

A beautiful face can make up for a few extra pounds, but if she's hiding behind filters or deceptive angles, that's a red flag.

Spotting Fake or Deceptive Profiles

Women are masters of illusion when it comes to online dating. Here's how to see through the BS:

- Watch for heavy photo editing. I know from my fashion photographer friend that you can completely transform someone with the click of a mouse.
- Insist on a full body shot. If she doesn't provide one, she's probably hiding something—and that something is usually a lot of extra weight.
- Look for consistency in photos. If her face looks like a supermodel in one picture but completely different in another, she's catfishing you.
- Pay attention to group photos. If she's always posing with a friend, she might be the less attractive one.

Character Over Looks—The Hard Lesson I Learned

I once dated a stunning woman from the UK—Indian, perfect body, and incredible augmented breasts. She was externally flawless, but in side? A nightmare.

- Zero empathy
- No warmth or caring
- Completely transactional—she wanted an ATM, not a partner.

This was in my weaker days, so I put up with her for a while. But once I reached my limit, I ghosted her without hesitation. Lesson learned: A beautiful woman with a bad heart is uglier than an average-looking woman with a beautiful soul.

Should You Be Selective?

If you're going to be picky, make sure you're bringing something to the table. If you're an 8.5 or higher, you can afford to be highly selective. If you're not?

- Get professional photos. They can move you up two full points in attractiveness.
- Stay fit, dress well, and improve yourself.
- Be realistic about what you're attracting.

Also—don't lie about your age, height, or weight. And don't tolerate women lying, either.

If she says she's "curvy" and shows up 100 pounds heavier than her pictures, she wasn't curvy—she was dishonest. Honesty is the best policy in dating.

You attract what you put out.

Final Thoughts

Choose wisely. Because a bad personality in a pretty package is still poison

THE REALITY OF DATING SITES AND PROFILES

Choosing a Dating Site—They're All the Same

I've used numerous dating sites and apps over the years—some better than others, but none drastically different. There are dozens, maybe even hundreds, of dating sites, all promising you love, happiness, and the partner of your dreams. Reality?

- They all function the same.
- They all yield similar results.
- They all cost about the same.

Some cater to specific age groups (like *OurTime* for older daters), while others are more hookup-oriented (*Tinder, Bumble*). But in the end, you'll meet the same kinds of people on any of them.

Avoiding Scams & Fake Profiles

If you spend enough time on dating apps, you **will** run into frauds. It's just **part of the game.**

Some sites, like Match, Tinder, and Bumble, do a decent job of filtering out scams. Others, like Facebook Dating, are completely overrun with fake profiles—easily 80% of them are scammers.

Red Flags for Scammers:

- Too-good-to-be-true pictures – Flawless skin, perfect everything? Likely AI-generated or stolen.
- No bio or minimal effort in the profile.
- "Hey, handsome." – I know I'm decent-looking, but the last woman who called me handsome was my mother. *Real women don't open like that.*
- Suspicious location – If a profile is exactly 72 miles away from me, that means *Miami*, and she's probably on a VPN

(virtual private network), which means she can be anywhere in the high scam probability. She's probably in a scam room somewhere in Asia, planning to help you start investing in crypto or gold options. If she's a trader, her next trade is probably going to be you and your bank account.

Most scammers use free trial accounts because they're not going to pay to scam you. So, subscription-based sites tend to be safer than free ones.

The Truth About Dating Profiles—It's ALL About Emotion

Your dating profile's only job is to spark **an emotional response.** That's it. A good profile makes a woman think:

- This guy is exciting.
- This guy is different.
- What would a date with him feel like?

What to Include:

- Just enough to grab attention.
- Don't overshare—leave some mystery.
- Show you're financially stable (without bragging).
- Unpredictability = Excitement – But don't come off as a potential serial killer.

Dating Profile Picture Strategy—Why They Matter More Than Anything

Let's be real—pictures are 80% of the game. You can have the best-written bio in the world, but if your pictures suck, you're getting swiped left.

What NOT to Do:

- **Shirtless gym selfies** (unless your body is insane).
- **Holding a fish** (seriously, why do guys do this?).
- **Standing in front of expensive cars** (you'll only attract gold diggers).

How I Cracked the Code on Photos

For years, my pictures were just okay. Then, I reconnected with a woman I had briefly dated—a world-class fashion photographer.

She took 7-8 shots on her iPhone, did some minor color correction and lighting adjustments, and the results were unbelievable. At the time, she made me promise not to use them for dating apps. I agreed. But when she moved on and found someone else? The deal was off. I uploaded them to my profiles and immediately noticed something:

- Responses doubled.
- Women started commenting on my "amazing" eyes.
- My match rate tripled.

That's when I had an epiphany: If billion-dollar companies spend fortunes on packaging, why wouldn't I? I hired her to do a fully professional photo shoot—multiple outfits, different lighting, various backgrounds. When she was done, I looked at the photos and thought, *Damn…if I were gay, I'd date me.* They were that good.

And guess what? It worked. Suddenly, I was getting more attention than I could handle. I started canceling dating app subscriptions; I didn't need them anymore. Now, I am on just one app and get more traffic than a cop on 42nd Street.

Final Tips for Maximizing Dating Profile Success

1. Get Professional Photos Taken

- No overly staged shots.
- Natural, well-lit, high-quality pictures that capture your best angles.
- A good photographer will bring out your best self.

2. Rotate Your Photos Regularly

- If you use the same profile pics for months, **you'll start getting ignored**.
- Change your first photo every so often to refresh your profile.

3. Take Planned Breaks from Dating Apps

- If responses slow down, hide your profile for a month or two.
- When you return, you'll show up as a "new" user, leading to a fresh wave of interest.

4. Stick to 1-2 Apps at a Time

- With my new photos, I cut down to just one dating app.
- I could easily go on a date every night, but I don't have the time or interest.

Final Thoughts: It's a Numbers Game

With bad pictures, you might get one match for every ten swipes. With great pictures, you might get three or four out of ten. Dating is a numbers game—and your profile is your packaging. Make it look good, and the game changes entirely.

WHY WOMEN HATE WEAK MEN: THE FUNDAMENTAL TRUTH ABOUT STRENGTH, RESPECT, AND ATTRACTION

Nature abhors weakness. Across the animal kingdom, weakness is often synonymous with death. The slowest gazelle in the herd gets picked off by the lion. The runt of the litter often struggles to survive. Predators target the sick and the weak because they are the easiest to take down. This is an undeniable reality that has governed survival since the dawn of life itself.

But then, there's humanity—a species that, at first glance, seems to defy these natural laws. Humans protect the weak, uplift the vulnerable, and create societies based on ideals of fairness and compassion. We champion the underdog and celebrate stories of overcoming hardship. But beneath this social veneer, the natural aversion to weakness remains hardwired into our DNA—especially when it comes to attraction, relationships, and gender dynamics.

Women, in particular, have an instinctive, biological, and psychological aversion to weakness in men. This isn't a cultural phenomenon. It isn't about societal conditioning. It is evolutionary. A woman's survival—both in ancient times and even in modern ones—has always depended on her ability to select a strong, capable, and competent mate. A man who exudes confidence, control, and security is biologically preferable to one who is timid, indecisive, and fearful.

The Duality of Weakness in Human Nature

When we enter this world as infants, we are the embodiment of weakness. We are completely dependent on caregivers for food, shelter, and survival. Unlike most animals, human babies take years—sometimes decades (especially millennials)—to reach full independence.

171

And yet, while we inherently love the weakness of babies—their innocence, their vulnerability, their absolute need for protection—we resent that same weakness in adults, especially in men.

Why? Because weakness in adulthood signals incompetence, helplessness, and an inability to navigate the world effectively. We despise it in ourselves, and we certainly don't want to see it in a partner—especially from a man who is supposed to lead, protect, and provide. Women, consciously or unconsciously, react to weak men with disdain, contempt, and often, outright rejection.

Weakness, however, is not inherently negative. In its rightful place, it serves a purpose. It drives growth, challenges us to improve, and pushes us to develop skills, courage, and resilience. But when a man embraces weakness instead of overcoming it, when he allows fear to dictate his actions, when he becomes emotionally needy, fragile, and insecure—he loses a woman's respect. And without respect, there can be no attraction.

The Feminine Need for Strength

To understand why women loathe weak men, we must first understand the fundamental masculine and feminine dynamic. Throughout history, men and women have played distinct roles in human survival. Women have traditionally taken on nurturing roles—raising children, maintaining the home, and ensuring emotional bonds remain strong within a community. Men, on the other hand, have historically been the protectors, the providers, the problem-solvers.

This dynamic isn't just a relic of the past—it is deeply ingrained in our psyche. While modern society has changed many external factors, human instincts have not evolved nearly as fast. Women still look for strength in men. They still crave security, stability, and a sense of direction. This doesn't mean that a man has to be rich, powerful, or physically dominant to be attractive. Strength is not about material wealth or brute force—it is about a man's ability to remain calm, assertive, and in control of his emotions and circumstances.

The Difference Between Vulnerability and Weakness

Before going further, we need to distinguish between vulnerability and weakness because many men confuse the two. Vulnerability is not the same as weakness. A strong man can show vulnerability in a way that does not diminish him. If a man has a difficult moment, shares a personal struggle, or expresses his emotions in a way that demonstrates self-awareness and maturity, it does not make him weak. Women can respect and even admire this kind of vulnerability because it reflects authenticity, confidence, and trust.

Weakness, however, is a lack of control over one's emotions, an inability to face challenges, and a tendency to be overly reactive, indecisive, or dependent. A weak man is a man who collapses under pressure, allows fear to dictate his decisions, and expects a woman to take on the emotional burden of leading the relationship. Crying in front of a woman is seldom a good thing.

Fear and Neediness: The Death of Attraction

One of the greatest weaknesses a man can display in a relationship is **fear-based behavior.**

Fear of losing her.
Fear of upsetting her.
Fear of being alone.
Fear of confrontation.
Fear of making a decision.

A fearful man second-guesses himself at every turn, always looking for validation, always needing reassurance, always worried about what others think of him. And nothing turns a woman off faster than a man who is afraid to stand up for himself, assert his desires, or risk rejection. Women despise neediness in men because it forces them into a role they don't want to play—the dominant, decision-making leader of the relationship. If a man is constantly seeking approval, asking permission, or deferring decisions to her, she will resent him for it. Even if she doesn't immediately recognize it, her instincts will push her away from him.

The Contempt Women Feel for Weak Men

A woman must respect a man in order to feel attraction for him. If she does not respect him, she will eventually resent him. Contempt is the natural response to consistent weakness. A man who cannot command respect in his relationship will inevitably be treated with disdain. His woman will test him, argue with him, nag him, and push him to see if there's any strength left in him at all. If he fails these tests, if he continues to give in, appease, and retreat from conflict, she will stop seeing him as a man altogether.

It is a slow death of attraction. First, she stops listening to him. Then, she stops taking him seriously. Then, she stops wanting him sexually. Then, she stops caring if he leaves. And by the time a weak man realizes what has happened, it is already too late.

The Solution: Strength Through Self-Respect

So, what's the answer? How does a man cultivate strength and avoid the fate of being seen as weak and undesirable? The solution is **self-respect.**

- Stop living from fear. Understand that life is uncertain, relationships are unpredictable, and you cannot control everything. A strong man accepts this and moves forward anyway.
- Become independent. A man should never build his entire life around a woman. He needs his own mission, his own passions, and his own sense of purpose.
- Master your emotions. It's okay to feel fear, sadness, or anxiety, but a strong man does not let these emotions rule his actions. He controls his reactions and makes decisions from a place of logic, not desperation.
- Develop unshakable confidence. Women are drawn to men who exude confidence—not arrogance, but a deep, quiet

assurance that they are in control of themselves and their circumstances.

- Establish boundaries. Weak men let women walk all over them because they are afraid to set limits, because inevitably they believe that acting strong will drive them away, how the opposite is true. A strong man knows his worth and does not tolerate disrespect. When a woman finds this out, she will become more attracted to him or she'll leave. Either outcome is positive.
- Never chase validation. A man who constantly seeks approval and reassurance will never be respected. A strong man validates himself.

Final Thoughts: The Truth About Attraction and Respect

Women loathe weak men not because they are cruel or shallow but because they are biologically wired to seek strength and security. It is a fundamental law of nature. If a man wants to be respected by his woman—if he wants to maintain attraction, admiration, and desire— he must embody strength, both in action and in mindset. This doesn't mean being aggressive or controlling. It means being grounded, confident, and decisive. It means standing firm in your beliefs, setting clear expectations, and refusing to let fear dictate your behavior. Because at the end of the day, no woman truly wants to be with a weak man. And deep down, no man truly wants to be a weak man.

Women Will Overlook Weakness—For a Time —If Resources Are Provided

There is one major exception to the rule that women loathe weak men: money. A man with substantial resources—a provider, a high-income earner, or someone with wealth—can buy himself time. He can mask his weakness temporarily. If he showers a woman with gifts, takes her to expensive dinners, flies her to exotic destinations, and spoils her with luxury, she will tolerate his weakness—for a while. But make no mistake: this is not attraction. It is a transaction.

At best, she sees him as a means to an end. She may convince herself that she loves him because of the comfort, security, and ease he provides. She may convince herself that she is attracted to him because she enjoys the finer things in life. But deep down, the foundation of their relationship is not respect, not desire, but dependency. And one day, that will no longer be enough.

When a Woman Wakes Up and Realizes She's Not Satisfied

For a while, the man with money can create an illusion of strength. His wealth gives him the appearance of being a high-value man. He's paying the bills. He's taking her to five-star restaurants. He's buying her designer handbags. He's covering her rent, her car payments, or maybe even her entire lifestyle. For a woman who is primarily seeking financial security, this might be enough to keep her around. But the moment she realizes that she does not respect him, the clock starts ticking.

- She will begin to feel an internal discomfort—a vague dissatisfaction she may not even fully understand.
- She will start noticing other men—men who have confidence, presence, and control, even if they don't have as much money.
- She will lose sexual attraction to her provider—his touch will no longer excite her, and she may start avoiding intimacy.
- She will test him harder than ever before, looking for some shred of strength beneath his wealth.

At first, she may not even consciously realize what she is doing. She may still go through the motions, still smile at dinner, still tell herself that she's in a great situation. But instincts don't lie. Attraction is not a choice. And once her instincts tell her that the man she's with is not someone she truly respects, it is only a matter of time before she leaves—or before she cheats.

Men Who Rely on Money to Attract Women Are Inherently Weak

A man who leads with money is a man who knows, deep down, that he has nothing else to offer. He is insecure. He is afraid. He knows he is only a prize for what he can give, not for who he is. And this is why I never rely on flashy displays of wealth to attract women. I have money. I live well. I have nice things. But I do not use them as bait. I do not lead with wealth because the moment you do, you are telling a woman, "This is the only thing that makes me valuable."

And worse—you are inviting the wrong kind of woman into your life.

The women who chase wealth first and foremost are the least desirable women to pursue seriously. They are the most fickle, the most easily bored, and the most likely to leave the moment someone with a bigger bank account comes along. They are not looking for love.

They are not looking for a deep connection. They are looking for a deal. And once the terms of that deal no longer feel exciting, once they feel safe and comfortable but uninspired, they will seek passion elsewhere.

The Fatal Flaw of "Provider Game"

There are two ways a man can attract women:

1. Through who he is. His confidence, his presence, his charisma, his ability to create emotional highs and lows.
2. Through what he can give. Money, gifts, luxury, and financial support.

The first type of man will always command respect and attraction. He could lose all his money tomorrow, and women would still chase him because they are addicted to how he makes them feel. The second type of man? He only commands attention as long as the money keeps flowing. If he lost his wealth, his cars, his house—his woman would leave in an instant. Why? Because she was never truly with him in the first place. She was with his lifestyle. She was with his financial support. She was with the fantasy he could provide. And once the illusion breaks, once she no longer needs him—the game is over.

Final Thoughts: Why Strength Will Always Matter More Than Wealth

Women will tolerate a weak man for a time if he provides. But the day will come when she realizes that she does not respect him. And when that day comes, she will leave. This is why true high-value men do not rely on wealth alone. They understand that their power comes from their confidence, their presence, their ability to command respect—regardless of their bank account. Wealth is a tool, nothing more. But strength? Strength is everything.

THE ONEITIS TRAP: HOW THE ILLUSION OF "THE ONE" DESTROYS ATTRACTION

There is no "one." There never was, and there never will be. This is one of the hardest lessons a man can learn when it comes to women, dating, and relationships. Even those of us who have dated hundreds of women—who have studied attraction, mastered seduction, and built a lifestyle where women come and go—can still fall into the **oneitis trap**. I know this because I have. And so has every guy I know. What is *oneitis*? Oneitis is the delusion that a particular woman is "the one." She is perfect, flawless, the answer to your prayers. You've met plenty of women before, but something about her—her beauty, her energy, her intellect, her smile—makes you believe she is different.

It happens fast. You meet her, and suddenly, your behavior shifts. You don't act like yourself anymore. You become careful with your words, worried about making the wrong impression. You prioritize her over your own needs. You start putting her on a pedestal, elevating her to a status she hasn't earned. And the moment you do that? You've already lost.

How Women Trigger Oneitis

Women know. They can tell when you've been infected with oneitis. They see it in your eyes, hear it in your voice, sense it in your energy. They can feel when they have a hold over you. And while they might enjoy the initial attention, it doesn't take long before the attraction they felt starts to wane.

Women are biologically wired to test men. They probe for weaknesses, looking for signs of strength or vulnerability. If a man displays too much neediness or desperation—if he appears too eager to please—he signals that he is beneath her in value. And no matter how much a woman may claim to want a man who worships her, the truth is, she cannot respect a man she has conquered too easily.

This is where most men fail. They mistake a woman's attention and beauty for worthiness. They believe that just because she is stunning, she must also be rare. They let their emotions dictate their actions rather than standing firm in their own sense of self-worth.

My Own Battle with Oneitis

Even as a seasoned dater—someone who has been with countless women, who understands female psychology inside and out—I still find myself susceptible to oneitis from time to time. Most recently, it happened with a woman 15 years younger than me. She was stunning. I mean, jaw-droppingly gorgeous, with a personality to match. She was smart, elegant, and seemingly kind. In my mind, she was everything I had been looking for.

And because of that, I made the one mistake I swore I would never make again. I told her I loved her before she said it first. That was all it took. From that moment on, the dynamic changed. She no longer had to work for my affection—I had handed it to her on a silver platter. And suddenly, I was the one putting in all the effort. The excuses started. She was "too busy" to see me. She "couldn't drive 50 miles" to meet up. She was "overwhelmed with work."

Let me tell you something: If a woman is truly into you, she will cross mountains, oceans, and time zones to see you. She will make the effort. She will want to make the effort. But I had given her certainty too soon. And certainty, for a woman, is the killer of desire. Eventually, the relationship fizzled out. And when it did, I looked back and realized something obvious: She was never "the one." She was just one of many.

Why Oneitis is an Illusion

Oneitis is a mind trick. It convinces you that this one woman is different from all the rest, that she is special in a way no other woman could be. It blinds you to her flaws, makes you ignore the red flags, and turns you into a weaker version of yourself. But the truth is, there is no "one." There are many. Many beautiful women. Many incredible connections. Many opportunities. And the moment you forget that? The moment you believe that this woman is the only one for you? You have already given away your power.

The Fatal Mistake of Pedestalization

The core issue with oneitis is that it leads to pedestalization—treating a woman as though she is above you, better than you, more valuable than you. But let me ask you: Why? Why do you assume that this woman is more important than you? Why do you treat her like she is a prize to be won instead of realizing that you are the prize? The irony is that women don't even want to be put on a pedestal. Sure, they like admiration. They enjoy being desired. But the moment they feel like a man is placing them too high above himself, they lose respect. As previously stated: "When you put a woman on a pedestal, she has no choice but to look down on you." And that is exactly what happened to me.

How to Kill Oneitis Before It Kills Your Game

So, how do you fight back against oneitis? How do you stop yourself from falling into the trap?

Here's the playbook:

1. Understand That There Is No One
   o Accept this truth now: There is no single perfect woman. The idea of "the one" is a Hollywood fantasy designed to keep you weak.
2. Maintain an Abundance Mindset
   o Women are everywhere. If you lose one, there are ten more waiting. Never operate from a place of scarcity.
3. Wait for Her to Earn It

- Never shower a woman with love, attention, or commitment before she has proven herself worthy of it. She should be chasing you, not the other way around.

4. Make Her Work for It
   - If a woman feels like she doesn't have to put in any effort, she will not value you. She must feel that she is winning you over, not the other way around.

5. Focus on Your Own Life First
   - The strongest men are the ones who have their own mission, purpose, and direction. Women are additions to your life, not the center of it.

6. Watch for Red Flags Early
   - If a woman is making excuses, flaking, or acting lukewarm, cut her off immediately. A woman who truly wants to be with you will make it obvious.

7. Never Say "I Love You" First
   - This is one of the golden rules of dating. The second you say those three words before she does, the dynamic shifts. Let her come to that conclusion on her own.

Final Thoughts: You Are the Prize

When it comes to oneitis, the most important thing to remember is this: You are the prize. You are the man. You bring value. You have options. And the moment you start acting like you don't—the moment you pedestalize a woman and treat her as if she is the best you'll ever get—you become disposable in her eyes. The reality is, she was never The One. She was just one of many. And the sooner you internalize that, the stronger, more attractive, and more in control you will become.

MASTERING REJECTION:
THE KEY TO SUCCESS IN DATING AND LIFE

Rejection is a universal human experience. It's something we all encounter, whether in our careers, friendships, or romantic pursuits. Yet, for many men, rejection in the dating world feels uniquely painful. Unlike a job application that gets ignored or a business pitch that gets declined, romantic rejection feels deeply personal. And that's because it is.

When a woman rejects you, she isn't just saying no to your offer—she's saying no to you. At least, that's how most men interpret it. But if you want to be successful in dating—and in life—you need to rewire how you process rejection. Because the truth is, rejection is never as personal as it seems. It's rarely about your intrinsic worth as a man and more often about factors that have nothing to do with you. Rejection is a test. It's a lesson. And more than anything, it's a filter—helping you weed out the women who were never meant for you in the first place.

Rejection in Dating vs. Rejection in Life

I remember taking a sales course where the professor said, *"When someone says no to you in sales, they're not rejecting you personally—they're rejecting your offer."* That simple distinction was meant to help salespeople separate their sense of self-worth from the outcome of a deal.

But here's the challenge: Dating is personal. When a woman turns you down, it's not just a product or an offer she's saying no to—it's you. Your face. Your personality. Your presence. Your energy. That's why rejection in dating stings far more than a failed business deal or a declined job interview. The trick is understanding that even though dating rejection is personal, it is never final. It is never the ultimate judgment on your desirability as a man. More importantly, it is never about just you.

Why Women Reject Men (And Why It's Rarely About You)

When a woman rejects you, your mind immediately jumps to conclusions:

- I'm not good-looking enough.
- She's just out of my league.
- I must have said something stupid.
- I'll never find someone like her again.

But the reality is, most of the time, rejection has nothing to do with you. Here's a hard truth: Women reject men for reasons they often don't even fully understand themselves. It might be something as trivial as:

- She's had a stressful day.
- She's still emotionally attached to her ex.
- She just started her period and is feeling irritable.
- She had a bad experience with someone who looked like you.
- She's overwhelmed with work or personal life issues.
- She's just not emotionally available at the moment.

And, yes, sometimes, she's just not attracted to you. And that's fine. Not every woman will be. Does that mean you're unworthy? Not even close. Does that mean you should dwell on it? Absolutely not. Think about it: Have you ever walked into a bar, restaurant, or social gathering and seen an attractive woman but just *weren't feeling it* that day? Maybe she had a great personality, a cute smile, but for whatever reason, you weren't in the mood. It's the same with women.

When you internalize this—when you truly believe that rejection is not about you but about timing, circumstances, and compatibility—you'll stop taking it personally. And when you stop taking it personally, rejection loses its sting.

The Power of Handling Rejection Like a Man

Women are **wired to test men.** They don't always do it consciously, but they are constantly **evaluating, screening, filtering.** One of the most powerful ways to pass a woman's subconscious test is **how you handle rejection.** Most men react **emotionally** when they get rejected:

- They get angry or resentful.
- They lash out, calling her names or questioning her judgment.
- They beg, plead, or try to convince her she's making a mistake.
- They sulk and wallow in self-pity, believing they're doomed to be alone.

All of these reactions are the hallmark of a weak man. A **strong** man, on the other hand, reacts like this:

- "No problem. Have a great day." (And he walks away.)
- "Totally understand. If you change your mind, you know where to find me."
- "Your loss." (Said in a playful, teasing way—not in a bitter, angry way.)

Rejection Becomes Attraction When Handled Right

Believe it or not, the way you handle rejection can actually make a woman more attracted to you. I've had women reject me at first, only to reach out later. Why? Because I handled rejection like a man.

- I didn't get bitter.
- I didn't get butt hurt.
- I didn't chase.
- I didn't beg.
- I walked away with confidence, indifference, and certainty.

And guess what? That's attractive. A woman expects a man to be wounded by rejection. But when you don't react the way she expects, you stand out. You become an enigma, a challenge, a man who values himself. Many women have come back to me after initially rejecting me, but by that point, I wasn't interested anymore.

Why? Because the way I see it, if a woman rejects me once, she has already shown me where I stand in her priority list. And if I wasn't her first choice before, why should I be now?

Here's a little story. I liked this lady. I had seen her at meetups. She was a solid 6.5 with the politics somewhere between Abby Hoffman and former New York City Mayor Bill DiBlasio. I told her I wanted to go out with her, and she said she was interested in someone else. I was still on the road to red pill mastery, but I acted dignified and quickly moved on. Six months later, she called me, *surprise*, wanting to know how to purchase a gun. Turned out my "competition" was a stalker, and he was making threats. Then, she indicated she would like to go out with me. Well, I had lost my appetite for this one. I wasn't sure why I was no longer interested in her, but now it's obvious.

I don't want to be a woman's Plan B. I don't want to be the guy she calls after she realizes her first choice was a mistake. And you shouldn't either.

Rejection is a Blessing in Disguise

Most men see rejection as a failure. But I see rejection as a filter. Every time a woman rejects me, she has just done me a favor. She has saved me time. She has saved me energy. She has saved me from investing in someone who wasn't right for me. Most men chase after women who have already rejected them because they believe there's something they can do to change her mind.

Don't be that guy. Quite simply, you are dealing with a woman. Even if you have the persuasion skills of Alan Dershowitz, you will never be able to convince a woman that you are the right person by making a logical argument. Remember, she's an emotional being that makes emotional decisions. Your logic wasn't made to work in such situations.

Instead, adopt this mindset:

- "She rejected me? Great. That means she's not the right fit, and I just dodged a bullet."
- "On to the next."
- "Every rejection gets me closer to the right woman."

Because that's the truth.

Your Expectations Shape Your Reality

One of the most profound lessons I've learned in life is this: What you expect is what you will receive. If you expect rejection, you will get it. If you expect success, you will find it.

Women are hypersensitive to a man's confidence—or lack thereof. If you expect to be rejected, you will subconsciously telegraph that through your body language, your tone of voice, and your overall energy. But if you approach every interaction expecting a **positive outcome**, you will be shocked at how different your results will be. Confidence is everything.

Final Thoughts: The Only Response to Rejection

So, what's the bottom line? Rejection is inevitable. It happens to everyone. It is a part of life. But it only defines you if you let it. The key to handling rejection like a high-value man is not to care, not in an apathetic way, but in an abundance mindset way. There are millions of women in the world. One woman's rejection means absolutely nothing in the grand scheme of things. So hold on tightly, but let go lightly. And remember: Every "no" gets you one step closer to a "yes."

They Always Come Crawling Back

There's a saying I live by when it comes to breakups: they always come crawling back. It doesn't matter how it ended, how nasty the final conversation got, or whether she swore on her life that she would never speak to you again. If you were the one to end it—if you were the one who walked away—there's an incredibly high probability that she will try to find her way back into your life.

Now, I'm not saying this to stroke my own ego. I don't believe I'm the greatest thing that ever walked the Earth, nor do I think every woman I've dated is desperately hoping to rekindle what we had. It's simply human nature, particularly when it comes to female psychology. Rejection is one of the hardest things for women to process. Most women, especially attractive ones, are used to being the ones who do the rejecting. They are accustomed to being chased, pursued, and desired. So when the script flips—when they are the ones being told "no thanks, I'm done"—it triggers something deep inside them. A mix of wounded ego, curiosity, and the basic human desire to be validated again.

Why Women Can't Handle Being Dumped

The world has conditioned women to believe that when it comes to relationships they are in control. They decide who gets access to them, filtering out the men who don't meet their standards, and choosing whether a relationship progresses or ends. And in many ways, this is true. Women hold the key to intimacy. A man can pursue all he wants, but unless the woman is interested, nothing is going to happen.

But here's the catch: while women control the initiation of intimacy, men control the commitment.

This means that while a woman can decide if she sleeps with a man, it is ultimately the man who decides if he's going to commit to her long-term. And that power dynamic is what drives women insane when they get dumped. They can handle turning a man down—hell, they do it all the time. But when a man turns *them* down, it creates a crack in their reality.

A woman who has been rejected by a man, especially one she thought she had wrapped around her finger, will often go through an entire psychological shift. At first, she may act indifferent, even relieved. She may tell her friends that it was for the best, that she wasn't feeling it anyway, and that she has plenty of other guys lined up.

But then, days, weeks, or even months later, it hits her.

She starts to wonder:

- Why did he leave me?
- What does he see in someone else that he didn't see in me?
- Was I not good enough?
- How could he walk away so easily?

This internal dialogue eats away at her. Even if she had no real emotional investment in the relationship at the time, the simple fact that you took away her ability to be the one in control of the breakup will drive her crazy. And that's when the slow creep back into your life begins.

The Different Ways They Come Crawling Back

There's a pattern to how women attempt to reinsert themselves into your life after a breakup. It usually plays out in predictable stages, and if you pay attention, you'll start to recognize these behaviors every time.

1. The "Casual" Check-In

This is the first and most common way she'll try to reopen the door. It might be a random text that says:

- "Hey, just saw something that reminded me of you. Hope you're doing well!"

- "I was just thinking about that amazing dinner we had at that Italian place. How have you been?"
- "I just found your sweater in my closet! Want me to drop it off?"

It's never anything overt or emotional—at least not at first. It's just a feeler. A way to gauge whether you'll take the bait.

2. The Social Media Lurking

If she's still following you on Instagram, Facebook, or any other platform, you'll start to notice an uptick in her engagement.

- She suddenly starts liking your old posts.
- She leaves a comment on a photo from weeks ago.
- She watches every single one of your Instagram stories without fail.

Even if she never reaches out directly, these are clear signals that she wants to be noticed.

3. The Drunk Text or Call

Ah, the classic. Few things reveal a person's true feelings more than alcohol. If she's been drinking and the right (or wrong) song comes on, expect your phone to light up.

- "I miss you."
- "I don't even know why we broke up."
- "You probably don't care, but I just wanted to say I'm sorry for everything."

Sometimes, she won't even have a coherent message—just a random, out-of-the-blue call at 1:30 a.m. Don't be surprised if she hangs up before you even answer. She just wanted to see if she could still reach you.

4. The Jealousy Play

If a woman truly believes she has lost her grip on you, she may attempt to trigger your jealousy. She might start posting more pictures with guys, going out more often, or making a show of how amazing her life is without you. But make no mistake—if she truly didn't care, she wouldn't feel the need to prove it. This is a last-ditch effort to get you to react. She wants to see if you'll reach out, if you'll show jealousy, if you'll try to get her back.

5. The Full-On Confession

This happens when enough time has passed, and she finally breaks. Maybe she realized that none of the guys she dated after you measured up. Maybe she thought she could do better and realized she was wrong. Either way, she'll reach out with a heartfelt message about how she misses you, how she regrets what happened, and how she wishes she could undo everything.

At this stage, it's not just about ego anymore—it's about genuine fear of losing you forever.

Should You Ever Take Them Back?

Here's the million-dollar question: if she comes crawling back, should you let her? It depends. If you ended things because she was toxic, disrespectful, or made you feel undervalued, then absolutely not. She is coming back because she realized she lost something good, not because she changed. And if you let her back in, you're just resetting the cycle for the same issues to repeat.

However, if the breakup was more circumstantial—bad timing, outside pressures, or misunderstandings—it *might* be worth considering, but only if you make her prove that she deserves another chance. The key is never to take her back on her terms. If she's coming back, she has to do the chasing this time. She has to show you that she recognizes where she went wrong and is willing to fix it.

Final Thoughts: You Hold the Power

The biggest takeaway here is that when you walk away from a relationship, you hold the power. Women are not used to being rejected. They are not used to being the ones left behind. If you carry yourself with confidence, maintain your abundance mindset, and refuse to beg or chase, you'll see the truth of what I'm saying: they always come crawling back. And when they do? The choice is yours.

FINALITY:
WHY I NEVER TAKE THEM BACK

For me personally, there is virtually no chance I would ever take a woman back. It's not about holding grudges, playing games, or proving a point—it's about a fundamental belief in **finality**. When I walk away, it's not for effect. It's not a strategy to make her miss me or to manipulate her into chasing me. It's because I have decided, with full clarity, that this is the end.

I don't believe in looking back. Once a decision is made, I move forward. No regrets. No second-guessing. No replaying scenarios in my head, wondering if things could have gone differently. Life is too short to dwell on relationships that didn't work. And if they didn't work the first time, chances are, they won't work the second time either.

I treat every woman I date with respect and dignity, and I make it clear from the start: if you think you can find better, there's the door. I'm not the kind of guy who begs for someone to stay, nor do I ever try to convince a woman that I'm the best option she has. I let her decide that for herself. And if she chooses to leave or shows signs of not valuing what I bring to the table, I have no problem holding the door open for her.

This mindset isn't about arrogance—it's about self-respect. I've seen too many men destroy their dignity by trying to win back women who have already written them off. They become weak, desperate, and willing to accept terms they never would have tolerated before. And for what? To get back into a situation that clearly wasn't meant to last? That's not me.

Why Finality is Power

One of the biggest mistakes men make after a breakup is leaving the door open. They may say it's over, but deep down, they're hoping she'll come back. They'll respond to her texts, check up on her social media, and secretly analyze every little move she makes to see if she still has feelings for them. I don't do that.

When it's over, **it's over**. I almost never stay friends. I don't keep in touch. I don't check in "just to see how she's doing." I don't respond to the random texts that come weeks or months later, designed to test the waters. I block, delete, and move on. Some people might see this as cold or unforgiving. But I see it as clarity.

I am a forgiving person in the sense that I don't hold onto anger or resentment. If a woman does me wrong, I don't dwell on it. I don't need closure or explanations. I don't need an apology. I simply accept what happened, learn from it, and never look back. Why? Because when you leave the past behind, you make room for better things ahead.

They Always Come Crawling Back—But I'm Not There to Catch Them

The irony in all of this is that my mindset only makes women more obsessed. They don't understand how I can be so detached, how I can walk away so cleanly without any visible emotion. They expect drama. They expect pleading. They expect a long, drawn-out process of "figuring things out." But with me, there's none of that. That's why they always come crawling back. Not because they truly want to re-kindle things but because they need to understand why I didn't fight for them. They need to feel validated again. They need reassurance that I still want them.

But by the time they reach that realization, I'm already gone. I'm no longer available for their emotional validation. I'm not an option an-ymore. And nothing frustrates a woman more than realizing that a man who once wanted her has moved on without hesitation. It's not a game. It's not about being heartless. It's about having the discipline to respect myself enough to never reopen doors that I intentionally closed.

Never Go Back—Here's Why

1. **If it was meant to work, it would have worked the first time.**
   Relationships don't fall apart for no reason. If there were fundamental incompatibilities before, they will still exist now. A few weeks or months apart won't change that.

2. **She didn't value you enough the first time.**
   If a woman walked away or let you go without a fight, it's because she believed she had better options. Do you really want to be someone's backup plan?

3. **She will never respect you the same way.**
   Women may come back, but they don't come back with the same level of respect they once had for you. If you let them go and then take them back, they now know that you are willing to accept whatever treatment they dish out.

4. **You set a precedent that she can leave and return at will.**
   If you take her back once, she'll assume she can do it again. It becomes a cycle. She pulls away when she wants, and you're always there waiting. That's not the kind of relationship dynamic I ever want to be in.

5. **You waste time that could be spent on someone better.**
   Every moment spent looking back is a moment you're not moving forward. There are too many incredible women out there to waste time trying to fix something that was already broken.

The Importance of Owning Your Decision

A lot of men struggle with finality because they let emotions cloud their judgment. They break up, but then they start reminiscing about the good times. They forget why it ended in the first place. They miss the comfort of having someone around. And before they know it, they're reaching back out, hoping to "try again." I don't do that.

When I make a decision, I own it completely. I don't second-guess myself. I don't entertain "what if" scenarios. I trust my instincts, and I trust the reality of the situation. This level of decisiveness is powerful. It's what keeps me in control of my own life, my own emotions, and my own future. And when a woman realizes that I'm not the type of man who will bend, chase, or reopen closed doors, it only amplifies the effect. She comes crawling back, but I'm not there to catch her.

Final Thoughts: The Strength of Never Looking Back

One of my core beliefs in life is that the past belongs in the past. I never look back. There's no need to. What's done is done. The best way to honor any experience—whether good or bad—is to learn from it and move forward. That's why I never take women back. It's not about proving a point. It's not about revenge. It's about maintaining my own sense of self-respect.

If a relationship ends, it ends for a reason. And if she realizes later that she made a mistake? That's her burden to carry, not mine. So yes, they always come crawling back. But by then? I'm already gone.

WHY WOMEN ALWAYS HAVE A BACKUP PLAN

"She thought she was Tarzan. What she didn't know was I cut the whole damn vine."

In today's dating world, one truth separates the players from the played: women always have options. Whether she's actively searching or just existing, there's always a swarm of guys circling—DMs, texts, "hey strangers—just waiting for a shot. Most men operate in scarcity mode, thinking quality women are rare. But women? They're in abundance mode, and that changes everything.

This is where the concept of monkey branching comes in. Monkey branching is when a woman secures her next relationship before exiting the current one—just like a monkey grabbing a new branch before letting go of the last. Sometimes it's conscious and calculated, other times it's just instinct. Either way, if she's acting cold, distracted, or less affectionate, it's not random—she's already scouting the next branch.

That's exactly why I live by a simple rule: if you think you can do better, there's the door. I don't close it, and I sure as hell don't block it. She's free to walk—because I'm not here to beg, bargain, or compete. And trust me, if she does leave, she'll eventually learn the new branch isn't as sturdy as it looked.

The first red flag is emotional distance. When a woman is into you, she's affectionate, engaged, and plugged into the connection. But when that spark fades—texts slow down, plans get canceled, conversations feel hollow—you're not imagining it. She's mentally moving on long before she physically does.

Next, you'll hear the classic excuse: "I've just been so busy." No, she hasn't joined NASA or taken on three jobs—she's just investing her time elsewhere. She stops making space for you, spontaneous hangouts vanish, and she's glued to her phone when you are together. That's not distraction—it's redirection.

Then comes the shift in future talk. A woman who sees you as long-term will naturally talk about what's ahead—vacations, holidays, even next weekend. If that chatter disappears and she starts dodging any plans beyond tomorrow, pay attention. She's not planning the future with you in it anymore.

Her phone behavior will change, too—and fast. Suddenly, her phone is face down, always on silent, and she takes calls in another room. If she wasn't secretive before, and now she's guarding that thing like it holds nuclear codes, something's up. And no, she's not "just checking work emails."

Monkey branching often triggers fights, too—pointless, petty ones. This is emotional sabotage designed to justify her exit. If she can convince herself that you're "always arguing," it makes leaving easier for her conscience. And it makes the breakup feel like your fault, not hers.

Social media becomes her soft-launch pad. She ramps up the selfies, deletes your photos, and starts posting cryptic captions like "letting go" or "new energy only." You'll notice new male followers and random guys liking everything she posts. She's not hiding it—she's warming up the crowd.

So, what do you do when you see the signs? First, you don't confront—you observe and act. Most women will deny monkey branching even with hard evidence. Don't chase answers—just match her energy and begin pulling back.

You start showing up less, replying slower, becoming unavailable. Let her feel the shift without the drama. The worst thing you can do is beg for clarity from someone who already checked out. If she's playing games, stop being on the field.

Always maintain an open-door policy—emotionally, not literally. If she thinks there's a better deal out there, let her go explore it. But don't stand in the doorway hoping she returns. Once she's gone, she's gone for good.

The one thing you should never be is a safety net. When she says, "I need space," it's usually code for "I'm trying someone else out, but I might circle back if it doesn't work." Don't let yourself become the Plan B while she beta tests Chad 2.0. Once she's out, remove the cushion and let her fall.

The most powerful response isn't revenge—it's improvement. Hit the gym, upgrade your style, focus on your money, and start dating someone new. Become so unbothered and dialed-in that she sees you thriving and feels the sting. Nothing ruins her rebound fantasy faster than watching you level up.

At the end of the day, women will always have options—and so should you. Hypergamy is real, and it's not going away. Some women are loyal and intentional; others swing from branch to branch like they're auditioning for a *Tarzan* remake. Your job isn't to stop them—it's to be the man they regret losing.

You are not her backup plan, her placeholder, or her emotional crutch. You're the prize, the mission, the upgrade. And when she decides to swing, let her. Just make sure you're not standing there when the next branch snaps.

Foodie Calls and Dinner Hoes: The Modern-Day Dinner Whores

There's an old saying: *There's no such thing as a free lunch.* But if you spend any time in the dating world, especially in places like South Florida, you'll find that for a certain category of women, free dinners are a way of life.

Back in the day, these women were called **"dinner whores"**—ladies who would happily accept an invitation to a fancy meal, enjoy the best food and drink a man's credit card could buy, and then vanish into the night, never to be seen or heard from again.

Today, the term has evolved. We call them **"foodie calls"** or **"dinner hoes"**—women who use dating apps and social opportunities not to find romance but to enjoy a lavish meal on someone else's dime.

It's a game they play and a game I've learned to play right back.

The Art of the Foodie Call

Women have always known they have something men want. And while sex is the primary currency in dating, attention and companionship are close seconds. Some women have realized that they don't even have to give sex or affection to receive male generosity. All they have to do is accept a dinner invitation, bat their eyelashes, engage in some small talk, and then disappear.

For them, this is transactional dating without the transaction. Now, let me make one thing clear: I have no problem taking a woman out for a nice meal. I enjoy good food, I love great conversation, and I don't mind spending money on a date. What I do mind, however, is being played. And in today's world, where dating apps are flooded with opportunistic women looking for nothing more than a free steak and lobster dinner, a man needs to recognize the signs early on.

How to Spot a Dinner Ho Before You Swipe Right

Most foodie calls follow a predictable pattern. Once you know the red flags, you can weed them out before you even send that first message.

1. She Avoids Personal Questions About You

A woman who is genuinely interested in a man will ask questions. She'll want to know about his life, his interests, his experiences. A foodie girl? She's all about the logistics.

- "What's your favorite restaurant?"
- "Where do you like to go for drinks?"
- "Are you more into sushi or steak?"

Notice something missing? You. She's not asking about you—she's planning her next free meal.

2. She Suggests Expensive Restaurants

This one is classic. You suggest meeting for a drink or coffee to feel each other out, and she immediately counters with a high-end restaurant.

- "Oh, I'd love to meet! How about Prime 112?"
- "Mastro's has the best seafood! We should go there!"
- "I've been dying to try Nobu. Wanna take me?"

If a woman is dictating where you should take her before you even meet, you can bet she's done this before—and she's not interested in anything more than the dinner.

3. She Orders Like a Queen but Acts Like a Pauper

A woman who appreciates your company will order a meal as if she were paying for it herself. A foodie girl? She sees your Amex as an unlimited buffet pass.

- She gets appetizers, an entrée, and dessert.

- She orders the most expensive thing on the menu.
- She picks the top-shelf wine or cocktail.
- And when the bill comes? She doesn't even pretend to reach for her purse.

A woman who orders without a second thought about cost is not considering you—because she has no plans of seeing you again.

4. She Mentions That She's "Really Traditional"

Translation? She expects the man to pay for everything. Now, I don't mind paying for dinner. I come from a generation where that's the norm. But there's a difference between a woman who values chivalry and one who views men as walking ATMs. The moment she says, *"I never pay on a first date,"* or *"A real man takes care of the bill,"* she's giving herself away. She's not looking for romance— she's looking for a free ride.

Turning the Tables on a Foodie Call

Like I said, I've been in this game a long time. I can usually see them coming from a mile away. But sometimes, I let them think they're playing me—because I enjoy playing back. See, here's the thing: most women assume they are in control. They believe they can dictate the outcome of the night by flashing a smile, sipping their wine, and keeping things "friendly." But if she's feeding off my Amex card? She better be nice. And she better at least pretend to be grateful.

Breaking Down the Barriers

A lot of guys get bitter about foodie calls. They feel used, taken advantage of, and humiliated. Me? I take it as a challenge. Here's what I've learned: Most of these women are playing the game because they've never met a man who could flip the script. I don't go on a date expecting anything, but I also know how to create opportunities when the moment is right.

Here's how it works:

- A couple of glasses of wine lower her inhibitions.
- The right conversation opens the door to flirting.
- A casual touch, a well-timed joke, a confident glance—suddenly, she's second-guessing her own game.

A foodie girl expects a simp—a guy who will sit there, pay for everything, and hope for a second date that will never come. She doesn't expect a man who knows exactly what he's doing. And when the night ends, it's not uncommon for her to end up in my car, my arms, or my bed. And here's the kicker—I never call them again. Why? Because these women are a dime a dozen.

The Foreign Factor: Russian, Ukrainian, and Eastern European Women

Now, let's talk about a particular breed of foodie girls: The Eastern European contingent. If you've spent any time in Miami, Palm Beach, or any other major city, you'll know what I'm talking about. These women are gorgeous, charming, and incredibly calculating. Many of them grew up in places where survival meant using their beauty as currency. They are experts at extracting resources from men without ever giving up anything in return.

They are also the biggest users of the foodie call strategy. But here's the secret: Many of them secretly crave a man who doesn't fall for their tricks. I've had more than one Russian beauty try the foodie call approach with me—only to end up chasing me when they realized I wasn't another desperate American man willing to pay for their lifestyle.

When you show them you understand the game, they start playing by your rules.

Why Foodie Calls Are Fading (For Most Women)

One thing I've noticed over the years is that foodie calls are becoming less common—at least among American women.

Why?

- **Dating app culture has changed expectations.** Women who want free dinners now go straight for men with money instead of wasting time on guys who might expect more in return.
- Men have wised up. Guys are less willing to spend big money on first dates, opting for coffee, drinks, or casual meetups instead.
- The rise of "situationships." More women are okay with casual dating than ever before, making traditional foodie calls less necessary.

That's not to say foodie girls are extinct—but they are more obvious now, making them easier to avoid.

Final Thoughts: Play the Game, Don't Get Played

Look, I get it—no man wants to feel like he's just another free meal ticket. But here's the truth: Women will always test men. Some will test you emotionally. Some will test you intellectually. And some will test you by seeing how easily they can get a dinner out of you. The key is knowing the game before you step onto the field. So, the next time a woman hints at an expensive restaurant before she even knows your last name? Just smile. Because if she thinks she's playing you, she has no idea who she's dealing with.

Shit-Testing: Why Women Test Men and How to Handle It Like a Pro

Women love to test men. Even the ones they admire and respect. And truthfully, I'm okay with it—to an extent. Why? Because I do the same thing to them. The difference is how and why we test each other.

Women test men to suss out weakness. They want to know if the man they are with is truly strong or if he is just playing the part. Early on, these tests serve a critical function: they help a woman determine if a man is worth her time, effort, and emotional investment. Women crave strength, leadership, and confidence.

But here's where things get tricky. Once a woman is with a man, she doesn't stop testing. The testing evolves. If a man starts slipping—if he loses his edge, his ambition, or his masculine presence—the tests increase. At first, they are trying to confirm if he is weak. But once they know for certain that he is weak, the testing takes on a different purpose: humiliation and contempt.

This is why a man must always be on his guard. Not in a paranoid way, but in a way that acknowledges this reality: A woman's respect for you is directly tied to your ability to handle her tests.

The Psychology Behind Why Women Shit-Test Men

A woman's biology, social conditioning, and evolutionary instincts compel her to test men. This is not necessarily something she does consciously—it is built into her nature.

Think about it like this: for thousands of years, a woman's survival depended on her ability to choose the right man. She needed a man who could protect her, provide for her, and ensure the survival of her offspring. Weakness in a man was dangerous—because a weak man could be overtaken by stronger men, killed in battle, or left unable to provide resources. Even today, in our modern world, where survival is no longer a daily fight against nature, these instincts remain. So, a woman will test a man's strength in many ways:

- To see if he is confident.
- To see if he is emotionally stable.
- To see if he can handle pressure.
- To see if he will bend to her will or stand his ground.

Every time a woman throws out a test, she is essentially asking: "Is this man strong enough to handle me?"

How Women Test Men in the Early Stages of Dating

When you first meet a woman, her tests are subtle but deliberate. If you know what to look for, you'll recognize them immediately.

1. The Compliment Reversal Test

This is when a woman *seemingly* compliments you, but in reality, she's seeing how you react to subtle criticism.

- "You're actually pretty good-looking for your age."
- "I usually date taller guys, but you seem cool."
- "You're not like most of the guys I meet… I think."

What is she doing? She's testing to see if you're insecure. If you get flustered, act defensive, or try to seek her validation, you fail.

2. The Flakiness Test

A classic. She cancels plans last minute or texts: "Oh, I made other plans because I didn't hear from you!" She wants to see if you will chase her. If you get upset, beg to reschedule, or shower her with attention, she now knows you're desperate—and her attraction drops.

3. The Indifference Test

She plays cold, stops texting as much, or suddenly acts distant. What she wants to know: Are you a man who gets needy when things seem uncertain? Or do you stay centered and unaffected? The right response? Ignore the behavior. If she's interested, she'll come back around. If not, she was never into you to begin with.

How Women Test Men in Long-Term Relationships

Women do not stop testing men after commitment. In fact, the longer a relationship goes on, the more intense the tests become—especially if she starts to sense that a man is slipping. Here's what a lot of guys don't understand: When a woman knows you are weak, her tests are no longer about assessing you—they are about punishing you.

1. The Emotional Rollercoaster Test

She picks a fight out of nowhere. She seems distant one minute and affectionate the next. She creates chaos—seemingly for no reason. What she wants to know: Can you remain calm? Can you hold your ground without getting sucked into the drama? Fail this test by getting overly emotional, apologizing too much, or trying to "fix" her emotions? She loses respect for you.

2. The Respect Test

She starts being openly disrespectful:

- Eye-rolling
- Cutting you off in conversations
- Dismissing your ideas
- Criticizing your ambitions

This is a major test. If she starts losing respect and you do nothing about it, you are sealing your fate. The only response? Call it out directly and set a boundary. If she continues, you walk.

3. The Other Men Test

Suddenly, she's talking about male friends. Or about some guy at work who's "so funny." Or she name-drops an ex. She's not doing this by accident. She's testing you. Do you get insecure? Do you become reactive? Do you start chasing harder? Or do you smile, stay confident, and subtly make her feel like she's the one who should be worried about losing you?

The Right Way to Respond to Shit-Tests

Some tests you pass by demonstrating strength. Others you throw right back in her face.

For example:

"Does this dress make me look fat?"

- The weak man: "No, you look amazing! I love everything you wear!" (FAIL)
- The strong man: "I think you look great, but you looked even sexier last week in that black one." (PASS—confident but not a pushover)

"Oh, I made other plans since I didn't hear from you."

- The weak man: *"Oh no, I'm so sorry! Let's reschedule. When are you free?"* (FAIL—now she knows she's your priority over everything else)
- The strong man: *"Cool. I was busy anyway. Have fun!"* (PASS—signals that she's replaceable)

The key to handling any shit test is not reacting emotionally. Women love to provoke emotions in men. It's how they assess strength. If she can throw you off balance with words alone, you fail.

Testing Women Right Back

Now, here's where it gets interesting. While women test men to look for weakness, I test them to look for compatibility.

I want to know:

- Is she sexually open and adventurous?
- Is she selfish?
- Does she have narcissistic tendencies?
- Does she lack empathy?

One of my biggest tests? How she talks about her father. A woman's relationship with her father directly affects how she treats men. If she has serious daddy issues, I run. Fast. Another test? How she handles small inconveniences. If a woman loses her mind over a slow waiter or a minor annoyance, she's emotionally unstable. If she can't handle small issues, how will she handle a real crisis?

Final Thoughts: Play the Game or Get Played

Here's the deal: Women will always test men. And they should. A man who fails these tests isn't fit to lead, protect, or inspire confidence. But as men, we should also be testing them. Not to look for weakness but to look for red flags, emotional stability, and compatibility. At the end of the day, dating is a game of strength and discernment. You either play the game or you get played. And trust me—you want to be the one setting the rules.

THE SECRET TO BEING A GREAT LOVER: A WOMAN ALWAYS COMES FIRST

There was once a book published by a somewhat eccentric psychologist titled *A Woman Always Comes First*. While the author may have been a bit of a wacko, the fundamental premise of the book wasn't wrong—it was just often misunderstood.

When I say a woman always comes first, I don't mean that you should put her happiness ahead of your own in all aspects of life. You were not born to be a martyr. No man should ever live in a way that suppresses his own desires, ambitions or needs just to make a woman happy. That kind of self-sacrifice leads to misery, resentment, and, ultimately, failure in relationships.

But there is one time and one time only when a man should prioritize a woman's pleasure over his own—in bed. This isn't just about being generous. It's not about impressing her or making her think you're some kind of god in the bedroom. It's about psychology, physiology, and what makes for a truly fulfilling sexual experience.

Why Prioritizing Her Pleasure Makes You a Better Lover

There's an undeniable truth in intimacy: if a woman doesn't climax, the experience feels incomplete for both partners. You can try to convince yourself otherwise. She may tell you, "It's fine. It still felt amazing," or "Not every woman can orgasm every time," but deep down, something feels off. Even if you had a great time, there's a nagging thought in the back of your mind—Did I really satisfy her? Did I measure up?

This isn't just about male ego; it's about understanding how intimacy works on a deeper level. When a man reaches orgasm, his role in the experience is effectively done. The endorphins kick in, the dopamine levels spike, and suddenly, he feels that wave of relaxation that comes after release.

For a woman, however, the path to climax is more complex. Women don't climax as easily as men do. Some do, sure—there are women who can achieve an orgasm with just the right kind of penetration, and some can come within minutes if they're highly aroused. But for most, it takes work—the right setting, the right foreplay, the right level of trust and comfort.

If she doesn't reach climax, the experience is unfinished for her. She may still enjoy it, but she's left with unfulfilled tension—like getting 90% through a great book and never reading the final chapter. And as a man, if you care about your own experience as much as hers, you'll recognize that her pleasure magnifies yours.

The Psychological and Emotional Benefits of Making Her Come First

Let's talk about the mental and emotional impact of prioritizing a woman's pleasure. When a woman reaches orgasm first, the dynamics of intimacy change completely. She lets go. Her body relaxes, her mind becomes uninhibited, and she becomes far more open to experiencing deeper levels of pleasure.

This does two things:

1. It amplifies her connection to you. Women are emotionally tied to their sexual experiences. The man who gives them the strongest orgasms is often the man they feel the most drawn to.
2. It enhances your own pleasure. When a woman is satisfied, she becomes more giving, more adventurous, and more eager to return the favor.

On the other hand, if a man finishes before his partner, she might not say anything, but the dynamic shifts. There's a subconscious disappointment—not because she's selfish, but because her own pleasure was left incomplete. A sexually satisfied woman is a happier, more engaged, and more loyal partner. When a woman consistently has powerful, mind-blowing orgasms with a man, she naturally wants more of him.

Mastering the Art of Holding Back

If you truly want to be a great lover, you need to master the ability to control your own orgasm so that she finishes first. This takes discipline. Some men struggle with premature ejaculation; others get too caught up in the moment and don't pace themselves. Either way, learning to control your release is a fundamental skill in great sex.

Techniques to Last Longer and Ensure She Comes First

1. Focus on foreplay first.
    - Women need buildup. Start with kissing, touching, and teasing. Don't rush to penetration. Make her crave it.
2. Use digital and oral stimulation.
    - Hands and tongue before penetration will virtually guarantee she reaches climax first. Many women need clitoral stimulation to orgasm—not just penetration.
3. Change positions strategically.
    - Slowing down, changing angles, and taking breaks to stimulate her manually or orally can help extend your endurance.
4. Train your body.
    - Practice edging—getting close to climax and then stopping—to improve control.
5. Breathe and stay mentally aware.
    - When you feel yourself getting too close, pause, slow down, and focus on her pleasure.

The Role of Substances: Alcohol and Weed in Sex

Many men and women use alcohol or weed to enhance their sexual experiences. These substances lower inhibitions, increase sensations and allow for more relaxed, open sexual encounters.

How Alcohol Affects Orgasms

- A drink or two can help a woman relax and become more receptive to pleasure.
- Too much alcohol, however, can numb sensitivity and make climaxing harder.
- For men, excessive alcohol can lead to delayed ejaculation or erectile dysfunction.

Weed and Orgasms

- Many women report more intense orgasms when they're high.
- Weed can help with anxiety and tension, making it easier to let go.
- The downside? It can also reduce lubrication in some women and cause delayed response time.

A moderate amount of either can enhance the experience—but always in balance.

When a Woman Struggles to Orgasm

Some women have a hard time reaching climax.

This could be due to:

- Mental blocks or stress
- Insecurity about their bodies
- Lack of experience or sexual trauma
- Poor communication with partners

If you encounter a woman who has difficulty orgasming, **your job is to guide her.**

- Reassure her. Let her know there's no rush.

- Encourage her to relax and focus on the sensations rather than the outcome.
- Take your time exploring her body and discovering what turns her on.

Some women require multiple experiences with a partner before they reach climax. Patience and skill make all the difference.

Final Thoughts: The True Secret of a Great Lover

Being a great lover isn't about having the biggest dick, knowing the craziest positions, or lasting for hours. It's about understanding how pleasure works. If you can control your own orgasm, understand female pleasure, and prioritize her climax before your own, you will be one of the rare men who actually knows what he's doing.

Women talk. They compare experiences. They remember the men who made them lose control. And trust me—if you're that man, she'll never forget you. So remember: A woman always comes first. Not in life, not in your priorities, but always in bed.

50 Ways to Leave Your Lover:
The Art of Breaking Up Without Chaos

Breaking up is never easy. Whether it's a casual relationship, a long-term romance, or even a marriage, there's no magic formula to ensure a clean, painless exit. The best possible breakup scenario—the rarest one—is a mutual decision where both partners calmly agree that it's time to part ways. No bitterness, no anger, no lingering resentment. Just two adults acknowledging that their paths no longer align. But let's be real—this almost never happens.

More often than not, breakups are messy, emotional, and filled with conflict. When there are shared assets, joint living arrangements, businesses, children, or close-knit social circles involved, things get even more complicated. In many cases, one person is more invested in the relationship than the other, and when that reality sets in, the one being left behind can lash out.

A breakup is, at its core, a power shift. The person who is emotionally or financially dependent will fight the hardest to maintain control, and the one who is willing to walk away holds all the cards. Whether you're ending a short fling or a long-term commitment, you need a strategy. Here's how to navigate the inevitable with as much dignity, control, and self-respect as possible.

1. Understanding the Power Dynamics of a Breakup

Before you pull the plug, understand one fundamental truth: the person who cares the least controls the relationship. This doesn't mean you should act cold, heartless, or manipulative, but you need to recognize that emotional attachment and financial dependence dictate how a breakup unfolds. The more someone needs you—emotionally, financially, or socially—the more volatile their reaction will be.

For this reason, it's critical to prepare for the fallout. If you've been dating someone who is emotionally unstable, financially reliant on you, or prone to outbursts, be especially careful about how you approach the breakup. Key things to consider before ending things:

- **Financial entanglements** – Does she rely on you for money, rent, or a business you run together?
- **Emotional stability** – Is she prone to breakdowns, irrational behavior, or manipulative tactics?
- **Your own safety** – Will she react with aggression or threats?
- **Shared assets** – Is there a lease, property, or car you both use?
- **Mutual friendships** – Are you socially intertwined, making the breakup more complex?

If the relationship is relatively casual and these concerns don't apply, you have a far easier exit. But if any of the above factors are in play, you need to tread carefully.

2. The Wrong Ways to End a Relationship

There are a hundred bad ways to break up with someone, and most people instinctively choose the worst ones.

Ghosting

Ghosting is a coward's move. Disappearing without explanation is juvenile and disrespectful—unless you're dealing with someone dangerous, in which case it's about self-preservation. If safety isn't an issue, ghosting is weak and leaves the other person without closure, which often leads to obsessive behavior or unexpected retaliation.

The Fade-Out

This is a slow, passive-aggressive version of ghosting. You text less, cancel plans, show less enthusiasm—essentially trying to make her break up with you by frustrating her. This rarely works because many women will cling harder when they sense distance.

The Public Breakup

Dumping someone in a public place or over social media is disrespectful and humiliating. If she has any dignity, she'll hate you forever. If she doesn't, she might cause a scene. Either way, it's a bad move.

Cheating Your Way Out

Some guys intentionally cheat as an "escape strategy." They figure if they get caught, she'll break up with them and save them the trouble. It's a low blow and destroys any remaining respect she might have had for you.

Blaming Her for Everything

Even if she was the problem, don't go out of your way to rip her apart on the way out. This invites unnecessary drama. Breakups don't have to be a blame game.

3. The Right Way to End Things: A Clean Break

If you've decided to move on, be direct, be firm, and don't drag it out.

Best Practices for Breaking Up Like a Man:

1. Do it in person (if safe to do so).
    - o Unless she's volatile or violent, the respectful thing to do is face-to-face.
2. Keep it short and simple.
    - o No long explanations or drawn-out conversations. Say your piece and let it end.
3. Don't get baited into arguments.
    - o She may try to guilt-trip you, cry, yell, or start a fight. Stay calm and detached.
4. Avoid saying, "Let's be friends" if you don't mean it.
    - o If you want a clean break, don't offer false hope.
5. Be clear that it's final.
    - o No mixed signals, no "maybe later." Women cling to hope—don't give it to her.

6. Set boundaries.
    o   If necessary, block her on social media and cut off contact to prevent drama.

4. The Legal and Financial Side of Breakups

If you were living together, own property, or have joint bank accounts, breaking up isn't just emotional—it's a logistical nightmare.

To protect yourself:

- Get a prenup if you're married or planning to be.
- Never add a girlfriend to your lease or mortgage.
- Keep separate bank accounts.
- If breaking up, don't leave her in a position to claim financial dependency.

If she refuses to leave your place, you may need legal action. Avoid letting her establish residency—in some places, if she's been living with you for a certain period, she can claim tenancy rights, making it hard to evict her.

5. The Emotional Fallout: Handling the Aftermath

Some women handle rejection poorly. Expect pushback.

Common Post-Breakup Behaviors Women Exhibit:

- Guilt-Tripping & Begging – "I can change! Just give me another chance!"
- Fake Pregnancy Claims – "I missed my period. We need to talk."
- Revenge Tactics – Trashing your name, making false accusations.
- Showing Up Unexpectedly – At your home, work, or gym.
- Suddenly Finding a "New Guy" – Posting him everywhere to make you jealous.

How to deal with it? Stay detached. The less reaction you give, the sooner she'll move on.

6. Moving On: Why She'll Always Come Crawling Back

If you were a strong, dominant, and confident man in the relationship, there's a high chance she'll come back. As stated before, women hate being rejected. Even if she wasn't that into you, the fact that you ended it on your terms will drive her crazy. But should you take her back? Probably not. Once you walk away, stay gone. I live by the saying, "I never look back." There's a reason you broke up in the first place. Reuniting just reopens old wounds.

Final Thoughts: How to Leave Without Drama

Breaking up isn't easy, but it doesn't have to be a disaster. The key is to be firm, decisive, and unemotional.

- If she's dangerous or emotionally unstable, break up in a safe, controlled setting.
- If she's just upset but not vengeful, keep it short and kind, but don't waver.
- If she tries to win you back, remind yourself why you left in the first place.

And most importantly?

Once you leave, don't look back.

The Last Thing You Should Do: Why Moving in Together is a Risk You Shouldn't Take Lightly

Moving in together is often seen as the natural progression of a serious relationship. But make no mistake—this is one of the most significant decisions you will ever make. It changes the entire dynamic between you and your partner, and if it goes south, a breakup becomes exponentially more difficult, messy, and traumatic.

So, should you ever move in with a woman? The short answer is yes, but only if under the right circumstances. And that's a big *if*. Too many men rush into cohabitation without fully understanding what they're getting into. They assume that moving in together is just a trial run for marriage or a way to spend more time with their girlfriend. In reality, it's much more than that. The decision to share a living space fundamentally alters the relationship's balance of power, financial responsibilities, and emotional expectations.

Before you take the plunge, you need to evaluate your partner carefully. You need to stress-test the relationship, determine if she is relationship material, and assess whether moving in together benefits you—or if it's simply a trap.

1. The Hidden Risks of Moving in Together

Living together may sound great in theory—more time together, shared expenses, increased intimacy—but in practice, it can become a minefield of potential problems.

Here's why:

a. Moving in Too Soon Creates a False Sense of Security

Many couples move in together before they truly know each other—and that's where the problems start.

- In the early months of a relationship, everything is fun and exciting. You're still getting to know each other, and your partner is still on her best behavior.
- But living together strips away the illusion of perfection. You start seeing her daily habits, her flaws, and her real personality.
- If you haven't stress-tested the relationship, you might wake up one day and realize you're living with someone you can't stand.

Too many men assume that moving in together is just "the next step." But it isn't. It's a massive commitment, one that binds you emotionally, legally, and financially.

b. Breakups Become Infinitely More Complicated

When you're just dating, breaking up is relatively easy. You have an argument, decide you're done, and go your separate ways.

But when you live together?

- Now you have to deal with a lease, bills, shared furniture, and possibly even joint assets.
- If your name is on the lease or mortgage, you might find yourself legally stuck in a situation you want to escape from.
- If she refuses to leave, you could be in for months of drama and legal headaches.

Even worse, many women use cohabitation as a power play. They move in with a man not because they want to build a life with him but because they see it as a way to secure financial benefits, create social pressure for marriage, or even trap him into an arrangement that benefits her more than it benefits him.

2. The Real Reason Some Women Want to Move In

a. Is She Trying to Lock You Down?

Women know that men are more likely to marry someone they live with. Moving in together often serves as a precursor to marriage, whether you want it to or not.

- Does she bring up living together constantly?
- Does she push the idea of getting a place together after only a few months?
- Does she use guilt or manipulation to convince you that it's time?

If so, proceed with extreme caution. You need to ask yourself: Is she really the right partner for you? Or is she just trying to secure a long-term commitment before you've fully tested the relationship?

b. Is She Financially Motivated?

Living together can drastically lower a woman's financial burdens—especially if you're paying the majority of the rent, utilities, or groceries.

- Does she suddenly start talking about money when discussing moving in?
- Does she assume you'll pay most of the expenses?
- Is she in financial trouble and looking for an easy way out?

A financially independent woman who genuinely wants a partnership won't need to rush into cohabitation. But a woman looking for a free ride might be eager to move in as soon as possible.

c. Has the Relationship Been Tested?

Before considering cohabitation, your relationship needs to go through real-world stress tests.

Ask yourself:

- Have you had serious arguments, and how did she handle them?

- Have you spent extended periods of time together under stressful conditions?
- Do you know her views on money, chores, and conflict resolution?
- Does she respect your independence, or does she try to control you?

If you haven't seen her under pressure, in financial situations, or in moments of true difficulty, then you have no idea who she really is.

3. The Legal and Financial Risks of Moving In

a. If It's Your Home, Protect Yourself

If you own the home, letting her move in could give her rights you never intended.

- In some states, a woman who lives in your house for a certain period may establish residency rights.
- If she contributes to home improvements, she could later claim part ownership.
- If you break up, she may refuse to leave, forcing you into legal battles.

b. Never Put Her Name on the Lease Unless You're Certain

If you rent, putting her name on the lease makes it just as much her place as yours.

- If she stops paying her share, you're still legally responsible for the full rent.
- If she damages the property, your credit could take the hit.
- If you break up, she has just as much legal right to the space as you do.

c. Don't Let Her "Invest" in Your Property

It may seem harmless to let her pay for renovations or contribute financially to your home. But once she's made an investment, she can argue for ownership rights.

- Let her pay rent or utilities—but never let her invest in your property.
- If she insists on contributing to big expenses, get a legal agreement in writing.

4. When Moving in Together Might Make Sense

Despite all these risks, moving in together isn't always a bad idea. If you're serious about marriage or a long-term relationship, cohabitation can be a logical step.

However, you should only do it under the following conditions:

- You've been together for at least a year and have been through real challenges.
- You have seen how she handles stress, money, and conflict.
- You are financially independent and have a legal plan in place.
- She respects your boundaries, your space, and your independence.
- You genuinely enjoy being around her for long periods.

If you move in together, make sure there are clear financial agreements to prevent problems down the line.

5. The Illusion That Moving in Will "Fix" a Relationship

One of the biggest mistakes men make is assuming that moving in together will solve relationship issues.

- If she's jealous or insecure, living together will make it worse.
- If you have communication problems, they will only intensify.
- If she's pressuring you for commitment, moving in will only delay the inevitable.

If a relationship isn't solid before you move in, it won't magically improve after. It's better to fix problems first—or walk away.

Final Thoughts: The Smart Approach to Moving In Together

Moving in together is not a casual decision. It has financial, emotional, and even legal consequences. Before taking that step:

- Know who she really is.
- Have clear financial agreements.
- Protect your assets and legal rights.
- Never let moving in be a way to "fix" an unstable relationship.

If you make the wrong decision, you could end up in a situation that is far more difficult to escape than you ever imagined.

Avoiding the Baby Trap:
Protecting Yourself from an Unwanted Pregnancy Scheme

Men of all ages have fallen victim to the baby trap—a deliberate pregnancy orchestrated by a woman to solidify a relationship or secure financial commitment. It's a scenario that has played out time and again, and if you think you're immune, you're mistaken.

Whether you're a young man just starting your dating life or an older man who believes he's beyond the risk, baby trapping can happen to anyone. Even if you thought you were "shooting blanks" for years, one unexpected pregnancy can change your life permanently.

This is why it is absolutely crucial to take the necessary precautions, set clear boundaries, and be aware of the warning signs. Your future—both financial and personal—depends on it.

1. Understanding the Baby Trap: Why Some Women Do It

Before we discuss how to protect yourself, let's break down **why** a woman might try to trap a man with a baby.

a. Financial Security

- A woman who sees a man as a financial provider may view having his child as an investment.
- In many jurisdictions, child support can amount to thousands of dollars per month, often lasting 18 years or more.
- Some women actively seek out high-earning men to secure a lifelong financial payout.

b. Relationship Leverage

- Some women believe that a baby will force a man to commit—either through marriage or long-term cohabitation.
- If a relationship is already failing, she may see pregnancy as a way to hold onto the man and prevent him from leaving.

c. Social and Emotional Fulfillment

- Some women want children regardless of the father's wishes and will deceive or manipulate to achieve that goal.
- If her biological clock is ticking and she hasn't found a committed partner, she may view an "accidental" pregnancy as a solution.

d. Pressure from Friends or Family

- Certain cultural or family pressures may push a woman toward pregnancy, especially if she comes from a background that values marriage and motherhood.
- If her friends or family members are all having babies, she may feel compelled to do the same—by any means necessary.

2. The Tactics Some Women Use to Trap Men

Most baby-trapping scenarios aren't random accidents. They involve deliberate deception or manipulation—and you need to know the warning signs.

a. The "Oops" Pregnancy

- The classic "I forgot to take my birth control" excuse.
- Claiming birth control failed (without proof).
- Swapping out condoms or sabotaging protection.

b. The "Don't Worry, I Can't Get Pregnant" Lie

- Some women will claim they have fertility issues or are on their period as a way to bypass protection.
- Others will say, "I'm on birth control," even if they're not.

- Never take a woman's word for it when it comes to contraception.

c. The Secret Baby Fever

- Some women pretend they don't want kids, only to suddenly change their mind once they believe you're emotionally invested.
- She may start "joking" about having a baby together or making subtle references to motherhood.

d. The Condom Disposal Trick

- Some women retrieve used condoms from the trash to inseminate themselves.
- It may sound extreme, but it has happened many times.
- Always dispose of used condoms yourself—flush them, tie them up, or take them with you.

3. How to Protect Yourself from the Baby Trap

a. Always Use Protection—And Handle It Yourself

- Never rely on a woman's claim that she's on birth control.
- Always use your own condoms (never trust one she provides).
- Dispose of used condoms properly. Don't leave them where she can access them.

b. Demand a Paternity Test Immediately

- If she claims she's pregnant, do not accept it at face value.
- Insist on a legally supervised paternity test as soon as possible.
- Do not sign a birth certificate until paternity is confirmed.

c. Be Clear About Your Stance on Children

- Make it known early in the relationship if you don't want kids.
- If she starts pressuring you about having a baby, it's a red flag.

d. Never Marry a Woman Just Because She's Pregnant

- Child support is often cheaper than a divorce.

- If the relationship was already unstable, marrying her will only make things worse.

e. Date Women Who Are Past Their Childbearing Years

- If you have zero interest in having kids, dating post-menopausal women eliminates the risk.

4. The Legal Side: Understanding Child Support and Your Rights

a. The Legal System Will Not Protect You

- Many men believe that if they were deceived, they shouldn't have to pay child support.
- Wrong. In most jurisdictions, the court does not care how the pregnancy happened.
- If you are the biological father, you are financially responsible—period.

b. The Child Support Trap

- Child support payments are often determined by income, not actual expenses.
- In some states, fathers can be forced to pay for private school, medical expenses, and even college tuition.
- If you fall behind, the state can revoke your driver's license, garnish your wages, and even put you in jail.

c. False Paternity: What Happens If You're Tricked?

- Some men unknowingly pay child support for years for a child that isn't theirs.
- In some states, even if a paternity test later proves you are not the father, you may still be financially responsible.
- This is why it is critical to demand a paternity test as soon as possible.

5. The Psychological and Emotional Toll

A baby trap isn't just about money. It's about control, stress, and emotional manipulation.

- Being forced into fatherhood against your will can destroy your peace of mind.
- You may be tied to a woman you dislike for decades.
- Your financial future may be permanently altered.

The best way to avoid this nightmare? Be vigilant, be smart, and never assume you're immune.

Final Thoughts: Taking Control of Your Future

Avoiding the baby trap isn't about paranoia—it's about being smart.

- Recognize the warning signs.
- Take control of contraception and disposal.
- Demand a paternity test immediately if she claims to be pregnant.
- Never let emotional manipulation force you into an unwanted commitment.

Your future, your finances, and your freedom are on the line. And remember: You can never lose what you never had. If a woman tries to trap you, walk away—and never look back.

How Many Times Per Week?
And What Happens When She Really
Doesn't Love Sex?

Sex is a crucial component of any romantic relationship. It's one of the fundamental ways that two people express their connection, passion, and intimacy. But how much sex is enough? Is there an ideal frequency, or is it purely subjective?

The reality is that there is no universal rule—it all depends on the couple, their individual sex drives, and their ability to communicate and compromise. For some, once a week is more than enough to feel satisfied and connected. For others, anything less than daily sex is considered a dry spell. And for a select few, an insatiable appetite for intimacy might indicate deeper psychological or emotional issues.

But what happens when you enter a relationship and the sexual dynamic shifts? What if, over time, the passion fades? More importantly, what if you find out that your partner never really loved sex in the first place—but only pretended to enjoy it at the start of the relationship? These are critical issues that every man must face, because sexual compatibility is non-negotiable in the long run.

1. The National Average vs. Personal Reality

Studies suggest that the national average for sexual frequency among married couples is about once per week. This might sound reasonable to some, but to others, it seems abysmally low. In the early stages of a relationship, known as the "honeymoon phase," many couples engage in sex multiple times per day. But eventually, that initial passion fades, and reality sets in.

The key question is: How much sex is the right amount?

a. The Importance of Sexual Compatibility

- If one partner is content with once per week and the other needs it daily, this is a problem.
- If neither partner feels deprived, then their frequency is "enough," regardless of what statistics say.
- Mismatched libidos can cause serious resentment over time.

b. The Gradual Decline: What's Normal?

- It's natural for sexual activity to decrease over time in a long-term relationship.
- But it shouldn't decline to the point where one partner is consistently frustrated.
- Busy lives, stress, and fatigue can affect frequency, but making time for intimacy is essential.

c. Beware of the "Bait-and-Switch"

- Some women initiate a relationship with frequent sex, only to withdraw once they feel secure.
- A drastic drop-in sexual activity could mean she never really loved sex—she only used it as a tool to secure the relationship.
- If this happens, don't ignore it—address it immediately.

2. The Woman Who Hates Sex: A Dealbreaker?

Let's talk about one of the most frustrating scenarios a man can experience: falling for a woman who secretly hates sex.

Imagine this:

- In the beginning, she was passionate, eager, and adventurous.
- **But over time, she becomes distant, uninterested, or even repulsed by intimacy.**
- You try everything—romance, foreplay, communication—but nothing works.

At this point, you have a serious decision to make.

a. Is This a Temporary Phase or a Permanent Issue?

- Temporary sexual issues can arise due to stress, medical problems, or hormonal changes.
- Permanent sexual disinterest often stems from deep-seated psychological or emotional blocks.

b. The Woman Who Pretended to Enjoy Sex

Some women fake enthusiasm in the early stages of a relationship because they know that men value sex highly.

- They act passionately to lock down a commitment.
- Once they feel secure, the mask drops.
- Suddenly, they claim they "never really liked sex" or they "just did it for you."

c. When to Try Therapy—and When to Walk Away

If you genuinely love the woman and believe her issue is resolvable, therapy might be worth exploring. But if her aversion to sex is fundamental to her personality, it will not change.

If you find yourself in this situation, you need to ask:

- Can I live the rest of my life in a sexless or low-sex relationship?
- Will I resent her if I stay?
- Am I willing to accept an open relationship if she refuses to meet my needs?

For many men, the answer is simple: Walk away.

3. Understanding Why Some Women Don't Love Sex

There are various reasons why some women have **low sexual desire** or seem uninterested in physical intimacy.

a. Psychological Blocks

- Upbringing: Raised in a conservative or religious environment where sex was viewed as shameful.

- Past Trauma: Sexual abuse, assault, or negative experiences in previous relationships.
- Body Image Issues: Feeling insecure about their appearance, leading to avoidance of intimacy.

b. Medical or Hormonal Issues

- Hormonal imbalances (low estrogen, testosterone, or thyroid issues).
- Certain medications (antidepressants, birth control, etc.).
- Chronic health problems affecting energy and libido.

c. Manipulation and Control

- Some women use sex as a bargaining tool to manipulate a man's behavior.
- Others withdraw sexually as a punishment or to assert dominance in the relationship.

Whatever the reason, you need to recognize the red flags early.

4. The Relationship Between Sex and Power

Sex isn't just about pleasure—it's about power dynamics in a relationship. The partner who desires sex more is often at a disadvantage because their needs are dependent on the willingness of the other person.

a. When She Controls the Sex, She Controls the Relationship

- If a woman realizes that sex is your weak spot, she may weaponize it against you.
- The more needy and desperate you seem for intimacy, the less attractive you become.
- A man who values himself will never tolerate a sex-starved relationship.

b. The Danger of Becoming Sexually Deprived

- Long-term sexual frustration breeds resentment.

- A man who is deprived of intimacy for long enough will either:
  - Cheat
  - Leave
  - Become emotionally dead inside

The worst mistake a man can make? Staying in a sexless relationship, hoping things will change.

5. How to Ensure You Never End Up in This Situation

a. Vet Her Sexuality Before Committing

- Pay attention to her attitude toward sex early on.
- Ask about her past relationships—if every ex was "controlling" or "sex-obsessed," that's a red flag.
- If she claims she "isn't that into sex" but expects a committed relationship, walk away immediately.

b. Set Expectations Early

- Make it clear that sexual connection is important to you.
- If she isn't enthusiastic about sex early on, it's only going to get worse.
- Don't ignore the warning signs.

c. Never Marry a Woman Hoping She'll Change

- If she has low libido before marriage, it will not improve later.
- Marriage often makes women feel more secure, meaning their motivation for sex may decrease even further.
- Never commit long-term to someone whose sex drive doesn't match yours.

Final Thoughts: Prioritizing Your Own Needs

Sex is not just an optional part of a relationship—it's a core foundation of intimacy and connection. If you find yourself with a woman who doesn't love sex, resents intimacy, or only engages to keep you around, you need to leave. The right woman for you is one who:

- Enjoys sex and is excited to share it with you.
- Matches your level of desire.
- Doesn't manipulate or withhold intimacy for power.

Your sexual happiness matters. Never settle for less than what fulfills you—because once you give up your right to passion, you give up a huge part of your masculinity and self-respect.

WOMEN FOR HIRE:
YOU'RE GOING TO DO IT ANYWAY, SO WHY NOT JUST HIRE AN EXPERT?

The debate about paying for sex is as old as time itself. Some men swear they'd never do it, while others see it as a simple transaction—the most efficient way to satisfy their desires without the complications that come with traditional dating. Whether you fall into one camp or the other, the reality is that sex work exists and has existed throughout history, making it "the world's oldest profession."

But why do some men choose to hire women for sex? What are the advantages and drawbacks of such an arrangement? And does it ultimately help or hinder a man's ability to form meaningful connections with women?

Let's break it down—the pros, the cons, and the social stigma surrounding this controversial topic.

1. The Evolution of the "Oldest Profession"

Prostitution has been part of human civilization for thousands of years. In ancient Rome, Greece, and China, courtesans were highly respected and often entertained the most powerful men in society. In Japan, the geisha culture, while not exclusively sexual, was rooted in the art of entertaining men through conversation, dance, and companionship.

Even today, in places like the Netherlands, Germany, and certain areas of Nevada, sex work is legal, regulated, and taxed, making it safer for both workers and clients. The argument in these places is simple: men have needs, and women have the power to fulfill them in a controlled, safe environment.

Contrast this with the United States, where prostitution remains illegal almost everywhere, driving the trade underground and creating risks for all parties involved. Despite its illegality, it thrives in back channels through escort services, sugar baby arrangements, and high-end courtesan services. The demand will never disappear, and where there is demand, there will always be supply.

2. Why Some Men Prefer the Transactional Route

a. The Efficiency Factor

For men who don't want to spend weeks or months chasing a woman—only to face rejection, manipulation, or disappointment—hiring an escort is a direct path to satisfaction.

- No games. No emotional rollercoaster. Just an agreement where expectations are clear.
- No worrying about texting the right way, planning elaborate dates, or playing the "does she like me?" guessing game.
- It's time-efficient, especially for high-powered professionals who don't have the luxury of navigating the dating market.

As Oscar Wilde once said, "Everything in the world is about sex, except sex. Sex is about power." Many men recognize that women wield an enormous amount of power in the dating market, and for some, removing that power imbalance by making the interaction transactional is preferable.

b. Avoiding Emotional Baggage and Drama

Relationships require emotional investment—and sometimes, that investment comes at a steep price. Arguments, mind games, manipulation, and the risk of being cheated on or ghosted can drain a man's energy and self-worth.

For those who hire professionals, there's no emotional entanglement, no uncertainty, and no heartbreak. It's a purely physical exchange, which some men find liberating.

c. Variety Without the Chase

Men are biologically wired for variety—a concept known as the Coolidge effect, which describes how males of most species tend to lose interest in the same mate over time but regain enthusiasm when introduced to a new one.

For men who have the means, hiring different women allows them to experience that variety without the effort of seduction. Instead of swiping endlessly on dating apps or spending hours trying to impress a woman over dinner, they simply select, pay, and enjoy.

d. Skill and Expertise

This is where things get tricky—because a man who indulges in professional companionship may find himself spoiled by the experience.

Let's be honest—many women in the dating pool lack sexual expertise or have hang-ups about sex due to upbringing, past experiences, or personal insecurities. A professional, however, knows exactly what she's doing.

Some men report that escorts or high-end courtesans provide far better experiences than any girlfriend they've ever had—because these women:

- Understand what men want without needing constant validation.
- Have mastered the art of seduction without emotional games.
- Take pride in delivering an unforgettable experience.

For some men, this raises the bar to an unattainable level, making them less willing to engage with "regular" women in traditional relationships.

3. The Downside of Paying for Sex

a. The Expense Factor

Let's not sugarcoat it—hiring an expert isn't cheap. High-end escorts charge anywhere from $500 to several thousand dollars per session, while exclusive courtesans can cost upwards of $10,000 per weekend, especially in Palm Beach.

This can add up very quickly, and for those who make it a habit, it can drain their finances faster than a high-maintenance girlfriend ever could.

b. The Emotional Deception

One of the biggest risks in hiring a woman is the illusion that she actually likes you.

- These women are professionals, meaning their job is to make you feel desired.
- The laughs, compliments, and intimacy you experience may feel real, but they are part of the service.
- You may start believing she has genuine feelings for you—but in most cases, she doesn't.

As **Jean-Jacques Rousseau** once put it, "The money you have gives you freedom; the money you pursue enslaves you."

The same concept applies to women for hire—if you're paying for their time and attention, you have freedom, but the moment you start pursuing something real with them, you're lost.

c. The Risk of Addiction and Detachment from Reality

Some men become dependent on transactional intimacy to the point where they lose touch with real-world relationships.

- They no longer want to put in the effort to build emotional bonds with women.
- They grow detached from normal social interactions because paid intimacy is easier.
- They may start avoiding regular women altogether, making long-term connections impossible.

While hiring an escort occasionally may not lead to this, those who make it a habit often find themselves disconnected from the dating world.

4. Legal and Social Stigma

Let's address the elephant in the room: **Prostitution is illegal in most places.**

This means:

- Legal risks if caught.
- Potential exploitation issues if dealing with underground operations.
- Moral and social judgment from others.

However, not all countries see it the same way. In the Netherlands, Germany, Japan, and Canada, sex work is decriminalized, regulated, and taxed—making it far safer and removing the criminal element.

The U.S., on the other hand, has a more Puritanical view of the subject, which forces the industry into unsafe, illegal territory.

Final Thoughts: Should You Hire an Expert?

At the end of the day, this is a personal decision. Some men will never pay for it, while others see it as a valid option when needed.

If you do decide to go down this road, remember:

- Keep it occasional—don't let it replace real human connection.
- Never fall for the illusion—these women are professionals, not potential girlfriends.
- Be mindful of your finances—it can become an expensive habit.
- Recognize the social and legal risks—know the laws in your area.

If you decide against it, remember:

- Sex is best when it's genuine.
- Building real connections with women takes effort but is more rewarding.
- You can develop your own game to attract high-quality women naturally.

In the end, as Mark Twain once said: "The lack of money is the root of all evil."

And when it comes to paying for pleasure, sometimes the cost isn't just financial—it's psychological.

NEVER BE A WHITE KNIGHT: WHY TRYING TO "SAVE" A WOMAN WILL ONLY DESTROY YOU

To paraphrase The Moody Blues, the problem with being a knights in white satin is that you never reach the end.

So many guys fall into the white knight syndrome—the belief that by rescuing a woman from her troubles, she will come to see him as her savior, appreciate his selflessness, and ultimately fall in love with him. But in reality? That's not how it works.

This is one of the most destructive mindsets a man can have in dating and relationships. White knights operate under the illusion that their kindness, generosity, and emotional labor will be rewarded with love, loyalty, and gratitude. Instead, they get used, discarded, and replaced by the very same woman they went out of their way to save.

The truth is that women do not respect men who sacrifice their dignity to save them from their own bad decisions. Worse, white knighting often attracts the very type of women who thrive on chaos, manipulation, and male servitude—leaving the man drained, frustrated, and bitter.

Let's dive into why white knighting is a losing game, why men fall into this trap, and how you can avoid becoming a woman's emotional tampon.

1. The White Knight Fantasy vs. Reality

At its core, white knighting is a form of covert contract thinking—a term coined by Dr. Robert Glover in his book *No More Mr. Nice Guy*. It's the belief that:

- If a man is kind, supportive, and emotionally available, a woman will reward him with love and loyalty.
- If he helps her through her struggles—be they financial, legal, or emotional—she will see his value and choose him over all the other men.
- If he proves himself as the best possible option, she will finally reciprocate his affections.

But in reality?

- Women do not fall in love out of obligation or gratitude—they fall for men they admire and desire.
- A woman who is attracted to chaos will continue to create chaos no matter how many times you rescue her.
- The more a man sacrifices for a woman, the less she values him.

White knights think they're playing the role of the **hero**, but in truth, they're often playing the **fool**.

2. The Emotional Tampon: When You Absorb Her Chaos

White knights don't just save women from their external problems—they also absorb their emotional baggage.

- She vents about her toxic ex. He listens for hours.
- She's stressed about her job, kids, or personal struggles. He offers solutions and reassurances.
- She talks about her dating problems. He secretly hopes she'll realize he's the better option.

Meanwhile, what does she do?

- She sees him as a friend, not a romantic partner.
- She continues dating other men who aren't bending over backward for her.
- She only calls him when she needs comfort, validation, or a favor.

The emotional tampon is the guy who absorbs all her stress, drama, and insecurities—but never gets the reward of a romantic connection.

By taking on this role, he lowers his own value because women aren't attracted to men who let themselves be emotional dumping grounds.

3. The Divorcee Trap: When Her Problems Become Your Problems

One of the most dangerous forms of white knighting happens when a woman is going through a divorce or a bad breakup.

The Red Flags to Watch For:

1. She's financially dependent on her ex.
   - She complains that her ex controls the money.
   - She subtly hints that she could use some help.
2. She constantly talks about her legal battles.
   - She shares every court update like you're her lawyer.
   - She asks you for legal advice or financial help.
3. She "leans on you" for emotional support.
   - She talks about how miserable her life is.
   - She tells you, "You're the only one who understands me."

The white knight swoops in, thinking, "I'll help her get through this, and once she's free, we'll be together."

But what really happens?

- She accepts his help, but never sees him as an equal.
- Once she's financially or emotionally stable, she moves on to a new guy.
- The white knight is left feeling used, bitter, and rejected.

This pattern repeats itself with men who believe "saving her" will make her love them.

4. The High Cost of Playing the White Knight

Being a white knight **never ends well**—and here's why:

a. You Become a Stepping Stone

- White knights help women level up, only to be left behind once she's back on her feet.
- She never saw him as a romantic partner—just a temporary emotional and financial crutch.

b. You Will Be Used and Discarded

- Once a woman knows a man is willing to rescue her, she loses respect for him.
- If he's always available, she starts taking him for granted.

c. You Waste Your Own Time and Resources

- White knights spend money, time, and energy on women who will never be theirs.
- Meanwhile, they ignore other women who might actually want them.

5. How to Avoid the White Knight Trap

a. Stop Trying to "Fix" Women

- A woman's problems are her own to solve—not yours.
- If she's in constant turmoil, she's probably addicted to it.
- Instead of saving her, let her prove that she's stable and capable.

b. Set Boundaries and Protect Your Time

- If she only calls when she's upset, she's using you as free therapy.
- If she's not reciprocating interest, cut the emotional support.

c. Prioritize Yourself Over Any Woman

- A high-value man doesn't put a woman's needs above his own.

- Focus on your goals, career, fitness, and finances.
- Let women earn your time and attention, not the other way around.

d. Date Women Who Don't Need Saving

- The best relationships come from two stable, independent people choosing each other.
- Avoid women who are constantly in crisis—they will never be stable.

Final Thoughts: Be a King, Not a Knight

A king doesn't rescue damsels in distress—he rules his own kingdom and lets the right woman earn a place beside him.

If you want a strong, healthy, and rewarding relationship, the answer is not in white knighting. It's in becoming the type of man who women desire—not out of desperation, but out of admiration. Never sacrifice your dignity to be a woman's hero. Because once you do? She'll never see you as one.

GIVERS AND RECEIVERS OF PLEASURE:
UNDERSTANDING THE DYNAMICS OF INTIMACY

I have a theory, one that has evolved over years of observing people, relationships, and my own experiences: people are either natural givers or receivers of pleasure. This doesn't mean that one is inherently better than the other or that one is completely incapable of fulfilling the opposite role. Rather, it's about inclination, preference, and an individual's natural tendency when it comes to intimacy and human connection.

Some people derive immense satisfaction from giving—whether it's sexual pleasure, emotional support, or even material generosity. Others feel most fulfilled when they are on the receiving end, soaking in their partner's attention, care, and efforts. Ideally, a balance exists where both partners transition between giving and receiving, but in my experience, most people have a dominant inclination.

So, where does this tendency originate? Is it rooted in childhood experiences, psychological conditioning, or perhaps even something deeper—something innate? While I don't have a definitive answer, I do have some observations that help clarify the dynamic.

The Psychology Behind Giving and Receiving Pleasure

The way a person interacts in intimate settings often mirrors the way they engage in life at large. Some individuals are hardwired to give. They are the nurturers, the caretakers, the ones who put others first. They take joy in seeing their partner's pleasure, sometimes even at the expense of their own. Their fulfillment comes not from their own physical gratification but from witnessing the response of their partner.

On the flip side, there are those who naturally prefer to receive. They crave attention and thrive on being the center of someone else's efforts and desires. It's not necessarily a selfish trait—at least, not inherently. Some receivers are deeply appreciative, knowing that their pleasure is a gift from their partner and reciprocating in other ways.

However, when the scales tip too far in either direction, problems arise. A relationship where one person is always giving and the other is always taking becomes unbalanced and, eventually, unsustainable. The giver may feel unappreciated, drained, and emotionally neglected. The receiver, on the other hand, may develop an unconscious sense of entitlement, taking their partner's efforts for granted.

To maintain a healthy and fulfilling connection, both partners must learn to step into the other's shoes—to give when needed and to receive when the moment calls for it.

The Giver: The Nurturer, The Pleaser, The Selfless One

Givers often come from backgrounds where they were expected to take care of others from an early age. Maybe they were the eldest sibling in a household where they had to raise their younger brothers and sisters. Perhaps they had a parent who was emotionally or physically dependent on them. In many cases, givers learned from an early age that love and acceptance came from being of service to others.

Sexually, givers are the ones who focus on their partner's experience more than their own. They pay attention to the little details—what makes their partner sigh, what movements elicit the strongest reactions, how to prolong pleasure. They take pride in knowing they have the ability to make their partner feel something extraordinary.

However, there is a downside. Givers, when taken for granted or unappreciated, can burn out. When they give and give without receiving in return, resentment can build. The very thing that once brought them joy—pleasing their partner—can become a source of frustration.

The most tragic part? Many givers are uncomfortable receiving. They've spent so much time focusing on others that when the spotlight is on them, they don't know how to relax into the moment. They might feel undeserving, guilty, or even anxious about being in a vulnerable position.

The key for a giver is to learn balance—to recognize that receiving is not selfish, that their pleasure matters just as much as their partner's, and that true intimacy is a two-way street.

The Receiver: The Indulger, The Center of Attention, The Sensory Seeker

Receivers are the ones who thrive on being pleasured, adored, and lavished with attention. They enjoy being on the receiving end of someone else's affection, whether it's physical, emotional, or even material. In many cases, receivers have a deep-seated desire to be desired. They crave that feeling of being wanted, of knowing that their partner is willing to go the extra mile to make them happy.

Sexually, receivers are the ones who melt under a partner's touch. They revel in the experience, letting themselves be taken care of and allowing their partner to take the lead. For many, this isn't about selfishness but about surrender—about letting go and fully immersing themselves in the pleasure their partner provides.

But just like with givers, there's a dark side. Some receivers become too comfortable in their role, expecting to be catered to without offering much in return. They may see their partner's giving nature as a given rather than something to be cherished and reciprocated.

The healthiest receivers are the ones who express genuine appreciation for what they receive. They make their partner feel valued, whether it's through words, gestures, or acts of reciprocity. They understand that while they love to be pleasured, their partner also deserves to feel wanted and adored.

For receivers, the challenge is to step outside of their comfort zone— to be the one who initiates pleasure, who takes the lead sometimes, who ensures that the giving is mutual.

Why Balance Matters: The Interplay of Giving and Receiving

A fulfilling relationship is built on the continuous exchange of giving and receiving. When both partners are able to switch roles—when the giver learns to receive, and the receiver learns to give—the result is a deeply satisfying, evolving connection.

In the best relationships, these roles are fluid. One night, one partner might take full control, lavishing their partner with attention and pleasure. The next night, the roles might reverse. There's an unspoken understanding that both people's needs matter and that true intimacy is about more than just physical gratification—it's about emotional connection, mutual respect, and shared experience.

When one person is always the giver and the other is always the receiver, stagnation occurs. The giver becomes drained, unfulfilled, and possibly resentful. The receiver, on the other hand, may start feeling guilty—or worse, entitled.

To avoid this imbalance, open communication is essential. Couples should talk about their needs, their desires, and their expectations. They should recognize when things start to feel one-sided and address it before it becomes a deeper issue.

The Takers: When Receiving Turns into Taking

There's a difference between being a receiver and being a taker. A receiver enjoys pleasure but also appreciates it. A taker, on the other hand, expects it—without reciprocation, without gratitude, without thought. Takers drain people emotionally and physically. They move from partner to partner, extracting as much as they can before discarding the person who has given so much to them.

Takers exist in every aspect of life, not just relationships. They're the ones who always expect favors but never offer to help. They're the friends who only call when they need something. They're the colleagues who let others pick up the slack.

Avoiding takers is essential for personal happiness. In relationships, being with a taker is a slow death of emotional exhaustion. The sooner you recognize the signs—the lack of gratitude, the expectation of service, the inability to give back—the better.

So, Are You a Giver or a Receiver?

The truth is, most people fall somewhere in between. Some lean more toward giving, others toward receiving, but ultimately, balance is what makes relationships thrive. The key is awareness—understanding your own tendencies and making sure that both you and your partner feel fulfilled.

Giving is an act of love, but so is receiving. Being open to pleasure, allowing yourself to be taken care of, and showing appreciation for your partner's efforts are all crucial aspects of intimacy.

The goal isn't to change who you are but to make sure that whatever role you naturally fall into complements your partner's needs. If you're a natural giver, make sure your partner values what you do. If you're a receiver, make sure you're showing your appreciation in return.

Because, at the end of the day, true intimacy isn't about who gives and who receives.

It's about making sure that both people feel wanted, needed, and deeply, undeniably satisfied.

Why I Have Written This Book

I look around, and I see a lot of men in pain. Not necessarily physical pain, but emotional pain—frustration, confusion, sometimes outright despair when it comes to dating, relationships, and navigating the ever-changing dynamics between men and women.

A lot of this pain comes from misunderstanding. Men don't always understand women, and women don't always understand themselves. I've learned, through thousands of interactions, that many women don't consciously know why they are attracted to a man. They might list their ideal traits—kind, caring, good job, responsible—but then turn around and give themselves fully to the man who doesn't check any of those boxes.

I wrote this book because I don't believe men should be in pain over something that can be understood, studied, and mastered. I don't claim to be the ultimate authority, nor do I think I've figured it all out. But I do have something that many others lack—extensive experience. And experience is the best teacher.

Through the years, I've gone on countless dates with an incredibly diverse array of women. I've learned what works and what doesn't. I've succeeded and failed, and I've analyzed every interaction—sometimes as a detached observer, sometimes with intense introspection—to understand what actually happens between men and women in the real world, not in some Hollywood fantasy.

And if my insights can help other men avoid years of unnecessary pain, self-doubt, or wasted effort, then this book has served its purpose.

Men Are Struggling, and No One Is Helping Them

It is no secret that men today are struggling when it comes to relationships. The modern dating landscape is vastly different from what it was just a few decades ago. The economic power dynamic has shifted, traditional gender roles have eroded, and women have more choices than ever before. Men who once had a clear path to a wife, children, and a stable family now find themselves lost, wondering where they fit in.

Some men react to this by checking out entirely. They walk away from relationships, choosing instead to focus on their careers, hobbies, or personal development. And I get it—dating, for many men, feels like a losing game. They pour time, effort, and money into women who seem indifferent at best and opportunistic at worst. They face rejection, confusion, and an overall sense that no matter what they do, they just can't get it right.

But is walking away really the answer?

I don't believe so.

Intimacy is a deep human need, one for which there is no true substitute. Some men try to fill the void with material success, fitness, or intellectual pursuits. Others bury themselves in work or dedicate themselves to their children. But no amount of money, muscle, or accolades will ever replace the fulfillment of being with a woman who is truly, deeply into you.

The Myth of the "Perfect Relationship"

A lot of men suffer in dating because they have bought into the idea that relationships should be easy, natural, and effortless. They believe in the Hollywood version of love—where you meet "The One," and everything magically falls into place.

But reality is much different.

In truth, relationships are a battlefield of emotions, desires, and unspoken expectations. Women test men—sometimes consciously, sometimes unconsciously. Attraction is fickle, often shifting based on factors even she doesn't fully understand. A man who enters the dating world expecting fairness and logic will soon find himself disillusioned.

That's why so many men get blindsided by breakups. They think that if they just provide, support, and show unwavering commitment, they will be rewarded with loyalty and affection. But that's not how attraction works. Women don't fall in love with a man because he's "nice" or because he's "always there for her." They fall in love with the man who triggers their deepest emotions, who makes them feel something raw, unpredictable, and real.

The sooner men understand this, the sooner they can take control of their dating lives.

What This Book Is (And What It Isn't)

This book is not a dating guide in the traditional sense. I'm not here to teach men how to send the "perfect text" or how to craft the ultimate online dating profile. I won't waste your time with cheesy pickup lines or "seduction techniques" that feel forced and unnatural.

Instead, this book is about understanding human nature—both yours and hers. It's about seeing past the illusions, learning from experience, and developing the mindset of a man who doesn't just attract women but understands them on a fundamental level.

If you read this book and still find yourself struggling with dating, then you either didn't pay attention or you are unwilling to let go of false beliefs that keep you trapped in a cycle of failure.

Because at the end of the day, dating success isn't about being the richest, the handsomest, or the smoothest talker. It's about mastering yourself, understanding the rules of the game, and having the discipline to walk away from situations that don't serve you.

Why This Book Helped Me More Than Anyone Else

I'll admit it—writing this book was just as much for me as it was for anyone else. Throughout my life, I've experienced deep frustrations in dating. I've suffered heartbreak, confusion, and even moments of self-doubt. I've questioned my own worth, wondered if I was good enough, and made mistakes that I now look back on with amusement.

But in writing this book, I have forced myself to confront those mistakes. I have analyzed my successes and failures with brutal honesty. And in doing so, I have gained an even deeper understanding of what works and what doesn't. I don't claim to be perfect. I still make mistakes. I still learn. But what I do know is this: I will never suffer from **oneitis** again. I will never pedestalize a woman. I will never chase or beg for attention. And I will never allow myself to be in a relationship that diminishes me as a man.

Because once you truly understand women—how they think, how they test, how they desire—you realize that the power was always yours. You were just conditioned to believe otherwise. To The Women Who Read This Book If a woman stumbles upon this book, I already know what her reaction will be. She will call me awful, sexist, arrogant, and a whole host of other names. She will claim I don't understand women at all, that I am bitter or jaded. She will dismiss everything I say as "toxic masculinity" or outdated nonsense.

But let's put that same woman across from me at one of Palm Beach's most exclusive restaurants. Let me feed her great food, pour her a glass of wine, and engage in playful banter that turns into light teasing, then flirting, then something even more. By the end of the night, more often than not, she will find herself in my car, in a pocket park, or back at my place, giving herself to me completely.

Because here's the truth that enrages women more than anything else: Women have no idea what actually attracts them to a man. They will tell you they want kindness, stability, emotional availability. But they will go home with the man who understands their triggers better than they do. They fall for the man who knows how to handle them, who makes them feel, and who takes control in a way that excites them.

And if you, as a man, understand this—if you truly grasp what makes women tick—then you will possess the keys to the kingdom.

Final Thoughts: The Path Forward

If you've made it this far, congratulations. That means you are willing to question what you've been taught, to step outside the lies and illusions that have been fed to you since childhood. My hope for you is simple: that you take these lessons and apply them. That you stop hoping women will like you and instead start understanding what actually creates attraction. That you never again find yourself lost, confused, or emotionally wrecked by a woman who was never worth your time to begin with.

Because once you **truly get it**, dating stops being painful. It becomes a game you enjoy playing.

And the best part? You never have to **chase** again. The women who are meant for you will come **to you**. And that, my friend, is what real power looks like. Happy dating and good luck.

DEALING WITH MANIPULATIVE WOMEN:
DON'T FALL FOR THE CROCODILE TEARS

Throughout life—whether in relationships, business, or any setting where you interact with people—you will inevitably encounter manipulators. These individuals, through experience and practice, have mastered the art of using emotions and emotional responses to get what they want. The problem? What they want is usually at the expense of others, including you.

Manipulative people are inherently dishonest, often very transparent if you know what to look for and have a blatant disregard for the feelings of others. They will blindside you when you least expect it. And that is exactly the point—manipulation works best when you don't see it coming. If you could see it clearly, you could defend yourself and avoid the situation altogether. That's why manipulators rely on subtlety, deceit, and confusion to keep you off balance and make you doubt your own instincts.

Some manipulators are benign, meaning they simply use persuasion and charm to get what they want without necessarily harming you. Others are malignant, and these are the ones you need to watch out for. They see life as a zero-sum game—where their gain is your loss, and they don't care how much damage they inflict as long as they get their way.

Women, as a rule, tend to be expert manipulators. And I don't mean this in a purely negative way—it is, at its core, an evolutionary survival strategy. Being the physically weaker sex, women learned thousands of years ago that their best weapon wasn't brute force but influence. They survived by bending men to their will, using sex, tears, kindness, anger, and emotional manipulation as tools in their arsenal. And guess what? It worked. It still works to this day.

Trust me, a man did not invent gaslighting, even though he did in the movie. But before we go any further, let's be clear about something: not all women are manipulators in a harmful way. Just like not all men are heartless players. The key is to recognize the women who use manipulation as a way to control you and stop them before they succeed. Let's break down what manipulation looks like, how to spot it, and—most importantly—how to shut it down.

The Different Types of Female Manipulation

Women manipulate in various ways, and the smartest ones adapt their strategies based on their target. If she senses you are weak in one area, she will attack there. If you're strong in another, she will avoid that battle altogether. But no matter what, the goal is the same: to bend reality to her advantage while making you believe it's your idea.

1. Emotional Manipulation (aka, Crocodile Tears)

This is one of the most classic forms of manipulation. She will use her emotions—crying, sulking, mood swings—to guilt you into submission.

- You tell her you don't want to take things to the next level yet. She cries and tells you how much she has sacrificed for you.
- You refuse to buy her that expensive handbag. She sulks for days and makes you feel guilty for "not caring about her happiness."
- You call her out on bad behavior. She flips the script and makes herself the victim, forcing you to apologize for daring to stand up for yourself.

The reality? Most of the time, the tears are fake.

Women know that men instinctively feel uncomfortable when a woman cries. They count on that discomfort, knowing most men will do anything to make it stop—even if it means giving in to her demands.

How to Handle It:

- Stay calm. The worst thing you can do is react emotionally. If you panic, she wins.
- Don't try to comfort her—this is what she wants. Instead, hold your ground and disengage.
- If she's genuinely upset, she will compose herself and talk to you like an adult. If she's manipulating you, she will escalate her theatrics.
- If she throws a tantrum, walk away. Let her cry alone. She will get over it.

2. The Sexual Manipulation Game

Women know that sex is one of the biggest motivators for men. So, naturally, it's one of their most powerful bargaining chips.

There are two primary ways women use sex to manipulate men:

1. Withholding Sex – She denies physical intimacy to punish you or control you.
2. Using Sex as a Reward – She only gives it when she wants something in return.

How to Handle It:

- Never let a woman use sex as a bargaining chip. If she starts withholding sex to get her way, make it clear that you will not tolerate it.
- Be willing to walk away. If you let her manipulate you with sex once, she will do it again and again.
- Understand that you have value too. Women often act as if they are granting you a privilege by sleeping with you. But attraction is mutual, and you are just as valuable as she is.

3. The "Damsel in Distress" Play

Many women, especially those who lack independence or financial security, will fake helplessness to get a man to take care of them.

Examples:

- She "doesn't know how" to manage her finances, so you step in and start paying for everything.
- She has "bad luck with cars," so you find yourself fixing her car, paying for repairs, or even buying her a new one.
- She's "not good with confrontation," so you end up handling all her difficult conversations for her.

At first, it feels good to help—after all, men love being the hero. But over time, you realize she's perfectly capable of handling these things herself—she just doesn't want to.

How to Handle It:

- Stop enabling her. If she can't figure out her finances, give her a budgeting book. If she can't manage her car, tell her to call a mechanic.
- Test her. The next time she plays the damsel, see if she makes any effort to solve the problem herself. You'll be shocked at how quickly she "figures it out" when you refuse to step in.
- Recognize that helplessness is often a form of control. The more dependent she makes herself, the more obligated you feel to stay and take care of her.

The Secret to Dealing with Manipulators: Stop Reacting

The biggest mistake you can make when dealing with a manipulative woman is engaging with her game. Why? Because manipulators thrive on emotional reactions. They need you to feel guilty. They need you to feel obligated. They need you to believe that if you don't comply, you are a bad person. If you refuse to play, they lose all their power.

How to Shut Down Manipulation Immediately:

- Stay emotionally detached. Never react with anger or guilt— both are weapons in her arsenal.

- Call out the manipulation directly. "I see what you're doing, and it's not going to work." Watch her scramble.
- Be willing to walk away. The only real leverage you have is your ability to leave. If she knows she can't control you, she will either stop the games or disappear.

Final Thoughts: Never Put Up With It

I learned the hard way that allowing yourself to be manipulated is the ultimate form of weakness. And guess what? Women despise weak men. My first wife was a consummate manipulator. I spent hundreds of thousands of dollars catering to her whims, breaking every time she pushed, often hating myself for my weakness. It took me years to realize that it wasn't her fault—it was mine. I allowed it.

But weakness, just like strength, is a learned behavior. Now, I see them coming a mile away. And when I do, I walk. Because if a woman needs to manipulate you to get what she wants, she's not worth your time. And trust me—there will always be another one waiting to take her place.

LET'S TALK MONEY:
WHY YOU SHOULD NEVER LEND TO WOMEN,
FRIENDS, OR FAMILY

If you go out with enough women for a long enough time, eventually, one of them is going to ask you for money. Maybe it will be framed as a one-time emergency—a sudden eviction notice, an unexpected medical bill, or an overdue rent payment. She might tell you that without your help, she will have to leave town, move back in with her parents, or worse, leave you.

It doesn't matter how the request is presented, the core issue remains the same: This is a special kind of shit test. Women test men constantly. Sometimes, it's to see if you're strong, confident, and self-assured. Other times, it's to gauge just how much control they have over you. And nothing reveals a man's strength (or weakness) faster than his willingness to part with his hard-earned money in response to an emotional plea.

This is not just a lesson in dating—it applies across the board to family, friends, and acquaintances as well. Lending money to individuals, especially in personal relationships, is one of the quickest ways to ruin those relationships forever. Why? Because when you loan money to people you know, you can be almost certain you will never see it again. It's a virtual certainty. And once money enters the equation, the dynamics of your relationship change permanently.

The Cold, Hard Facts About Private Loans

You don't have to take my word for it—there's hard data to back this up. Studies have shown that private, informal loans between friends and family members rarely get repaid in full.

Key Statistics:

- A study conducted by LendingTree found that roughly 60% of people who lend money to friends or family never get fully repaid.
- Another study from Bankrate indicated that more than 37% of people who lend money say it permanently damaged or ended the relationship.
- According to a survey by CreditCards.com, 43% of respondents who had loaned money said they regretted it, citing financial loss and broken trust.

These numbers prove what many of us have already experienced firsthand: lending money to people you care about almost always ends in disappointment.

How to Handle the Request for Money

When a woman—or anyone else—asks you for money, you have a few ways to handle it. Some responses will keep the peace, while others will send a clear message that you are not a fool to be taken advantage of.

1. The "Absolutely Not" Approach (Best for the Hard Ass)

This is the simplest and most effective strategy. When she asks, you simply say:

"No."

That's it. No explanation. No justification. Just no.

The mistake most men make is feeling the need to explain why they're saying no. The moment you start justifying your decision, you invite negotiation.

- "I just paid my taxes." She might respond, "That's okay, I don't need much."
- "I've had a lot of expenses lately." She will say, "I wouldn't ask if it weren't serious."

- "I can't afford it." She might argue, "But you just bought a new car last year."

If you refuse without explanation, you don't give her anything to push against. End of discussion.

2. The "Nice Guy Excuse" Approach (For Those Who Hate Confrontation)

If you're someone who struggles with flat-out rejection, you might prefer a softer approach. Instead of outright refusal, you can give her a reason that makes it impossible for her to argue:

- "I'd love to help, but I just paid my taxes."
- "I'm in the middle of a big investment, and all my money is tied up."
- "I made a promise to myself never to lend money to anyone because it always ruins relationships."

The key here is to make it about your personal policy, not about her. That way, she can't take it personally (though let's be honest, she probably will anyway).

3. The Secured Loan Option (For When You Want to Have Some Fun)

If she keeps pushing, you can turn the tables by offering a **secured loan**—a proposal that will likely scare her off immediately.

- "I'd be happy to lend you money. How much equity do you have in your home?"
- "Sure, I'll lend you $2,000—just leave your Rolex Daytona with me until you pay it back."
- "I can do it, but I'll need a signed contract at 15% interest, with collateral."

This is a beautiful way to weed out opportunists. If she was serious about paying you back, she should have no issue with collateral. If she balks? You just exposed her true intentions.

4. The Small "Test Loan" Trick (For Curious Minds)

If you truly want to see whether someone is trustworthy, you can do what I did when a friend asked me for $5,000.

Instead of saying no outright, I responded: "I can't do $5,000, but would $250 help?"

I already knew the money would never be repaid, but $250 was a price I was willing to pay to test his character. As expected, he never paid me back—but more importantly, he came back asking for more.

This is the real lesson: If you give someone money once, they will ask again.

The next time he asked, I changed tactics. Instead of giving him cash, I offered him work:

- "I need help moving. I'll pay you $25 per hour for ten hours of work."

He must have really needed the money because he agreed. And you know what? He was actually a big help. I gladly gave him the money after he earned it. But guess what? I never heard from him again. And that, my friends, is why you should never give money away for free.

The Russian Lady Who Asked for Money: Instant Ghosting

I once dated a Russian woman who seemed to have everything going for her—intelligent, stunning, charming. But one day, she dropped the "I need money" bomb on me. She made up some excuse, probably assuming that because I had money, I'd hand it over without question. I didn't even entertain the request. I ghosted her permanently and never spoke to her again. Lesson learned: If a woman asks you for money, she doesn't respect you. And if you give it to her, she never will.

Final Thoughts: Money and Power Go Hand in Hand

Money is more than just currency—it is power. It represents control over your own life, your decisions, and your self-respect. The moment you start giving it away freely, you are surrendering power. Women respect power. They may ask for money, but deep down, they don't truly respect the men who give in.

So, the next time a woman—or anyone—asks for money, remember these key rules:

- Never lend money you can't afford to lose.
- If you must lend, demand collateral.
- Understand that once you give, they will ask again.
- Never justify your refusal—just say no.
- If a woman asks you for money early on, walk away and never look back.

Because at the end of the day, money doesn't buy love, but it does reveal true character.

FIX-UPS AND OTHER DATING MISTAKES: WHY YOU SHOULD AVOID PLAYING MATCHMAKER ROULETTE

In my neck of the woods, I'm a very eligible bachelor. I've got a good lifestyle, an engaging personality, and the ability to attract women without any external help. Yet, for some reason, my friends and family have constantly tried to fix me up over the years, convinced they know what's best for me.

When I had a scarcity mindset, I used to jump at these so-called "opportunities." Huge. Huge. Mistake. I can't tell you how many overweight, unattractive, and incompatible women I went out with simply because someone I trusted said, "She's really beautiful and sweet." If I had been thinking clearly back then, my response should have been: "Okay, but how big are her tits, and how small is her ass?" Because, let's be honest—attraction is attraction. If she's not physically my type, then it's a complete waste of my time.

That doesn't mean I don't care about personality. It just means that if I'm not attracted to her, nothing else matters. The problem with fix-ups is you can't ask your friend or family member the real questions:

- How tight is her body?
- Does she take care of herself, or does she rely on "a great personality" to compensate?
- Is she actually looking for a relationship, or is she just trying to get free meals?

Your friend will never be able to answer those questions properly—because they don't see her the way you do. They see her potential, but potential means nothing when it comes to attraction.

So, let's talk about the many pitfalls of fix-ups and why you should avoid them like the plague.

Why Fix-Ups Are Usually a Terrible Idea

1. You're Stuck in a No-Win Situation

The biggest issue with fix-ups is that they put you in a social trap. If you don't like her, you risk offending both her and the person who set you up. If you do like her, but things go south, you risk damaging your friendship with the matchmaker. It's a lose-lose situation.

Here's a classic scenario:

Your friend says, "I know this amazing woman! She's beautiful, funny, and has a great heart. You have to meet her." You agree. The date happens. Within five minutes, you know this is going nowhere. Maybe she's overweight. Maybe she has a terrible personality. Maybe she's so boring that listening to her is like watching paint dry. But now you have to sit through an entire dinner, making polite conversation because you don't want to be rude.

Even worse? She might like you. Now you're in a situation where rejecting her will make you look like an asshole. And guess what? She's going to tell your friend EVERYTHING. "I thought we had such a great time, but he never called me back!"

Now, your friend thinks you're the problem, and your social circle starts whispering about how you're "too picky" or "not willing to give women a chance." See how this works? You've just lost your time, your energy, and possibly a friend—all because you agreed to a date you never should have taken.

2. The Matchmaker's Perspective is Totally Skewed

Most of the time, when someone is trying to set you up, they are not thinking like you are.

Your friends and family members don't understand your attraction triggers.

Instead, they focus on things like:

- "She's really nice!" (So what? Nice isn't enough.)
- "She's so sweet and caring!" (Still doesn't mean I want to sleep with her.)
- "She's been through a lot, and she deserves a good guy." (Not my problem.)

They think that because you're both single, you should give it a shot. But that's not how attraction works. I once had a woman try to fix me up with her "beautiful friend," who, as it turned out, was at least 50 pounds overweight and had a face that looked like she had lost a fight with a brick wall.

Did I appreciate the effort? Sure. Was I attracted? Not in the slightest. But now, because I trusted my friend's judgment, I was forced to have an awkward date, pretend to be interested, and then navigate the uncomfortable post-date follow-up. Lesson learned: Never trust someone else's definition of "beautiful."

3. The Risk of Insulting the Woman or the Matchmaker

Let's say you go on the date, and it's a disaster. Maybe she's rude, annoying, or just plain unattractive. What do you do?

- If you politely decline a second date, she might take it personally and badmouth you to the matchmaker.
- If you ghost her, you look like a jerk to both her and your friend.
- If you tell your friend the truth, you risk offending them.

I once made the mistake of being brutally honest after a bad fix-up. My buddy asked, "So what did you think?" I responded, "Dude, she's a solid 3. You really thought that was my type?" Needless to say, he never set me up again. So now, I take the easy route: I just say, "Hey, I didn't feel the connection, but I appreciate you thinking of me." No specifics. No insults. Just a polite deflection.

When Should You Actually Consider a Fix-Up?

There is only one time you should accept a fix-up: If she's breathtakingly gorgeous. That's it. If the woman being set up with you is so stunning that you would have approached her in a bar anyway, then maybe—MAYBE—it's worth the risk. Otherwise, it's not worth the hassle.

Because no matter how great her personality is, no matter how "sweet" she is, and no matter how much your friend swears you two are "perfect for each other," the reality is simple: If you're not attracted to her, it's a waste of everyone's time.

Final Thoughts: Don't Play the Fix-Up Game

I've learned my lesson the hard way: Fix-ups are almost always a disaster. Friends and family mean well, but they do not understand your attraction triggers. If you say **yes** to a fix-up, be prepared for:

- Awkward conversations
- Uncomfortable dates
- A social minefield if it goes badly

Instead, focus your energy on meeting women in ways that actually work for you. And if you do agree to a fix-up, just remember one thing: If something can go wrong, it will.

MEETING WOMEN IN BARS:
A RISKY GAME THAT CAN SOMETIMES WORK

I advise against it, but let's be real—sometimes, it works. There's something about the dim lighting, the alcohol flowing, and the charged atmosphere that makes bars an easy place for men and women to meet. The problem is that while it's easy to initiate, it's rarely the best place to build something meaningful. My first girlfriend? Met her at a bar in Greenwich Village, New York. I was 21, she was 19, and she walked in wearing no bra—which, to this day, remains one of my biggest weaknesses.

We had a couple of drinks—I've never been a big drinker—and one thing led to another. That meeting turned into a one-year relationship, a badly thought-out marriage proposal, and insanely good sex, which, at that time in my life, was exactly what I needed. She was completely insane.

She got into dropping acid, which I wanted no part of, and eventually cheated on me with a gay guy—but that's a story for another day. The fact that we met in a bar probably had very little to do with how things ended. But it made me start thinking: Is meeting women in bars really a smart strategy? Looking back, I can say with confidence that bars are the lowest common denominator for dating.

The Problem with Meeting Women in Bars

A guy I knew once told me, "Meeting women in bars is the absolute lowest effort way to get laid. It's all surface-level attraction, and there's no way to screen them properly." He was right.

When you meet a woman in a bar, here's what you don't know:

- Her real personality (she's probably tipsy, showing off, or just trying to have a good time with friends).

- What she's like in normal settings (you're only seeing her in "party mode").
- If she's looking for something real or just an ego boost.
- If she's single, taken, or on a break from her boyfriend/husband.
- If she's crazy (which you won't find out until much later).

What you do know:

- She looks good.
- She smells good.
- She's out to have fun.

That's it.

This is why bars are terrible for building relationships—everything is based purely on attraction.

Back in My 20s, Bars Were My Hunting Grounds

In my early 20s, I was scouring Manhattan bars—Greenwich Village, Soho, the Upper West Side, Upper East Side—you name it.

- I had a solid game.
- I looked good.
- I made decent money.
- I had zero approach anxiety.

And I hooked up a lot. Back then, one-night stands were way more common. The "hookup culture" was alive and well before dating apps turned the game into an online numbers game.

I had a decent success rate—probably one in ten approaches resulted in taking a woman home.

Not bad. But here's the thing: not a single relationship came out of it.

The Psychology of Women at Bars

Bars are a woman's playground.

- They're dressed to impress.

- They're competing with their friends for attention.
- They're on high alert for the "best deal" of the night.
- They're drinking, which can make them unpredictable.

A woman at a bar is not her real self—she's a heightened version of herself. You're not meeting Jessica from accounting, who loves hiking and reading. You're meeting Jessica, the tequila-fueled party girl. And Jessica, the party girl, doesn't want a serious conversation about life goals. She doesn't care about your values, your ambitions, or your career path. She only cares about how much fun she can have in the next few hours. And that's fine—if that's all you want, too.

Bar Women Are Not the Commitment Type

One of the biggest problems with meeting women at bars is that **most of them are there for fun, not for relationships**. I know, I know—some guys meet their wives at bars. It happens. But it's rare. Most of the time, bar women fall into one of these categories:

1. **The Party Girl** – She goes out multiple times a week, drinks too much, and her life revolves around socializing. She is not girlfriend material.
2. **The Attention Seeker** – She's there to get free drinks, flirt, and feel desired. She rarely goes home with anyone.
3. **The Heartbroken Rebound** – She just broke up with someone and wants to make herself feel better. Be careful with this one—she's unpredictable.
4. **The Girls' Night Out Type** – She's not even looking to meet guys. She's just there to dance, laugh, and post pictures with her friends.
5. **The Professional Gold Digger** – She's looking for a guy to buy her drinks, take her to an expensive after-party, and maybe even fund her next shopping trip.

I've seen all of them. And I've learned not to expect much.

Why I Stopped Taking Bars Seriously

At a certain point, I realized the ROI on bars was low. Yes, I had some great nights. But I also spent:

- Too much money.
- Too much time.
- Too much energy chasing women who were never serious.

It was fun, but it was also exhausting. And most of the women I met? They weren't relationship material. I'm at a point in my life where I don't need to chase. I'd rather have a steady rotation of high-quality women who actually like me for who I am—not some drunk girl I met at 2 AM who barely remembers my name.

When Bars Might Actually Work

Now, with all that said, there are some scenarios where meeting a woman at a bar can work:

1. **If You're at a High-End Lounge**

   o Dive bars? Forget it.
   o High-end cocktail bars, rooftop lounges, or hotel bars? Better odds.
   o The quality of women is higher, and they're less likely to be complete disasters.

2. **If You're at a Social Event That Just Happens to Be at a Bar**

   o Networking events, alumni meetups, or business mixers.
   o The environment is less about drinking and more about socializing.

3. **If She's There for a Chill Night, Not to Get Wasted**

   o Some women just grab a drink with a friend after work.
   o They're not trying to get hammered.

- o If she's nursing one drink and looks composed, she might actually be worth talking to.

4. **If You Meet Early in the Night**

- o By midnight, most people are drunk.
- o If you meet her at 8 or 9 PM, she's still in rational mode.

Final Thoughts: Should You Meet Women in Bars?

If you're looking for a fun night? Sure. If you're looking for a real relationship? Don't count on it. Bars are purely surface-level environments. It's a numbers game. You can win sometimes, but you'll spend a lot of time, money, and energy on women who aren't worth it. If you want high-value women who are worth dating, you're better off meeting them elsewhere—through hobbies, networking, fitness, or even online dating. But if you do choose to play the bar game, just keep your expectations in check. Because at the end of the day, most bar women are just looking for a good time, not a good man.

Meetup.com and Facebook Social Groups: Expanding Your Dating Pool Beyond Bars and Apps

When it comes to meeting new women, most men limit themselves to a few traditional methods: bars, dating apps, or through friends. But if you're serious about expanding your options—and you don't want to rely on pure luck—Meetup.com and Facebook social groups are two of the most effective ways to connect with high-quality women in a natural, social setting.

I've personally used both platforms, and they work. I met my last girlfriend at a Meetup event, and it was one of the best connections I've had in years (even if it didn't last). These platforms provide an organic way to meet women without the awkwardness of a cold approach or the artificiality of online dating.

If you're looking for a more effortless, low-pressure way to meet women—without spending a fortune on drinks or mindlessly swiping left and right—then Meetup.com and Facebook groups might be your best bet.

Meetup.com: What It Is and Why It Works

For those who aren't familiar with Meetup.com, it's a social networking platform that brings people together based on common interests. It has groups for just about everything:

- Happy hour groups
- Dinner groups
- Wine tasting gatherings
- Travel groups
- Fitness groups (running, hiking, kayaking, working out, etc.)
- LGBTQ+ groups
- Business and networking meetups

- Language exchange meetups

Meetup.com is international, and I've personally attended events in Florida, New York, California, Las Vegas, and more.

The beauty of Meetup.com:

- The people there already have a built-in common interest with you.
- It's not primarily a dating platform, so women aren't on high alert like they are on dating apps.
- It's far less intimidating than a cold approach in a bar or club.
- The women tend to be higher-quality, educated, and looking for more than just a random hookup.

My Experience: How I Met My Last Girlfriend at a Meetup Group

One night, I attended a happy hour Meetup at a popular bar and restaurant. She walked in, and I liked her right away. I struck up a conversation, got her number, and asked her out on a date. She said yes. The first date went great. We had chemistry, good conversation, and there was an obvious attraction. We discussed a second date for the following week, and I was looking forward to it. Then, the first red flag appeared. I texted her on Thursday to confirm our Friday plans.

Her response? "Oh, I didn't hear from you earlier, so I made other plans." I was pissed—not because she had other plans, but because she clearly expected me to chase her. I was less developed at the time than I am now, so it got under my skin more than it should have.

Instead of getting angry, I simply responded: "No problem, have fun." And I never contacted her again. Now, here's where things get interesting. A couple of weeks later, I went to another Meetup event, and who do I run into? Her. Within seconds, she was all over me—flirty, touching my arm, laughing at everything I said.

I should have walked away, but hey—I have an ego too. We ended up in a six-month relationship, which was frustrating as hell. Without getting into all the gory details, she wanted more than I could give her, and eventually, I ended things. To this day, she would hop back into the relationship in a heartbeat if I let her. She's actually one of the few women I've remained in contact with after a breakup, which is rare for me. Because she is that high quality of a person.

The Pros and Cons of Meetup.com for Dating

Like any method of meeting women, Meetup.com has advantages and disadvantages.

Pros:

- Higher-Quality Women – Unlike Tinder, where women can swipe a hundred guys a day, Meetup groups attract women who are social, friendly, and looking to expand their circles.
- No Pressure to Perform – Since it's not a "dating" environment, you can relax and just be yourself, which naturally builds attraction.
- Common Interests Create Easy Conversation – If you're at a wine-tasting event, talking about wine is a built-in conversation starter.
- You Meet Women in a Natural Setting – No awkward cold approaches, no pickup lines—just organic connections.
- Social Proof Works in Your Favor – If you regularly attend the same events, women will see that you're a normal, well-liked guy with a social life, which makes you more attractive.

Cons:

- You'll See the Same People Regularly – If you date someone and it doesn't work out, you'll probably run into her again.
- Some Women Just Want Socialization, Not Dating – Not every woman at a Meetup is looking to meet a guy—some are just there for the activity itself.
- Friend-Zone Risk – If you aren't flirting and escalating, you can easily end up being "just another guy in the group."

Facebook Social Groups: Another Hidden Gem for Meeting Women

Meetup.com isn't the only game in town—Facebook groups can be just as effective.

There are countless Facebook social groups that host:

- Happy hours
- Dancing events
- Weekend getaways and travel
- Themed parties

Facebook groups can actually be better than Meetup for one simple reason: The women in these groups tend to be more engaged and social. Many of them post pictures, comment on events, and interact before ever meeting in person, which makes breaking the ice easier when you show up.

The Facebook Group Scene: My Experience

In one of the Facebook social groups I'm in, there are dozens of attractive women who regularly attend our happy hours and events. One thing I've noticed? They drink a lot more than I do—which isn't ideal—but they also organize trips, game nights, and other activities, making it an excellent way to meet high-value women outside of bars and clubs.

One trick I've learned?

Be active in the group before you attend an event. Why? Because if a woman has already seen your name, read your posts, or interacted with you online, she's 10x more likely to talk to you in person. It removes the awkwardness and makes everything feel familiar.

The Verdict: Should You Use Meetup.com and Facebook Groups to Meet Women?

Absolutely.

But—like anything else in dating—you have to go in with the right mindset.

- Don't go in expecting to meet "the one."
- Don't try too hard—let things happen naturally.
- Be social, fun, and flirtatious.
- Escalate when the opportunity presents itself—don't just blend into the crowd.

Some of my best dating experiences came from Meetup and Facebook groups. Are they perfect? No. But they offer a level of social proof, quality, and natural connection that you'll never find on a dating app. If you're tired of bars, Tinder, and endless swiping, these social groups can be a game-changer. Because at the end of the day, dating is a numbers game—but it's a hell of a lot more fun when you meet women in ways that feel natural, effortless, and rewarding.

TOP 10 DATING RED FLAGS AND HOW TO HANDLE THEM LIKE A HIGH-VALUE MAN

After dating hundreds of women, I've encountered every type of red flag imaginable. Some are minor quirks that might be tolerable with the right person. Others? Absolute deal-breakers that will drain your time, energy, and resources if you ignore them.

The challenge for most men is recognizing these red flags early before getting emotionally (or financially) invested. Too often, guys ignore warning signs because they're blinded by a woman's beauty, charm, or sexual energy.

That's a rookie mistake. Red flags aren't just theoretical warning signs—they are patterns of behavior that will play out in your relationship sooner or later. And when they do, they will cause stress, frustration, and regret. This is why I've ranked the top 10 dating red flags, from minor annoyances (10) to absolute disasters (1), so you can spot them before they ruin your life.

10. She Has No Female Friends

What It Means: She doesn't get along with other women, which means one of two things:

1. She's too competitive, toxic, or self-centered to maintain female friendships.
2. She only seeks attention from men, which often means she thrives on male validation and is constantly keeping "options" open.

How to Handle It: Ask about her friendships. If she says, "I don't get along with other women," dig deeper. If she's been discarding female friends for years, she'll likely do the same to you once you no longer serve her purpose.

9. Overly Attached to Pets

What It Means: Owning a pet is normal—but treating it like a human child or romantic partner? Big red flag.

Signs she might be obsessively attached to her pet:

- The pet sleeps in her bed every night, and there's no room for you.
- She cancels plans because her dog "feels anxious."
- She refers to herself as "Mommy" when talking about her pet.

How to Handle It: If you're competing with a pet for attention, prepare for a lifetime of frustration. If you're cool with it, fine. But if you're not, walk away.

8. She Drinks Too Much

What It Means: If she can't enjoy a night out without getting wasted, she might have a drinking problem or be using alcohol to mask deeper emotional issues.

Common signs of excessive drinking:

- She gets hammered on every date.
- She brags about blacking out or "crazy" nights.
- She "needs" alcohol to be fun or relaxed.

How to Handle It: Pay attention to her drinking habits. If every night involves excessive alcohol, she's probably bringing chaos and bad decisions into her life—and yours.

7. Financially Irresponsible

What It Means: If she's constantly broke, in debt, or complaining about money, she likely has zero financial discipline.

Watch out for these red flags:

- She talks about credit card debt but keeps buying designer bags.
- She asks for money early in the relationship.

- She expects you to fund her lifestyle.

How to Handle It: If she's financially reckless, she'll eventually expect you to bail her out. If you're serious about your own financial future, this is a no-go.

6. The Drama Queen

What It Means: Her life is one crisis after another—always caused by someone else.

Common signs:

- Every ex was toxic, abusive, or a narcissist.
- Her friends are always "backstabbing" her.
- She feeds on arguments and chaos.

How to Handle It: If every relationship in her life is filled with drama, yours will be too. Exit while you can.

5. Testing Your Boundaries Early

What It Means: If she pushes your limits, disrespects your time, or acts entitled, she's seeing how much she can get away with.

Common tests include:

- Being late for dates without apology.
- Flirting with other guys to make you jealous.
- Playing games with communication (ghosting, ignoring texts).

How to Handle It: Women test men to see if they're strong or weak. The moment you let one boundary slide, she'll keep pushing further. Shut it down immediately.

4. Constantly On Her Phone

What It Means: If she can't put her phone down, she:

- Lacks respect for your time.
- Has low social awareness.
- Might be texting other guys while on a date with you.

How to Handle It: Give her one warning—if she still doesn't put her phone away, end the date early.

3. She Trash Talks All Her Exes

What It Means: If every ex was the problem, she takes zero accountability for failed relationships.

Signs of this red flag:

- She calls every ex a "narcissist" or "abuser."
- She never admits fault in past breakups.
- She still talks about her ex—often.

How to Handle It: Expect to be the next villain in her story. If she never takes responsibility, she never will.

2. Entitlement & Princess Mentality

What It Means: If she expects to be treated like royalty without offering much in return, you're dealing with a taker, not a partner.

Common signs:

- She demands luxury dates but never offers to contribute.
- She expects you to fund her lifestyle.
- She complains when things don't go her way.

How to Handle It: If she's expecting to be treated like a queen, cut her off immediately unless she treats you like a king in return.

1. She Asks for Money

What It Means: The biggest red flag of all. If a woman asks for money early on, she sees you as a wallet, not a man.

Common phrases to look out for:

- "I'm behind on rent—can you help?"
- "I just had an unexpected expense..."
- "I hate to ask, but I really need [X amount]."

How to Handle It: Immediately block and move on. No exceptions.

Final Thoughts: Protect Yourself Like a High-Value Man

Women will test you, push your limits, and see what they can get away with. That's just reality. Your job is to set strong boundaries, recognize red flags early, and walk away from bad deals.

Key Takeaways:

- Trust your gut. If something feels off, it probably is.
- Respect yourself. If she disrespects you early on, it will only get worse.
- Set strong boundaries. Women respect men who don't tolerate nonsense.

Remember, you can never lose what you never had. If she's throwing up red flags, don't stick around hoping she'll change. Walk away like a man who knows his worth.

Top 10 Green Flags in Women:
From Least to Most Important

When dating, it's easy to focus on red flags—the warning signs that tell you a woman is bad news. But what about the green flags? The signs that tell you she's a keeper, a quality woman, someone worth investing your time and energy into?

Green flags are just as important as red flags—if not more. Because if you only focus on avoiding the wrong women but don't recognize when you've found a great one, you'll keep missing out on truly valuable relationships.

Here are the top 10 green flags, ranked from least important to most important when dating a woman.

10. She's Polite and Shows Good Manners

At first glance, this might not seem like a big deal—but it is.

A woman who says "please" and "thank you," treats waitstaff with respect, and generally shows good social etiquette is someone who was raised right. It reflects well on her upbringing, her sense of respect for others, and her ability to treat people well even when they have nothing to offer her.

How a woman treats people who can't do anything for her is a strong indicator of her character. If she's kind and respectful to strangers, odds are she will be kind and respectful to you as well.

How to Test It: Pay attention to how she interacts with service workers—waiters, bartenders, Uber drivers, store clerks. If she treats them well, it's a green flag.

9. She's Emotionally Stable and Handles Stress Well

Everyone has bad days. But a quality woman knows how to handle stress, disappointment, and frustration without taking it out on others.

Women who constantly blame others, play the victim, or explode in anger over small issues should be avoided at all costs. On the other hand, a woman who can face difficulties with grace and keep a level head is a great partner.

How to Test It: Notice how she reacts when plans change unexpectedly. Does she roll with the punches, or does she throw a tantrum?

8. She Takes Care of Her Health and Appearance

This isn't about looking like a supermodel—it's about having self-respect and discipline.

A woman who eats well, exercises, and maintains her hygiene is someone who values herself. She understands that looking good isn't just about vanity—it's about feeling good, being healthy, and showing up in the world as the best version of herself.

How to Test It: Does she take care of herself, dress well, and maintain good hygiene? Or is she sloppy, careless, and indifferent about her health?

7. She Respects Your Time and Effort

A high-value woman doesn't waste your time. She doesn't flake, cancel at the last minute, or keep you as a backup option. She appreciates the time you invest in her and reciprocates with her own time and effort.

A woman who respects your time values you as a man. She won't play games or make you chase her for validation. She will be clear, honest, and consistent in her communication.

How to Test It: If she says she's going to call or text, does she? If she agrees to a date, does she follow through? If she's always flaking, making excuses, or giving half-hearted effort, she's not serious about you.

6. She's Supportive of Your Goals and Ambitions

A woman who believes in you and supports your vision is priceless. She doesn't discourage you from chasing success or tell you that your dreams are "too big." Instead, she **wants to see you win**.

She won't nag you for working too hard or try to distract you from your mission. She understands that a man needs purpose, drive, and ambition—and she encourages you to pursue it.

How to Test It: Tell her about a goal you're working on. Does she show excitement and encouragement, or does she dismiss it and try to change the subject?

5. She Can Disagree Without Being Disrespectful

Disagreements are natural in any relationship. But **how** she handles them tells you everything about her emotional maturity.

A good woman will express her concerns without screaming, insulting, or trying to manipulate you. She will argue fairly, listen to your perspective, and work toward a solution.

A bad woman will start fights for no reason, twist your words, and create drama for entertainment.

How to Test It: Next time you disagree, see if she can have a calm discussion or if she immediately resorts to insults, sarcasm, or emotional manipulation.

4. She Brings Peace, Not Chaos

A woman should add value to your life, not make it harder. If she's constantly picking fights, creating drama, or making your life stressful, she's a liability, not an asset.

A high-value woman makes your life easier, not more difficult. She's your safe space, not a source of anxiety.

How to Test It: Do you feel calm and happy around her, or do you feel drained and exhausted?

3. She's Loyal and Trustworthy

Loyalty is non-negotiable. A woman who is loyal to you, speaks highly of you in public, and doesn't entertain attention from other men is a rare find.

If she flirts with other guys, keeps male "friends" in the background, or hides things from you, she's not worth your time.

How to Test It: Does she avoid unnecessary attention from men? Does she openly communicate and prioritize your relationship, or does she keep secrets and act shady?

2. She Has a Great Relationship with Her Father

How a woman treats and respects men often stems from her relationship with her father.

- If she has a loving, respectful bond with her dad, she's more likely to respect men.
- If she hates her father, has "daddy issues," or constantly complains about men, she may have deep-seated resentment that will eventually be directed at you.

How to Test It: Ask her about her father. If she smiles and speaks fondly, that's a green flag. If she rolls her eyes, gets defensive, or starts ranting about how terrible men are, proceed with caution.

1. She's Happy on Her Own—She Doesn't Need a Man to Be Happy

This is the most important green flag of all. A woman who is genuinely happy, confident, and fulfilled on her own is someone who will be a true partner—not a burden.

A low-value woman looks for a man to fill the void in her life. She uses relationships as emotional crutches and expects you to fix her problems.

A high-value woman already has a great life—she just wants to share it with someone who matches her energy.

How to Test It: Does she seem genuinely happy and content with her life, or does she seem desperate for validation, attention, and constant reassurance?

Final Thoughts: Recognizing the Right Woman

Finding a high-value woman isn't just about avoiding red flags—it's about recognizing the green flags when they appear. If you find a woman who checks off most or all of these green flags, hold on to her—because quality women are rare and valuable. And remember: It's not about finding a perfect woman—it's about finding a woman whose flaws you can live with and whose strengths make your life better.

REVENGE IS A DISH BEST NEVER SERVED

When you've been hurt in a relationship—whether it's a romantic partnership, a marriage, a business deal, or even a deep friendship—the initial inclination for most people is to strike back. The betrayal stings. It ignites anger, pain, and a deep sense of injustice.

This is especially true when you catch your girlfriend or wife cheating. The overwhelming urge to make her pay for her disloyalty, to show her what she lost, or to make her suffer as much as she made you suffer is powerful. But revenge is a dangerous game.

It often backfires. It keeps you chained to the past. It prevents you from moving forward. It makes you emotionally dependent on someone who no longer deserves a place in your life. This is why revenge is a dish best never served. Because the real revenge, the only kind that truly matters, is success and self-improvement.

The Immediate Emotional Reaction: The Urge for Revenge

Let's be real. When you've been wronged—especially when someone cheats on you or betrays your trust—the rage is natural. You're not crazy for feeling the way you do.

You want to lash out. You want to make her regret it. You want to destroy the new guy she cheated with. You want to expose her lies to the world.

But here's the thing:

- Any reaction you have is exactly what she expects.
- Any effort you put into revenge just gives her more power over you.
- Any attention you give her—positive or negative—keeps you locked in the past.

Let's say you do go after revenge. Maybe you try to embarrass her publicly. Maybe you sleep with one of her friends to get back at her. Maybe you message the new guy she's with and try to warn him or ruin their relationship.

What does that really accomplish?

- It makes you look weak. Women thrive on emotional reactions. If you explode in anger, she knows she still has a hold on you.
- It makes you look petty. Instead of rising above, you're dragged down to her level.
- It stops you from healing. The more energy you pour into revenge, the less energy you invest in your own growth.

This is why self-discipline is key. It's why the strongest, most high-value men in the world don't waste time with revenge—they focus on leveling up instead.

The Real Revenge: Leveling Up

There's an old saying that our current president has mentioned many times: "Success is the best revenge." And it's absolutely true. The best way to "get back" at someone who wronged you?

- Live an incredible life without them.
- Become stronger, smarter, richer, healthier, and happier than ever before.
- Date better women, build a better body, make more money, and live with complete confidence.

This is what's known as leveling up. Because every setback is an opportunity for a comeback. How do you do it?

Step 1: Allow Yourself to Grieve, but Set a Deadline

Yes, you need to grieve.

- If you got cheated on, it hurts.
- If a long-term partner betrays you, it's painful.

- If you were used, manipulated, or discarded, it stings like hell.

A strong man doesn't deny his emotions—he processes them, but he doesn't dwell in them forever. Set a time limit for your grief. Maybe one week. Maybe two weeks. During this time, go ahead and feel your emotions:

- Get drunk for a night or two if you must.
- Let yourself be sad.
- Write out everything you're feeling in a journal.
- Go see a therapist if needed.

But when that deadline is up—you make a decision. You will never let this betrayal define you.

Step 2: Hit the Gym and Get in Peak Shape

The most immediate, most tangible, and most satisfying way to turn your pain into power is to hit the gym like your life depends on it.

Because it does.

- Lifting weights isn't just about strength—it's about rebuilding yourself.
- Running isn't just about cardio—it's about proving your endurance.
- Transforming your body isn't just physical—it's mental.

Every time you lift heavier, every time you push harder, you're not just working out—you're erasing the weak version of yourself that allowed this betrayal to happen.

Imagine this:

- You run into your ex six months later at a bar.
- She cheated on you because she thought she could upgrade.
- But now, you look better than ever—leaner, stronger, more confident.
- You don't even care about her anymore.
- She realizes she made a mistake.

That's real revenge.

Step 3: Build Your Wealth and Status

Nothing screams "I've moved on" louder than financial success. Money is not everything, but it is a tool that opens doors. Use this time to:

- Upgrade your career or start a business.
- Invest in yourself through courses, skills, and new knowledge.
- Improve your financial discipline and stop wasting money on useless things.

A man with options is a dangerous man. And nothing gives you options like money, status, and independence.

Step 4: Start Dating Again—But Choose Better This Time

The worst thing you can do after being cheated on or betrayed is to jump into another toxic relationship too soon.

Instead, you date smarter.

- You set higher standards. No more settling for manipulative, weak, or low-value women.
- You recognize red flags faster. No more ignoring obvious signs of disrespect or disloyalty.
- You take your time. No more rushing into relationships with women who haven't earned it.

And here's the best part… If you do everything right—if you hit the gym, level up your finances, and become the best version of yourself—your ex will almost always try to come crawling back. But by then…you won't care. Because you've outgrown her.

Final Thoughts: The Power of Walking Away

One of the hardest lessons you will ever learn in life is this: Sometimes, the best move is simply walking away.

- Not looking back.
- Not seeking revenge.

- Not wasting time on people who never deserved you.

Because the strongest man in the world is not the one who gets even—it's the one who refuses to be controlled by the past.

Final Rule: If someone cheats on you, betrays you, or tries to manipulate you, they are not worthy of your energy. Move on, level up, and become the man they wish they never lost. That's the real revenge.

You've Got Her Number— Now What?

You did it. You managed to have a good conversation, made a connection, and she gave you her number. Maybe you met her at a bar, at a social event, or through a mutual friend. She seemed into you, smiled at your jokes, and when you asked for her number, she gave it without hesitation.

Now, most guys—especially those who have been conditioned by Hollywood romance movies and outdated dating advice—would immediately call or text her as soon as they get home. Maybe they'll even send a long, heartfelt message the next morning, trying to "lock in" her interest before someone else does.

Big mistake. If you're doing this, you're already setting yourself up to fail. Why? Because you're showing too much availability, too much eagerness, and ultimately, too much neediness. Attraction is **not** built through constant attention and reassurance—it's built through uncertainty, intrigue, and a sense of scarcity.

Don't Be Like Every Other Guy

Most guys think the best way to get a woman interested is to show her how much they like her. They call right away, text non-stop, and make it their mission to prove they are interested. They believe that by giving her all their attention, they will win her over.

But here's the truth: Women don't want a man they can easily predict or control. They want a man who already has options—or at least behaves as if he does. When you call her the very next day, she immediately knows that you're sitting around thinking about her. That you're too available. That you probably don't have a lot of other women interested in you. And what does that do? It kills attraction.

Instead of making you seem desirable, it makes you seem easy to get. And anything that is easy to get is rarely valued.

Create Uncertainty—Make Her Think About You

If you want to separate yourself from the countless other guys blowing up her phone, you need to play it smart. Here's the golden rule: Wait at least two or three days before contacting her. That's right. Let the anticipation build. Let her wonder about you. Let her check her phone a few times, expecting to hear from you—only to find nothing. This does something incredibly powerful: It makes her start chasing you.

When you're not constantly reaching out, she starts asking herself questions:

- *Why hasn't he called yet?*
- *Did I misread his interest?*
- *Does he have other women he's talking to?*
- *Is he not as into me as I thought?*

This is exactly the position you want to be in. Because the moment a woman starts questioning your availability, her attraction grows.

The First Call—Keep It Short and Focused

After you've let a few days pass, it's time to reach out. But don't text her just to chat. That's what weak men do. Instead, call her—yes, actually use the phone to make a real call. Why? Because most guys today rely on texting, which makes an actual phone call stand out as something more masculine and intentional. When you do call, keep it short—no more than five minutes. The goal here isn't to have a deep conversation; it's simply to set up a date.

Here's an example of how it should go:

You: "Hey [her name], it's [your name]. How's your week been?"

(Let her respond.)

You: "Cool. Listen, I had a great time talking to you the other night, and I'd love to see you again. How about we grab a drink this Thursday at 7?"

That's it. Short, confident, direct. No long conversations, no explaining yourself, no unnecessary texting back and forth.

If she's interested, she'll say yes. If she hesitates, stay cool and say something like:

"No worries. Let me know when you're free, and we'll make it happen."

Then, end the call.

This does two things:

1. It puts the ball in her court. She now has to decide whether she wants to see you again rather than you chasing her for a date.
2. It maintains your value. You're not begging or trying too hard. You're a busy guy with options, and she either makes time for you—or she doesn't.

Playing It Cool After the First Date

Let's say she agrees to go out. You meet up, have a great time, and there's clear chemistry. So what do you do next? The same strategy applies—don't over-pursue. After the date, let her be the one to reach out first. If she doesn't, you can send a simple message the next day: "Had a great time last night. Hope you have a good day." No emojis. No over-the-top compliments. Just a simple, confident message. Then, wait.

If she's into you, she will respond enthusiastically, and at that point, you can start planning the next date. If she gives a lukewarm response or takes forever to reply, move on—she's not interested enough to make it worth your time.

Why This Works—The Psychology Behind It

The reason this approach is so effective is that it flips the script on the usual dating dynamic. Instead of you chasing her, she starts chasing you. Most men operate from a scarcity mindset. They think, "I have to lock this down before she loses interest." But high-value men never rush. They act as if they already have plenty of options—and women pick up on that energy. A woman wants to feel like she has to earn a man's attention. If she feels like you're too eager, she instinctively sees you as less valuable. But if she feels like she has to work for your time, your approval, and your presence, her attraction for you skyrockets.

Building Long-Term Attraction

If things progress and you start seeing her regularly, the key is to maintain the frame.

- One phone call per week. Let her reach out more. Keep yourself busy.
- One date per week. If she wants to see you more, let her bring it up.
- Stay emotionally centered. Don't get too attached too soon.

When a woman sees that you're not overly available, she naturally wants to lock you down. She will start texting first, trying to schedule more dates, and making sure you're not spending time with other women. And at that point, **you've won.**

Final Thoughts: You Are the Prize

The key takeaway here is this: You are the catch. Too many men make the mistake of thinking they need to prove their worth to a woman. But the reality is, she should be proving her worth to you. By creating uncertainty, delaying contact, and keeping your interactions brief and confident, you send a clear message: You are a man of value. Women are naturally drawn to men who have options, who aren't desperate, and who make them work for attention. When you master this, you'll find that you never have to chase women again. Instead, they'll be the ones chasing you.

WHY SO MANY WOMEN GO FOR THE BAD BOYS

We've touched on this before, but it bears repeating. It's one of the most frustrating and confusing aspects of dating and attraction—why do so many beautiful, accomplished, and seemingly intelligent women gravitate toward the bad boys? You know exactly the type I'm talking about. The guy who can't hold down a regular job. The guy who doesn't care about his appearance. The guy who treats women like an afterthought, like disposable entertainment. And yet, these men always seem to have women chasing after them.

The question is, why?

I remember this guy from high school. He was objectively ugly—one of the most unattractive people around. And yet, he always had the hottest girls hanging off of him. Part of it was his car—a Corvette, then later a Pontiac Trans Am with a massive 454 engine. But it wasn't just the car. He had that aura of danger, that mysterious edge that so many women crave.

But here's the kicker: he wasn't just a bad boy in the fun, rebellious way. He was a predator. Years later, I learned that he was the class rapist. A friend of mine had witnessed one of his assaults. Another woman confronted him about it, calling him out for not just her attack but many others.

This was 50 years ago. Back then, victims rarely went to the police. They were often blamed, ridiculed, or shamed into silence. And yet, despite his disgusting behavior, women still pursued him. Why? Because he embodied a certain kind of energy that many women are drawn to—an energy that overrides logic, reason, and even basic self-preservation.

Let's break it down.

Your Kids, Her Kids—What Should You Do?

At a certain stage in life, it's almost guaranteed that the people you date will have kids—whether they are grown, living independently, or still at home. Unless you're exclusively dating younger women, navigating relationships where children (hers, yours, or both) are involved is something that needs careful consideration.

Some men, especially those who have never had kids of their own, assume that once children become adults and leave the house, they are no longer a factor in a relationship. That's a big mistake. Grown children still influence their parent's dating life, especially if they're protective, judgmental, or financially dependent.

So, how do you navigate this situation? What are the red flags, the green flags, and the non-negotiables? Let's break it down.

Scenario 1: Both of You Have Grown Kids Who Live Independently

If both of you have adult children who are out of the house and self-sufficient, congratulations—this is the easiest scenario to deal with. You can date freely without worrying about a ready-made family dynamic.

That said, her kids (and yours) will still be part of the equation. If she is close to her children and expects you to integrate into her family life, you need to decide if that's something you want.

- Are her kids friendly and accepting, or are they territorial and cold toward you?
- Do they resent their mother dating again, seeing you as a threat to their family dynamic?
- How much does she involve them in her decision-making? If she's always running things by her kids before making relationship decisions, be wary.
- If you have children of your own, how will they feel about you being in a new relationship?

Key Takeaway: If you're dating a woman with adult kids who are independent and well-adjusted, it's usually not a dealbreaker. Just be mindful of how much family involvement she expects and whether you're willing to participate.

Scenario 2: She Has Grown Kids Who Still Live with Her

This is a major red flag. If her kids are over the age of 25 and still living at home, you need to ask why.

There are some valid exceptions:

- They are in grad school or professional school (medical school, law school, etc.), which can temporarily require financial support.
- They had temporary setbacks, such as recovering from an illness or going through a major life transition.
- They are helping care for an elderly parent (though even this can be a slippery slope).

But in most cases, an adult child living at home is a problem. It could mean:

- "Failure to launch" syndrome—they're not self-sufficient and rely on their mother to survive.
- Financial dependence—they live off their mother's resources, meaning your money may eventually become involved too.
- A codependent or unhealthy dynamic—if she has coddled them for too long, they may resent you stepping in.

If you enter into a relationship with a woman whose adult kids still live at home, be prepared for a battle. If she enables them, you will always come second.

Key Takeaway: Think carefully before getting involved with a woman whose grown children are still dependent on her. This is a sign of bigger issues that will become your problem.

Scenario 3: She Has Younger Kids or Teenagers

This is where things get really tricky. If she is younger than you and still raising children, you need to think this through very carefully.

Here's the reality:

1. Her kids will always come first. If you expect to be her top priority, you will always be disappointed.
2. Dating a single mom means you are dating her kids, too. Are you ready to be a stepfather figure? Even if you don't plan to raise them, your time, energy, and emotional bandwidth will be affected.
3. You'll have to deal with her ex. If she shares custody, you will be involved in her past relationship drama, whether you like it or not.
4. Your freedom will be limited. If you're used to spontaneous trips, weekend getaways, or having full control over your schedule, forget about it. Her availability will be dictated by parenting responsibilities, not your desires.
5. Are you ready to help raise another man's kids? Even if you think, *I'll just date her and not get involved with her kids*, that's not how it works.

Most single moms will eventually expect some level of investment in their children's lives. If you're unwilling or unable to do that, don't start down that road in the first place.

Key Takeaway: Unless you are 100% on board with raising or helping raise another man's children, avoid dating single moms. It's a commitment you shouldn't take lightly.

Your Kids & Her Relationship with Them

Now, let's flip the scenario. If you have grown children, how does she interact with them?

- Is she warm and welcoming, or does she seem indifferent?

322

- Does she get along with them, or does she create unnecessary tension?
- Is she jealous of the time and attention you give your kids?
- Does she resent that you provide for your children financially (if applicable)?

If you're serious about a relationship, your partner needs to at least be civil with your children. If she's dismissive, rude, or resentful toward them, you have a problem.

Some women compete with a man's children for his attention. This is especially true if she doesn't have kids of her own. If she makes you choose between her and your kids, always choose your kids. A woman who tries to drive a wedge between you and your family is dangerous.

Key Takeaway: If she doesn't get along with your children or resents your relationship with them, walk away.

Final Verdict: What's the Right Choice?

Here's the brutal truth:

1. If her kids are independent, great. But make sure she isn't overly enmeshed in their lives in a way that affects your relationship.
2. If her grown kids live with her, question why. And proceed with extreme caution.
3. If she has younger kids, you need to be ready to take on a stepfather role. If you aren't, don't even start.
4. If she competes with your kids or resents them, leave immediately.

At this stage in life, you don't need unnecessary complications. Choose a partner whose family dynamic aligns with your goals and lifestyle. And as always, never compromise out of scarcity. If you think, *She's amazing, but her kids are a mess,* move on. There are plenty of women out there who won't bring unnecessary baggage into your life.

Final Thoughts

If a woman's family situation isn't right for you, don't try to "make it work." Relationships should enhance your life, not complicate it.

Let's Talk About Body Counts: Why It Matters (or Doesn't) to You

The topic of body count is a minefield in modern dating, especially for men who are red-pill aware or have spent any amount of time studying female nature. The common belief—one frequently echoed by Strong Successful Male (SSM) and others—is that when a woman gives you a number, you should multiply it by three and still assume she's underestimating.

Why? Because society shames women for having too many partners, and they instinctively downplay their past. On the flip side, men (with the exception of guys who have been truly successful in dating) tend to inflate their numbers—unless they're actually experienced, in which case they don't care enough to keep track.

The Double Standard: Why Men and Women See Body Count Differently

It's a cliché, but clichés exist for a reason:

- Men judge a woman based on her past.
- Women judge a man based on his future.

Women aren't particularly interested in how many women you've slept with—unless you're a virgin or completely inexperienced. If anything, they tend to view a man with a high body count as a sign of social proof—if other women wanted him, he must have value.

For men, however, a woman's past matters. And whether or not it should matter is irrelevant—because it does. It's instinctual, just like a woman's preference for strong, confident men who have resources and options.

A woman who has had many partners might be seen as:

- Less capable of pair bonding
- More likely to compare her new partner to past lovers
- More likely to cheat or have trouble staying faithful
- More jaded about relationships in general

Meanwhile, men with experience tend to be seen as attractive, dominant, and desirable. A man with options is considered a catch. A woman with a long list of past partners, however, is often seen as someone with less stability, higher risk, and more baggage.

This isn't misogyny—it's biology and social conditioning at work.

Should You Ask a Woman About Her Body Count?

Here's the truth: If you ask, you're not going to get a straight answer. And if you need to ask, you probably already suspect the answer won't be good. Most women will lie or downplay their number, not necessarily out of malice but because they know men judge them for it. If a woman tells you she's been with three guys, you can almost guarantee it's more like nine (and possibly much higher).

I personally don't ask. Why? Because if I like the woman, I'd rather focus on the present than dig into the past. However, there are red flags that indicate whether she's been around the block more times than she's letting on:

1. **She's highly skilled in bed—too skilled for her age or experience level.**
   - There are certain things a woman just doesn't learn from books or rom-coms. If she can perform high-level techniques in the bedroom, you have to wonder how she picked them up.

2. **She gets uncomfortable or defensive when discussing past relationships.**

- o If she dodges the question, laughs it off, or suddenly changes the subject, she doesn't want you to know the answer. And usually, that's because it's higher than you'd like.

3. **She has a history of short-term relationships, flings, or "crazy exes."**
   - o Women with high body counts often have commitment issues **or** a pattern of bouncing from one guy to the next.

4. **She's hypersexual and always talks about sex.**
   - o A woman who centers her identity around sexuality is probably more promiscuous than she lets on.

5. **She hangs around with a lot of other promiscuous women.**
   - o The phrase, *birds of a feather flock together*, exists for a reason.

If I really like a woman but suspect she's had a wild past, I pay attention to how she treats sex now. Is she still partying? Still running with the same crowd? Still entertaining multiple guys? If the answer is yes, I'm not interested.

What If She's a Former Sex Worker or Has a High Body Count?

For me, this isn't a hard one.

I don't care how attractive or talented a woman is in bed—if she's been in escort work, porn, OnlyFans, or anything of that nature, I'm out.

Here's why:

1. You never really know how she feels about you. Women in that world are trained to manipulate men's emotions for money. It's part of the job.

2. There are too many unknowns. What kind of people has she been with? How many guys? How does she view relationships?

3. She's seen too much. A woman who's been in that industry has seen and done things that change the way she views men, sex, and relationships.

I've been with highly skilled women before—some were great, some weren't worth the trouble. But if I found out she was in that world, I would walk away.

The Truth Has a Way of Coming Out

Even if a woman downplays her past, the truth has a funny way of surfacing. Maybe you'll overhear a conversation with her friends. Maybe an old social media post resurfaces. Maybe she slips up and says something about a wild past you didn't expect. One way or another, you'll know.

If she's comfortable enough with you, she may even admit later on that she lied. At that point, it's up to you to decide if you can live with it or not. For me? I don't dwell on it. If I enjoy a woman's company, I don't go digging through her history. But I watch for signs and let my instincts guide me.

Final Thoughts: Does It Matter?

This is where personal preference comes in. Some men say, "As long as she's with me now, that's all that matters. Others say, "I could never respect a woman who's been with too many guys."

For me, it's about self-respect. I don't want to be with someone who has zero sexual discipline or a messy past that will affect our future. At the end of the day, it's your choice. But make sure that you're honest with yourself about what you can and cannot accept. Because one thing's for sure—whatever number she tells you, it's probably not the real one.

HER FAMILY:
WHY THEY MATTER MORE THAN YOU THINK

A woman's family dynamics tell you more than she ever will. You can have chemistry. You can have attraction. You can have great sex. But if her family situation is a disaster, it's only a matter of time before that chaos seeps into your relationship. This is a hard-earned lesson from years of dating, relationships, and marriage. If a woman doesn't respect her parents, has a history of family drama, or carries unresolved baggage, you will inherit those issues—whether you want to or not. And no matter how much you care about her, you won't be able to fix it.

The Most Important Relationship: Her Father

A woman's relationship with her father is the biggest predictor of how she will relate to men—especially you. If she respected her father, she will likely respect her partner. If she had a loving father, she will be less needy, more secure, and better at long-term relationships. If her father was absent, abusive, or weak, she may have severe trust issues, difficulty with male authority, or an inability to commit. I've seen this play out over and over again.

The "Daddy Issues" Factor

I was married to a woman whose father was a reformed alcoholic.

- When she was young, he was abusive and destructive to his family.
- Then, when he hit rock bottom, and his wife served him with divorce papers, he turned his life around.
- He never drank again and became a leader in AA, mentoring and saving countless lives.
- When he died, over 200 people attended his funeral, sharing stories of how he had helped them.

It was one of the most moving things I had ever seen. And yet, despite his years of redemption, my ex-wife never forgave him. Even though he had become a saintly figure, even though he had done more good than most people do in a lifetime, she still held on to her anger.

And that anger seeped into our marriage. She couldn't forgive him. And in time, she couldn't forgive me for anything either. I should have left the moment she told me she could never forgive him. If she couldn't forgive her father, what chance did I ever have?

The Gold Standard: A Strong Father-Daughter Bond

If a woman had a great father, she will likely:

- Respect and admire men
- Have realistic expectations in relationships
- Be loyal and loving
- Trust easily and communicate well

If a woman had a terrible father, she may:

- Have major trust issues
- Test you constantly to prove your love
- Sabotage healthy relationships
- Be drawn to toxic or unstable men

It's not a guarantee, but it's a huge indicator of how she will treat you in the long run.

What About Her Mother?

While her father shapes how she views men, her relationship with her mother is also important—but in a different way.

- If she respects and admires her mother, she will likely be a nurturing, strong, and emotionally stable woman.
- If she hates her mother, she will probably have issues with other women, struggle with insecurity, and create unnecessary drama.

What If She Had a Bad Mother?

A bad mother doesn't always mean she will be a bad partner.

- If her father was strong and loving, he may have compensated for her mother's issues and given her a healthy foundation.
- If her mother was a narcissist, abusive, or cold, she might struggle with self-worth and trust—but she may have worked through it.

The key is to watch how she treats other women.

- Does she constantly badmouth female friends or coworkers?
- Does she sabotage friendships and call all her ex-friends "crazy"?
- Does she compete with other women instead of supporting them?

These are red flags. They signal deep-seated insecurities that will come out in your relationship sooner or later.

Her Relationship with Her Kids

If she has children, pay attention. If her kids love and respect her, that's a great sign.

If her kids are distant, resentful, or don't speak to her—that's a massive red flag. Here's the thing: Good mothers are usually good partners. But if she alienated her own children, what do you think she'll do to you? If her kids are grown and independent, great.

If her kids are still living at home well into adulthood, ask yourself why:

- Are they in school and working toward something?
- Or are they codependent, jobless, and leeching off her?

A woman who lets her kids take advantage of her will let them take advantage of you, too.

Her Family's Drama Becomes Your Drama

If she doesn't talk to her parents or her family is full of dysfunction, be careful. It's one thing to have a complicated family history—most people do. But if she's constantly dealing with fights, legal battles, or emotional baggage, guess what?

That becomes your life, too.

- If her parents are manipulative, they will meddle in your relationship.
- If her siblings are dramatic, they will pull her into their chaos—and take her attention away from you.
- If her family relies on her financially, you will eventually be expected to contribute too.

Family matters more than you think.

Final Thoughts: What to Watch For

A woman doesn't have to have a perfect family—none of us do. But how she handles her family relationships will tell you everything you need to know about her.

- A woman with a great father and a healthy family will make a great partner.
- A woman with a bad father but a strong will can still be amazing—if she has worked through her issues.
- A woman who is full of resentment, anger, or unresolved trauma will bring that into your relationship.

Trust me on this one.

When you meet a woman, pay attention to:

- How she talks about her father
- How she gets along with her mother and siblings
- What her relationship with her kids is like
- Whether she is surrounded by love or drama

Because no matter how much she likes you, if her family is a wreck, your relationship will be, too.

Choose wisely.

AGE DIFFERENCES:
DO THEY MATTER MORE FOR ONE PARTY THAN THE OTHER?

Age differences in relationships have always been a topic of debate. Society has long accepted older men dating younger women, but older women dating younger men has only recently gained broader acceptance. So, does age really matter? And if so, who does it matter more for?

Let's break it down.

Why Younger Women Go for Older Men

Throughout history, women have been attracted to older men. It's not random—it's evolutionary.

Older men typically have:

- More financial stability
- More life experience
- Greater emotional maturity
- More confidence

Women are biologically wired to seek security. They need to ensure that their partner can provide, protect, and lead.

That's why you often see:

- A 25-year-old woman dating a 40-year-old man
- A 30-year-old woman marrying a 50-year-old CEO
- A model linking up with a successful entrepreneur or celebrity

It's not just about money—although that helps. It's about stability, power, and wisdom. But let's be real: It's also about attraction. Many women find confidence sexy—and older men, who have already built their careers, social status, and self-assurance, naturally radiate that.

335

Why Older Men Go for Younger Women

Just as women are wired to seek security, men are wired to seek youth and beauty.

Younger women typically have:

- More fertility
- Higher energy levels
- Less emotional baggage
- A natural glow of youth and vitality

It's not about shallow preferences—it's about biological programming.

Men subconsciously look for signs of fertility and health.

That's why:

- A 45-year-old man might date a 30-year-old woman
- A wealthy man might marry a woman half his age

It's not that older women aren't attractive—it's that youth is highly valued in men's natural selection process.

The Challenges of Age Gaps

Of course, large age gaps come with challenges.

Different Life Stages

A 50-year-old man dating a 25-year-old woman may have completely different priorities.

- He's thinking about retirement; she's just starting her career.
- He's ready to settle down; she's still exploring life.

Cultural Differences

- A man in his 40s or 50s grew up in a different era than a woman in her 20s.
- They may have different values, music tastes, and social circles.

Family Pressure & Social Stigma

- Friends and family may not approve.
- Older women dating younger men often face harsher judgment than the reverse.

Energy Levels & Lifestyle Differences

- A younger partner may want to travel, party, and stay out late.
- An older partner may prefer a quiet evening at home.

What About Older Women Dating Younger Men?

Historically, older women dating younger men was rare—but it's becoming more common. There's even a term for it: The Cougar Effect.

Older women who date younger men typically have:

- More confidence
- Greater financial independence
- Less drama and emotional games
- Sexual experience that younger women lack

Younger men who date older women tend to like:

- Emotional and financial stability
- A lack of immaturity and head games
- The experience and wisdom an older woman brings

But here's the reality:

Most younger men don't want long-term relationships with older women.

Many younger men enjoy the excitement but eventually seek younger partners.

Older women face declining fertility, which may be an issue for men wanting a family.

There are exceptions, of course. Some younger men genuinely fall in love with older women and build lasting relationships. But in most cases, the relationship has a built-in expiration date.

Do Age Differences Matter More for One Party Than the Other?

Yes. Age differences matter more for women than they do for men.

Why?

1. Men age better in the dating market.

- A wealthy, confident 50-year-old man can still attract 30-year-olds.
- A 50-year-old woman dating a 30-year-old man is much rarer.

2. A woman's sexual market value (SMV) declines faster.

- A man's value tends to peak in his 40s and 50s (money, power, confidence).
- A woman's value peaks in her 20s and declines with age.

3. Older women face more competition from younger women.

- A 50-year-old man with money and confidence can still compete with younger men.
- A 50-year-old woman has a much harder time competing with younger women.

This is why you often see older men with younger women—but rarely the reverse.

Final Thoughts: Should You Date Outside Your Age Group?

Age gaps can work—but they come with challenges.

If you're an older man dating a younger woman, be aware of maturity differences.

If you're a younger man dating an older woman, understand that the relationship may have an expiration date.

338

If you're dating someone significantly younger or older, it's essential to communicate your expectations early.

At the end of the day, age is just a number—but biology is real.

Make sure you're dating someone compatible with your life stage, values, and long-term goals.

THE PSYCHOLOGY BEHIND THE ATTRACTION

There are a few key reasons why bad boys capture women's attention, even when it's obvious they're no good for them.

1. They Signal Strength and Confidence

Bad boys operate from a place of absolute self-certainty. They don't second-guess themselves. They don't seek approval. They don't hesitate.

Women are biologically wired to be drawn to confidence—it signals dominance, capability, and protection. A man who is too eager to please, who seeks validation from others (especially women), comes off as weak and uncertain.

Women don't want a man who needs them. They want a man who chooses them but would be perfectly fine without them.

Bad boys ooze this energy. They give off the impression that they don't need anyone. And paradoxically, that makes women want to be the one who tames them.

2. They Are a Challenge

Women love a challenge. The moment they know they have a man wrapped around their finger, they lose interest.

Bad boys never make it easy. They don't respond to texts right away. They don't shower women with affection or reassurance. They might disappear for days at a time. They create uncertainty—and uncertainty is one of the biggest triggers of obsession in the human brain.

The less available someone is, the more valuable they seem. It's the same reason people want exclusive, hard-to-get items more than something readily available at Walmart.

Scarcity = Desire.

A bad boy never hands a woman his attention on a silver platter. She has to earn it. And that makes it far more addictive when she finally gets it.

3. They Are Unapologetically Themselves

Bad boys don't filter themselves to be politically correct. They don't tiptoe around their opinions. They don't beg for approval.

In a world where men are constantly told to suppress their masculinity, bad boys reject all of that and embrace who they are.

They don't give a damn about societal expectations. They live life on their own terms. They do what they want, when they want.

And that kind of unshakable authenticity is magnetic.

Even if a woman knows she shouldn't be with him, she can't help but admire how he doesn't care what anyone thinks.

The Role of Evolution in Attraction

Attraction isn't logical. It's biological. For most of human history, a woman's survival depended on being with a man who could protect her and provide for her. Women are wired to seek dominant, strong men—men who wouldn't hesitate to fight off a threat, who wouldn't back down, who exude the confidence of a natural leader.

In modern society, physical danger is rare. Women don't need a man to physically protect them in the same way they did thousands of years ago. But the instincts are still there. And bad boys trigger those instincts. They give off the impression that they can handle themselves in any situation, that they can navigate danger, that they are strong, independent, and fearless.

Women feel this energy more than they consciously think about it. And that's why, despite knowing better, they keep going back to these types of men.

The Dark Side of the Bad Boy

Of course, the flip side to all this is that most bad boys aren't quality men.

- They cheat.
- They manipulate.
- They are emotionally unavailable.
- They can be abusive, both physically and mentally.

But women don't see this at first.

All they see is the mystery, the challenge, the dominance. By the time they realize they've fallen for someone toxic, it's already too late. Many women waste years chasing bad boys, hoping to be the one who finally tames them. They believe they can change him, that if they just love him enough, he'll finally commit and treat them right. Of course, that never happens.

So What's the Alternative?

If you're a good guy reading this, you might be frustrated. You might think: *So, should I just act like a bad boy to attract women?* The answer is no—but you should adopt some of their best traits. How to Attract Women Without Being an Asshole.

1. Develop True Confidence – Stop seeking validation. Build yourself up so that you genuinely don't care what people think.
2. Be a Challenge – Don't be too available. Make her earn your attention. Create uncertainty by not always responding right away.
3. Set Boundaries – Never let a woman walk all over you. Bad boys never tolerate disrespect—and neither should you.
4. Pursue Your Own Mission – Women are drawn to men who have a purpose beyond them. Don't make her your whole world.

5. Be Authentic – Speak your mind. Have strong opinions. Don't be afraid to disagree with her.

You don't have to be a bad boy. But you do need to adopt the masculine energy that makes them so attractive.

Final Thoughts

Bad boys aren't a new phenomenon—women have been chasing them for centuries. They represent strength, unpredictability, confidence, and challenge—all qualities that trigger deep, primal attraction. But real men—men of character, ambition, and discipline—can have the same effect without resorting to toxic behavior. If you can master confidence, emotional detachment, and self-respect, you'll find that you don't need to be a bad boy to have women chasing you. You just have to be a man worth chasing.

Don't Be a People Pleaser: Why Nice Guys Never Finish First

We've all heard the saying *nice guys finish last.* But the truth is, nice guys don't finish at all. Not in relationships, not in life, and certainly not in the game of attraction. They linger in the background, frustrated, confused, and feeling perpetually shortchanged by the world.

But let's get one thing straight—nice guys aren't really all that nice. They're not virtuous saints, misunderstood romantics, or the last noblemen in a world full of bad boys. No, nice guys are insecure, unfulfilled, and lacking a strong sense of self. They operate from a place of fear—fear of rejection, fear of not being liked, fear of confrontation, and most of all, fear of being alone. They bend over backward to accommodate others, not out of genuine kindness, but because they hope to be *rewarded* for it. And women? Women see right through it.

The People Pleaser Trap

Nice guys operate under a fundamental misunderstanding of attraction. They believe that if they just do enough for a woman—if they're polite, accommodating, and always available—then she'll recognize their efforts and reward them with love, sex, and commitment. But that's not how attraction works.

Women aren't attracted to men who need them. They're attracted to men who don't need them, but choose them. A man who puts a woman on a pedestal instantly lowers his own value in her eyes. And once that happens? She may use him for attention. She may keep him around as an emotional tampon. She may even let him orbit her life like a devoted little puppy. But she won't respect him. She won't desire him. She won't *choose* him.

The Real Problem with Being "Too Nice"

When I was younger, I fell into the nice guy trap , just like so many men do. I thought I had to shower women with gifts, compliments, and constant availability. I thought being a *good guy* meant always being there to help them pick up the pieces when their bad-boy boyfriends broke their hearts. I genuinely believed that if I just proved myself to women, they would eventually realize my value and choose me. Of course, that never happened.

All I got in return was:

- Women who saw me as a friend, not a romantic interest.
- Women who took advantage of my kindness but never reciprocated.
- Women who ran straight back to the toxic guys who mistreated them.

And what did I get out of it?

Resentment.

I hated myself for being weak. I hated women for not appreciating me. And worst of all, I hated the fact that deep down, I knew I was being inauthentic. Because here's the thing: Nice guys aren't actually nice. They're dishonest. They don't say what they really think. They don't set real boundaries. They don't stand up for themselves. They put on a fake, overly agreeable persona in the hope of getting something in return. And when that doesn't work? They get bitter. They curse their bad luck. They spiral into the dangerous mindset of *women only want assholes.*

How I Stopped Being a Nice Guy

So how did I change?

It didn't happen overnight. It took **years** of trial, error, and self-improvement. But I can tell you exactly what worked for me.

1. I Stopped Seeking External Validation

One of the biggest mistakes nice guys make is looking for validation outside of themselves. They base their self-worth on how others perceive them. If a woman laughs at their joke? They feel good. If a woman ignores them? They feel worthless. This is a recipe for disaster. Because when you depend on external approval, you give away all your power.

The first thing I had to do was develop an unshakable sense of self-worth. I started setting goals for myself—not for women, not for anyone else.

- I hit the gym to feel strong.
- I pursued my passions to feel fulfilled.
- I built my own success, so I never had to depend on validation from others.

When I stopped needing approval, everything changed. Suddenly, women started chasing me. Why? Because I was no longer desperate for their attention.

2. I Stopped Over-Accommodating Women

Nice guys over-give in relationships. They think the more they do for a woman, the more she'll appreciate them. Wrong. When you over-accommodate a woman, she loses respect for you. It's not about being an asshole—it's about setting boundaries. Once I stopped saying "yes" to everything... Once I stopped dropping everything to be available… Once I stopped putting women before my own needs… I saw a dramatic shift in how they treated me. The women who once strung me along? The women who kept me in the "friend zone"? Suddenly, they were the ones chasing me.

3. I Adopted the Mindset of a Bad Boy—Without the Toxicity

I wasn't about to become an asshole just to get women. But I did study what bad boys did right. And I learned that their biggest advantage wasn't their looks, money, or status. It was their mindset.

They:

- Didn't seek approval.
- Put themselves first.
- Were a challenge.
- Didn't over-pursue.
- Had boundaries.

So, I adopted those traits—without losing my integrity. I stopped putting women on pedestals. I stopped being overly available. I stopped caring so much about their reactions. And what happened? Women respected me more. Women pursued me more. Women saw me as a leader, not a follower.

The Final Evolution: Becoming the Man I Always Wanted to Be

Looking back, I can confidently say that I transformed my entire approach to life and relationships. It took time, effort, and brutal self-honesty. But eventually, I became a man who:

- Knows his worth.
- Doesn't chase women—he attracts them.
- Puts himself first—without apology.
- Never seeks validation from others.

And here's the best part: If I did it, so can you. You don't have to stay stuck in the nice guy trap. You don't have to live your life pleasing others at your own expense. You don't have to hate yourself for being weak. Because strength can be learned. Confidence can be built. And once you make that transformation, you will never look back.

MATCHMAKERS:
A WASTE OF TIME AND MONEY

If you've been in the dating game for a while and have a few bucks to spend, you might have considered hiring a matchmaker. After all, they promise to find you the *perfect* partner—someone who fits all your criteria and is looking for the same things you are. Sounds like a great deal, right?

Wrong.

For the vast majority of men, matchmaking services are an overpriced scam. They are no better than a high-end dating app with an expensive price tag and a lot of sales fluff. Most of them deliver subpar results…if any at all. I know this firsthand because I hired one in a moment of supreme stupidity, because I knew better.

I convinced myself that spending thousands of dollars would put me in a different league of dating, that it would connect me with women who were serious about relationships and would be the right fit for me. Instead, I got a series of disappointment, frustration, and outright deception.

The Illusion of Matchmaking "Expertise"

Most matchmakers are women. That's not necessarily a bad thing, but as we've discussed before, most women don't even fully understand what they are attracted to in a man. They'll tell you they want a kind, successful, family-oriented guy—but then they turn around and date the aloof, unavailable bad boy who excites them. So how is a matchmaker, who doesn't truly understand attraction at a deep level, going **to set you up for success?**

The short answer: she's not. She's going to set you up based on what sounds good on paper. She'll find someone in your "age range," your "career level," and who "wants a relationship." But chemistry? Attraction? Actual compatibility? These things can't be manufactured.

Matchmakers rely on checklists and vague compatibility assessments, but they don't actually know what makes relationships work. They're selling you a fantasy of exclusive dating, but they're using the same flawed process as dating apps—just without the convenience or volume.

My Experience with a Matchmaker: A Total Scam

I decided to give matchmaking a shot after getting tired of the games, swiping, and general nonsense of modern dating. I found a reputable service that claimed to have a "high success rate" and "extensive screening." They assured me that they would find me the *exact* type of woman I was looking for—someone at least five years younger than me, fit, attractive, and with aligned values. Sounds great, right? Except that's not what happened.

Every woman they sent my way was older than me. Some were nice, but I didn't pay thousands of dollars for "nice." When I pointed out that they were not meeting my requirements, they tried to guilt-trip me into considering their picks. They gave me the whole speech: *"You're being too picky." "These women are amazing catches." "Age is just a number."*

Let me tell you something—age is NOT just a number. A five-year difference is reasonable for a man in my position. I wasn't asking for a 22-year-old supermodel. I was asking for a woman within a perfectly normal range for an established, high-value man. But instead of delivering what they promised, they pressured me to settle.

The Lies They Tell You

Matchmakers will sell you on a dream. They'll tell you:

They have a pool of amazing, high-quality, relationship-ready women.

They do all the work for you, so you can skip the frustration of dating apps.

They guarantee results.

Here's what they don't tell you:

- They don't actually have a huge pool of candidates. Most of them recruit women AFTER they sign you up, meaning you're just another name in their system with no real matches waiting for you.
- They pressure you to "expand your criteria." If they can't find what you're looking for, they'll guilt you into lowering your standards instead of admitting they failed.
- They count ANY relationship as a success. Even if you go on three dates and realize it's not working, they'll use it as a "success story" to boost their marketing.
- They do NOT offer refunds. No matter how terrible their service is, once they have your money, good luck getting it back.

I actually tried to dispute the charge with Amex, but they wouldn't refund me because matchmakers offer a "service," not a tangible product. Later, the company got bought out, and the new owners gave me a few free "disaster dates" as a way to make up for it. That's thousands of dollars down the drain.

The "Success Fee" Con

There's a guy in Florida who runs a matchmaking service where you pay a success fee if you're with a woman for more than six months. It sounds fair, right? Except here's the thing:

It's still a scam. Why? Because he's no better than tossing darts or flipping a coin. His success rate is no higher than chance. And yet, if by some miracle one of his matches works out, you now owe him even more money for what was ultimately your own effort in making the relationship work. That's like a personal trainer taking credit for your weight loss six months after you joined a gym. Absurd.

Better Alternatives to Matchmaking

So, if matchmaking is a waste of time, what's the better alternative?

1. High-End Dating Apps: If you're going to pay for dating, you might as well use a service with actual volume and options. Apps like The League, Raya, and Luxy cater to successful men and offer way more potential matches than any matchmaker ever could. Unlike matchmakers, these apps let you screen women yourself instead of relying on someone else's flawed judgment.

2. Personal Networking: If you're looking for high-quality women, they're usually not hanging out on Tinder. Instead, you can attend exclusive social events and galas, join high-end hobby groups (sailing, wine tastings, art shows), and network through mutual friends. The best women tend to run in certain social circles—find those circles.

3. Building an Abundance Mindset: At the end of the day, attraction isn't about finding the "right" woman—it's about being the right man. The most attractive men don't chase matchmakers or dating coaches. They focus on improving themselves, creating options, and attracting women naturally.

Final Verdict: Matchmakers Are a Joke

Matchmaking services sell you a fantasy. They promise a shortcut to love, but in reality, they're just charging you a premium for something you could do yourself. They don't have a secret formula. They don't have magic powers. They don't know what women really want any better than you do. If you want real results in dating, skip the middleman. Take control of your own dating life, build yourself into a high-value man, and watch as the right women come to you. Because at the end of the day? No matchmaker will ever care about your success as much as you do.

WHERE I AM HEADING:
THE NEXT CHAPTER AFTER A LIFETIME OF DATING

After all the dates, all the women, and all the experiences, I have a crystal-clear idea of the kind of woman I'm seeking. I could keep playing this game until I'm using a walker or confined to a wheelchair. I have no doubt that if I wanted to, I could continue the dance of seduction well into my twilight years. But that's not where my mind is anymore.

I recognize now that what I truly want is the right woman—a partner with whom I can share life's joys, challenges, and unexpected twists. I don't want just any woman; I want the right woman. One who appreciates the man I have become, who understands and complements me, and who makes the idea of settling down feel like an upgrade rather than a compromise.

The Journey So Far: Lessons in Love, Lust, and Self-Discovery

It's been an incredible ride. I've learned more about women than I ever thought possible, but more importantly, I've learned about myself. Every experience, every moment of connection, and every fleeting romance has shaped me.

When I look back, I see a man who has evolved—not just in how he understands women, but in how he understands his own desires, strengths, and weaknesses. It's been a process of refinement. I've made mistakes. I've had my share of disappointments. But I've also had moments of pure exhilaration, moments that made the journey worth every second.

I've taken women to places they never knew existed—not just physically but emotionally and intimately. That's been one of the most rewarding aspects of this journey. It's not just about my own pleasure or satisfaction; it's about guiding someone into a deeper level of experience, helping them unlock aspects of themselves they didn't even realize were there. It's an ego boost, sure—but it's also a responsibility.

How Dating Has Made Me a Better Man

Through dating, I've improved in ways I never expected. I've sharpened my ability to read people. I've learned how to communicate—not just with words but through actions, energy, and presence. I've become more emotionally intelligent and more attuned to the nuances of attraction, desire, and human connection.

But more than anything, I've been forced to look at myself **squarely in the mirror.** I've had to take a hard, unfiltered look at the kind of man I am. The strengths I possess. The weaknesses I've needed to work on. The patterns I've repeated. The lessons I've had to learn the hard way.

Through it all, I've refined my sense of self. I've stripped away any illusions I once had about what relationships are supposed to be and what women actually want. I've cultivated a deep understanding of human nature—one that I wouldn't trade for anything.

Regrets? Not Really—But If I Had to Do It Again...

Would I change anything? Maybe. Sure, I'd love to have back all the money I've spent on dating. If I had that sitting in my bank account, I might have invested in a few more ventures, taken a few more trips, or learned to be an elite-level pickleball player. Maybe I would have devoted myself more to other hobbies or interests. But at the same time, I don't regret a single second of the journey.

Because this wasn't just about dating, it was about **understanding people.** It was about learning the intricacies of human relationships—how we connect, how we push each other away, and how we navigate the delicate balance of attraction and attachment. This has been one of my life's greatest studies, one of my most profound pursuits. I've treated it with the same curiosity and dedication that I've applied to business, law, and everything else I've built in my life. And that's why I wouldn't trade it for anything.

What I Want Now: The Woman Who Completes the Picture

At this stage, I'm looking for something different. Not just another beautiful woman. Not just another exciting night. Not just another conquest. I want someone who matches my energy. Someone who is just as confident, just as self-aware, and just as grounded in who she is as I am. Someone who doesn't play games because she doesn't have to. A woman who has been through her own journey of discovery and knows exactly what she wants.

I've reached a point where I don't need to be validated by another date, another seduction, another conquest. That phase has served its purpose. It has given me everything it was meant to. Now, I want something more substantial. Something built on mutual respect, deep attraction, and a shared sense of purpose. That doesn't mean I want to lose my edge. I don't ever want to be one of those guys who "settles" because he's tired of the game. If I'm going to be with someone, it's going to be because she makes my life better, not just easier.

The Next Chapter: A Life Well-Lived, With or Without Her

If I find the right woman, fantastic. If I don't? That's fine too. I've built a life I love. I have adventures to pursue, passions to explore, and experiences yet to be had. Whether I do them alone or with someone by my side is secondary to the fact that I am in control of my own happiness.

I refuse to be one of those men who enter a relationship out of fear— fear of being alone, fear of getting older, fear of running out of time. That's not who I am, and that's not who I will ever be. If I meet a woman who matches my ambition, my passion, and my intensity for life, she'll have a place beside me. But she won't be my purpose—she'll be an addition to an already fulfilling existence.

That, I believe, is the key. To know that you are already complete. To never need someone, but to welcome them if they enhance your journey. So where am I heading? Forward. Always forward. With a lifetime of experience behind me, a world of possibilities ahead, and the confidence that whatever comes next, I am ready.

FINAL THOUGHTS:
A NEW CHAPTER BEGINS

As I bring this book to a close, I find myself at the beginning of something new—a relationship with a woman who, for the first time in a long time, makes me pause and wonder if I might have finally found someone truly special. She is ten years my junior, hardworking, intelligent, and kind. She is not from the U.S., which, in many ways, adds to her allure. There is something refreshing about a woman who wasn't raised in the American dating culture, someone whose values seem to align more closely with my own.

We have been seeing each other for only a short time—just five dates—and yet, there is already a sense of mutual understanding, of chemistry, and of anticipation. She has officially become my girlfriend, a title I don't take lightly. I didn't rush into seduction as I might have in the past. Instead, I have savored the process, letting attraction build gradually, enjoying the dance of courtship without feeling the need to rush toward a physical connection.

This has been a deliberate choice. Not because I lack desire—far from it—but because I understand the value of anticipation, of letting things unfold naturally, of giving space for emotional connection to grow alongside physical attraction. I flirt with her mercilessly, and she responds in kind. We kiss, we dance, we touch. She melts into me when I hold her on the dance floor, her body pressing against mine, signaling what's to come. The attraction is undeniable, and I have little doubt about where we are heading.

Why I Haven't Told Her About This Book (Yet)

For obvious reasons, I have not told her about this book. Not yet. The contents would undoubtedly scare her off, at least at this early stage. I can imagine her reaction: disbelief, curiosity, maybe even a bit of outrage at my bluntness about women, dating, and seduction. I know she would ask, "Am I just another experiment? Another chapter in your story?"

The answer, of course, is no. She is not just another woman.

But I also recognize that revealing too much, too soon, would disrupt the natural flow of our connection. This is something many men fail to understand. Women crave mystery, intrigue, and the thrill of uncovering layers of a man over time. Telling her everything upfront would rob her of that journey.

This is an important lesson for all men: A woman should never feel like she has you completely figured out. There should always be a sense of discovery, of wondering what lies beneath the surface. Women are drawn to the unknown, to a man whose depths take time to explore.

So, for now, this book remains my secret.

The Evolution of a Man

Looking back on my journey, I realize that I wasn't always this self-aware. There was a time when I let emotions dictate my actions, when I fell into traps that I now see from miles away. I have been the nice guy, the simp, the one who put women on pedestals, who believed in the fairy tale romance sold by Hollywood and Disney. And I have been burned for it, over and over again.

But every misstep, every heartbreak, every lesson learned the hard way has shaped the man I am today. It has brought me to this point, where I can confidently say I know my worth. I understand what I bring to the table, and I refuse to settle for anything less than a woman who appreciates, respects, and cherishes me.

This new relationship feels different, not because I have suddenly become a romantic idealist, but because I approach it with clarity, experience, and a firm sense of self. I am not looking for validation. I am not seeking love out of loneliness. I am simply enjoying the company of a woman who excites me, challenges me, and makes me want to explore where this might lead.

The Beauty of the Unknown

The most thrilling part of any new relationship is the uncertainty. That sense of not knowing exactly what will happen next. Will she be the one? Or just another lesson along the way? I don't need the answer right now. For the first time in a long time, I am completely at ease with the process. There is no anxiety, no rush, no desperate need to define things immediately. I look forward to our next date, to the deepening of our connection, to the moments of laughter, seduction, and intimacy that lie ahead. But if, for whatever reason, this relationship does not work out, I will be perfectly fine.

That is the true power of experience—the knowledge that, no matter how things turn out, I will always land on my feet.

Lessons Earned and Lessons Shared

This book has been a journey of self-reflection as much as it has been a guide for others. Writing it has helped me solidify certain truths about myself, about women, and about the nature of relationships. I do not claim to be the ultimate authority on dating and attraction. But what I do offer is hard-earned wisdom, gained through thousands of experiences, both good and bad. If even one man reads this book and avoids the mistakes I once made, then my mission is accomplished.

As the saying goes, "An intelligent man learns from his own mistakes. A truly wise man learns from the mistakes of others." If you take even one lesson from this book, let it be this: Never stop improving. Never settle. Never become dependent on any one woman for your sense of happiness or self-worth.

Dating is a journey, not a destination. There is no final level, no ultimate achievement where you finally "win" at relationships. There is only growth, learning, and the ability to adapt to whatever life throws your way.

Finding the Right Woman

If you are fortunate, one day you will meet a woman who cherishes your presence, respects your being, brings joy to your life, and fulfills your deepest desires. She will be your equal, your partner, your complement. But until that day comes, enjoy the journey. Date without fear. Love without losing yourself. And always remember that you are the prize.

To those who have followed my journey through these pages—good luck in your own dating adventures. May you find a woman who is truly worthy of you. And if not, may you always have the strength to walk away with your head held high. And if this book has had any impact on your life, perhaps made a difference or you just want to talk or want me to coach you, write to me at:
JohnnyDepth1000@gmail.com. I answer all.